WAR AND SOCIETY IN EAST CENTRAL EUROPE:
THE EFFECTS OF WORLD WAR II
Vol. IX

Kálman Janics

CZECHOSLOVAK POLICY AND THE HUNGARIAN MINORITY, 1945-1948

With An Introduction by Gyula Illyés
An English Version Adapted From The Hungarian

By

Stephen Borsody

Social Science Monographs
Distributed by Columbia University Press
New York
1982

EAST EUROPEAN MONOGRAPHS, NO. CXXII

ATLANTIC STUDIES

Brooklyn College Studies on Society in Change No. 18
Editor-in-Chief Béla K. Király

CONTENTS

FOREWORD

The present volume is one in a series which, when completed hopes to present a comprehensive survey of the many aspects of War and Society in East Central Europe during the past two centuries.

These volumes deal with the peoples whose homelands lie between the Germans to the west, the Russians to the east and north, and the Mediterranean and Adriatic seas to the south. They constitute a particular civilization, an integral part of Europe, yet substantially different from the West. Within the area there are intriguing variations in language, religion, and government; so, too, are there differences in concepts of national defense, of the characters of the armed forces, and of the ways of waging war. Study of this complex subject demands a multidisciplinary approach; there, we have involved scholars from several disciplines, from universities and other scholarly institutions of the USA, Canada, and Western Europe, as well as the East Central European socialist countries. The author of the present volume is a Czechoslovak citizen.

Our investigation focuses on a comparative survey of military behavior and organization in these various nations and ethnic groups to see what is peculiar to them, what has been socially and culturally determined, and what in their conduct of war was due to circumstances. Besides making a historical survey, we try to define different patterns of military behavior, including the decisionmaking processes, the attitudes and actions of diverse social classes, and the restraints or lack of them shown in war.

We endeavor to present considerable material on the effects of social, economic, political, and technological changes, and of changes in the sciences and in international and interethnic relations on the development of doctrines of national defense and practices of military organization, command, strategy, and tactics. We shall also present data on the social origins and mibility of the officer corps and the rank and file, on the differences between the officer corps of the various services, and above all, on the civil-military relationship and the origins of the East Central European brand of militarism. The studies will, we hope, result in a better understanding of the societies, governments, and politics of East Central Europe, most of whose peoples are now members of the Warsaw Treaty Organization.

Our methodology takes into account that in the last three decades the study of war and national defense systems has moved away from narrow concern with battles, campaigns, and leaders and has come to concern itself with the evolution of the entire society. In fact, the interdependence of changes in society and changes in warfare, and the proposition that military institutions closely reflect the character of the society of which they are a part have come to be accepted by historians, political scientists, sociologists, philosophers, and other students of war and national defense. Recognition of this fact constitutes one of the keystones of our approach to the subject. The present volume concentrates on interethnic relations, and the Czechoslovak government's policies toward the minorities as related to their concept of national defense.

Works in Western languages adequately cover the diplomatic, political, intellectual, social, and economic histories of these peoples and this area. In contrast, few substantial studies of their national defense systems have yet appeared in Western languages. Similarly, though some substantial, comprehensive accounts of the nonmilitary aspects of the history of the whole region have been published in the West, nothing has yet appeared in any Western language about the national defense systems of the area as a whole. Nor is there any study of the mutual effects of the concepts and practices of national defense in East Central Europe. Thus, this comprehensive study on War and Society in East Central Europe is a pioneering work.

The present volume investigates the plight of the Hungarian minorities in Czechoslovakia. Czechoslovakia, as a multi-national state, was established as one of the consequences of the First World War. The Czechoslovak effort during and after World War II to transform their state into a Slavic nation state negatively affected the fate of the minorities of Czechoslovakia. The study of Dr. Kálmán Janics thus exposes a problem which is deeply rooted in the effects of both world wars, thus the book is a welcome addition to our series.

Brooklyn College Studies of Society in Change

PREFACE TO THE ENGLISH VERSION

This book is "a first." It is about the persecution of the Hungarian minority in Czechoslovakia after the Second World War, a topic nobody wrote a book about before. It covers the years between Czechoslovakia's liberation from the Nazis in 1945 to Czechoslovakia's conquest by the Communists in 1948. During these "homeless years," as Kálmán Janics calls them, the Hungarians had been the target of a policy formulated by Czechoslovak exiles during the war: the liquidation of national minorities. The Czechoslovak policy was only partially successful against the Hungarians mainly because of American opposition, but the anti-minority mentality in Slovakia against the Hungarians survives. This persecution is almost entirely unknown to the world at large. Moreover, to the Western reader, it may come as a surprise that such a persecution ever existed in democratic Czechoslovakia after 1945—and, even more of a surprise, that this persecution ended only when the Communists destroyed that democracy in 1948.

Kálmán Janics, the author of the book, is a medical doctor and a sociologist. He is one of the few Hungarians of the older generation with a higher education who survived the calculated expulsion of the intelligentsia, first the general target of persecution of the Hungarian minority in postwar Czechoslovakia. Well known, both at home and abroad, as a Hungarian writer on minority problems, Dr. Janics has recently been forced into retirement as a physician. He lives in his hometown, in one of Slovakia's still predominantly Hungarian regions.

Gyulla Illyés, author of the introductory essay on Hungarian minorities in general, is an internationally known Hungarian poet and writer. At the age of 79, he is the grand old man of contemporary Hungarian literature. Although recipient of several official prizes, the Communist authorities suppressed Mr. Illyés's recently published book of essays because of his outspoken views on the Hungarian minorities. Of Calvinist peasant origins, he is regarded today as the voice of Hungarian national conscience, both in Hungary and by Hungarians everywhere.

3

If the world at large is hardly aware of Hungarian minority problems, all the greater is the Hungarian interest in them. Evidence of that is the extraordinary success of Dr. Janics's book, both among the million or so Hungarians living all over the world and among the fourteen million or so Hungarians in the Danube region. The latter know of it mostly by hearsay only, or from foreign broadcasts, since the book is banned in Hungary and in the surrounding Communist countries with Hungarian populations. It was published in Munich under the auspices of the Hungarian Protestant Free University in Europe with headquarters in Bern, Switzerland.

The success of Dr. Janics's book among Hungarians is easy to understand. It speaks out on an issue which lies heavily on the Hungarian mind but cannot be freely discussed in public back home. Although the Hungarian minority survived the postwar Czechoslovak assault, its survival is a precarious one. And the Hungarian minority in Czechoslovakia is just one of several. The largest Hungarian minority is in Rumania; two smaller ones are in Yugoslavia and in the Soviet Ukraine. Altogether over three million Hungarians, one in every four, are exposed to the vicissitudes of minority existence today. Concern for their survival is aggravated by the Hungarian Government's apparent indifference toward them. The Communist regime regards the concern for the Hungarian minorities as a relic of bourgeois nationalism, which was discredited by the Horthy era's revisionist policy. Furthermore, according to the Communist theory of "common fatherland," the Hungarian minorities are well taken care of in the neighboring Communist countries since they are governed in the spirit of "proletarian internationalism." However, the truth of the matter is that, despite "fraternal" Communist Party demonstrations, national tolerance in the Danube region does not seem to flourish at all under Communist internationalism.

Understandable as the Hungarian interest in Dr. Janics's book may be, why should it be published in an English version?

The significance of Dr. Janics's book is that it speaks of a universal phenomenon: man's inhumanity to man under the dehumanizing influence of nationalist frenzy. Moroever, what is specifically noteworthy in this particular case is that it happened in a country with a democratic reputation. Furthermore—and this may reflect on the state of the Western democratic world itself—the brutalities committed in postwar Czechoslovakia against the national minorities did not seem to harm at all the

country's democratic prestige. The story of Czechoslovak policy to liquidate the country's Hungarian minority has never been told in any appreci-
able detail, which is another reason why this book deserves international
attention beyond the Hungarian language barrier. Its topic has so far been
subject to that "ugly silence" the British writer Nikolai Tolstoy spoke recently of in his book on the forciable repatriation of Soviet citizens by the
West (*Victims of Yalta;* in American edition, *The Secret Betrayal*) at the
end of World War II.

The historical setting of Dr. Janics's topic briefly stated is this: During
World War II, taking advantage of the West's feeling of shame over Munich,
and of the worldwide indignation over Hitler's cruelties, Edvard Beneš,
President-in-exile of Czechoslovakia, launched a punitive campaign that
advocated the expulsion of the German population from Czechoslovakia.
Soon he advanced a general theory, flimsy but successful, that national
minorities are the cause of war and a threat to peace. Thus, in order to
make Czechoslovakia into a homogeneous Slav nation-state, the Hungarian minority too has been declared guilty of treason and dangerous to
both the security of Czechoslovakia and to European peace. An "ugly
silence" of a special kind was necessary to make Dr. Beneš's wartime
anti-minority theory stick. Above all, silence had to be maintained about
the clearly visible fact that the Slovaks themselves—from whose half of
Czechoslovakia the Hungarians were to be expelled—had betrayed the
Czechoslovak State and gained, for the first time in their history, separate
national statehood with Hitler's help.

Hitler's crimes nothwithstanding, it was quite extraordinary that Dr.
Beneš should embrace the idea of an ethnically pure Slav state. Czechoslovakia after all had been founded following World War I, with Western
democratic assistance, as a multinational state with the expressed promise
to become—in Beneš's own words—"a sort of Switzerland," a fair replace-
ment, that is, of the defunct Habsburg Empire. Why things did not work
out according to Czech plans and promises, has skillfully been obfuscated
by Czech propaganda. Dr. Janics reveals a few points concerning this matter, worthy of Western attention. Mr. Illyés elaborates the theme on a
universal level. Their joint message is: peace cannot be built on falsehood
and injustice.

Despite blatant historical incongruities in his revised statemaking ideas,
Beneš was singularly successful during World War II in getting Allied

approval of his plans for expelling the Germans from Czechoslovakia. He was less successful, however, in adding the Hungarians to his list of national minorities deserving liquidation. It is to the credit of the United States that, by opposing Beneš and his Soviet Russian allies, the total expulsion of the Hungarian minority did not materialize. With Soviet support, Beneš did everything he could think of (and he was quite resourceful) to overcome or circumvent American opposition. His tactical moves, as well as the horrors the Hungarian minority went through while Beneš's campaign was conniving against them, is told with impressive documentation (mainly from Czechoslovak sources) by Dr. Janics's book.

Since Dr. Janics's narrative ends with the Communist coup of 1948, marking the "end of the nightmare," a note is in order to clarify the Soviet role in Beneš's policy against the Hungarian minority. Credit should not be denied to the Communists for ending the indiscriminate persecution of the Hungarians in postwar Czechoslovakia. On the other hand, not unlike everywhere else in the Soviet orbit of power, in Czechoslovakia too, Communist policy had been utterly cynical, serving no other purpose but to facilitate Soviet postwar conquest. After some hesitation, Stalin during the war approved Beneš's plan to expel the Hungarians, and the Communists took the lead in the postwar persecutions of the national minorities in Czechoslovakia. This ensured Beneš's continuous praise of Soviet policy, thus playing into the Soviets' hands during the critical postwar years—not unlike during the war, when Beneš kept assuring the Western democracies of Stalin's good intentions. When, in 1948, Czechoslovakia's turn came to be transformed into a "people's democracy," as the last one in a series, the Communists switched sides. They restored to the Hungarians their citizenship rights and denounced their postwar persecution as the work of "bourgeois nationalists." This is the technique of "ugly silence," Soviet style.

I should reveal at this point that, although I am far removed geographically, the minority affairs of the Danube region are very close to my heart. I grew up in Czechoslovakia as a minority Hungarian. In fact, had good fortune not lifted me out of my place of birth, I would have shared the misfortunes my fellow Hungarians have suffered in Czechoslovakia. I would have hardly escaped the charges of "treason," and other indignities, for belonging to a "fascist nation" as the haughty Slovaks—sitting among the victors, thanks to the Czechs—started calling the defeated Hungarians

after World War II. Speaking of Slovak thanks to the Czechs, there is another aspect of "ugly silence," receiving attention by Dr. Janics. It is the
story of how the Slovaks, while Hitler's protégés, expelled their Czech
benefactors from post-Munich Slovakia.

Although geographically far removed, the Czechoslovak vindictive campaign against minority Hungarians did catch up with me. At the Paris
peace conference in 1946, Jan Masaryk, Czechoslovakia's Foreign Minister, singled me out (I was then Press Attaché of the Hungarian Legation
in Washington) as an example of incurable "revisionism," in his vocabu-
lary a capital crime. I committed this crime in a rather unexpected way.
In a flurry of postwar idealism, born out of wartime necessity, I wrote a
book in 1945 on reconciliation between Czechoslovakia and Hungary.
Among many other propositions to clear the air of hostility between us,
I suggested that Czechoslovak propaganda was wrong in maintaining that
Hungarian revisionism (as far as criticism of the post-First World War
territorial settlement is concerned) was tied to Hungarian feudalism. A
democractic Hungary—I wrote— would probably have collaborated with
her neighbors after World War I, in a hope of securing the rights of Hungarian minorities, and of creating a favorable atmosphere for an eventual
revision of frontiers. However—I concluded—it is impossible to imagine
how any Hungarian Government could have renounced the idea of a revision of the Treaty of Trianon. To Mr. Masaryk, this was an evidence
that post-World War II Hungary, under a "make-believe democracy," is
unwilling to give up "her old and notorious revisionist policy which, as
always, is directed against Czechoslovakia." To this way of thinking, which
is as hypocritical as it is unrealistic, a "democratic" Hungarian is always
supposed to side with Czechoslovakia against Hungary.

Not long after the Paris peace conference, I met Jan Masaryk in the
United States. He pretended not to remember what he had said in Paris,
but his friendly eyes seemed to tell me: "Look, I did not mean it. . . ."
He considered, I guess, that his patriotic and filial duty was to serve Beneš,
co-founder of Czechoslovakia with the late T. G. Masaryk, father of Jan.
He served Beneš to the very end. But, in the last agonizing moments of
his life, Jan Masaryk might have been thinking, perhaps, not merely of his
own nation's tragedy but also of the tragedies that Beneš's policy had
caused to other nations. Humane as he was, Jan Masaryk could hardly
have believed in the rightfulness of Beneš's revolting theory which declared

Czechoslovakia's national minorities collectively guilty of treason, deserving expulsion from their homelands under the false pretext of peace and security. Personally, I wish to dedicate this English version to the victims of Beneš's vindictive campaign against Czechoslovakia's Hungarian minority. And specifically, because it is so insidiously buried in that "ugly silence," I would like to call attention to what Dr. Janics says about the tragic fate of János Esterházy, representative of the Hungarian minority in the National Assembly of the Slovak State during World War II. Esterházy's lonely vote in 1942 against the Slovak law authorizing the deportation of Jews is of particular interest, not merely as a measure of Esterházy's personal morality and political courage, but also for reasons related to the principal moral and political issues discussed in this book.

The Allied backing Beneš received in his campaign against Czechoslovakia's national minorities was due mainly to world-wide indignation aroused by Hitler's inhumanities against the Jews—not against the Slovaks. That the Slovaks, by demanding expulsion of the Hungarian minority from Slovakia, should claim benefits indirectly derived from Hitler's persecution of the Jews is truly the outrageous irony of the tragedy of which Dr. Janics is giving a polemical yet balanced account.

Janics and Illyés, authors of the Hungarian original, have expressed the wish that their book should be published in "world languages." Their book, however, is so specifically Hungarian as to make translation not merely difficult but impossible. A straight translation into English had been made and proved unfit for publication. An adaptation, which is different in form yet identical in substance with the original seemed to be the only solution. Such a radical operation entailed of course not merely stylistic changes but a rewriting and rearrangement on a scale which resulted in a book with its own character. Changes of sequences have been made, passages have been omitted and added. To indicate the many changes that were made in the English version would be technically impossible. I did it only in two instances: In Chapters 4 and 5, in sections on the Potsdam conference and the Paris peace conference. I added material there and expressed opinions which are my own. Otherwise, I have altered phrasings throughout the book, and made many minor and major adjustments, but never tinkered with underlying views. I had no reason to do so. I identify myself entirely with the authors of the Hungarian original, with their views, with their concerns. As author of the English version I had only one aim: To communicate the subject matter in English as effectively as the original succeeded in doing in Hungarian.

It was one thing to wish that the Hungarian original should be published in a "world language" and another to make the wish come true. Credit for the latter is due to Professor Béla Király, Director of the Brooklyn College Studies on Society in Change. Also, acknowledgements are due to the Hungarian-Americans (their wish is to remain anonymous) whose contributions made the publication in the Brooklyn College Series possible. In 1956, very young, they fought in the Hungarian Revolution. They lost their country's bid for freedom, but not their interest in the cause of freedom—nor their concern for the least free among their compatriots today: the over three million minority Hungarians living in the countries of Hungary's neighbors.

The preparation for publication of this English version owes a great deal to Mrs. Dorothy Meyerson, Editorial Assistant of the Brooklyn College Studies on Society in Change. Her efficiency is as unparalleled as her good humor—a delightful combination. Also, I wish to express my coming the often awesome-looking barriers between two such different English translation (in manuscript); his work was helpful to me in overcoming the often awesom-looking barriers between two such different languages as English and Hungarian. However, I alone bear responsibility for the text of the English version. And I ought to stress emphatically— lest the authors of the Hungarian original are accused of "collaboration with foreign enemy"—that neither Dr. Janics, living in Slovakia, nor Mr. Illyés, living in Hungary have collaborated with me. Without their knowledge or consent, by preparing an English version, I alone collaborated with them. I did it with the conviction that such an odd collaboration is a duty rather than a crime, for it upholds the indivisibility of the Republic of Letters in a politically divided world.

Wellfleet, Massachusetts   *Stephen Borsody*
August 20, 1981

BEYOND AN INTRODUCTION TO A BOOK

By GYULA ILLYES

"The Homeless Years"* needs no introduction. The book's very first pages impress the reader deeply. The author, Kálmán Janics, M.D., cuts right *to the core,* not only of his subject. He reveals the hidden feelings and painful needs of millions of his people. My words here serve as a commentary of sorts—as an addition. As a man of letters I am adding my data to the data of a man of science.

When cultural contacts between the nations of Central Europe reopened after the Second World War, the honor befell upon me to represent in Prague the Hungarian Writers' Union at the invitation of the Czech Writers' Union. At the same time a Czech writer was being received in Budapest. It was a part of a kind of exchange program. The people who had suffered so dreadfully through the war and under Fascism were now extending their hands to each other through their artists. This included opera singers and dancers. Their performances demonstrated their talents very successfully. Now the artists of the word were called upon to prove their talents with words.

One reason I had been chosen was that before the war, together with Attila József and Lőrinc Szabó, I translated Czech and Slovak poetry into Hungarian. It was for an anthology that Anton Straka, prewar Press and Cultural Attaché at the Czechoslovak Legation in Budapest, had helped us to edit with mutual enthusiasm, several years before his martyrdom at the hands of the Nazis. We became true friends in the course of this collaboration.

A reception combined with an author's soirée was given at the Prague headquarters of the Czech Writers' Union, all in the context of a truly

---

* This is the title of Dr. Janics' book in the Hungarian original—*"A hontalanság évei"* (The Homeless Years).

exceptional hospitality. A distinguished audience gathered. Vitězslav Nezval, the most celebrated Czech poet of that time, was also present.

I had translated more than a dozen of Nezval's poems into Hungarian, including five or six of his ballads. He sat in the front row, next to me; a tall heavy-set man, he stepped forward, and with some effort, onto the podium which served as a stage. By way of opening the evening's program, he read an eight-line poem of mine which he had translated from my works into Czech, evidently as a matter of friendly reciprocation for this occasion. On his way down from the podium, he handed me his manuscript; we shook hands—and even embraced, adding warmth to the ceremony.

Amidst lively applause, the program continued with speeches. None of the speakers missed mentioning that the two peoples—the Czechoslovaks and the Hungarians—whose rulers had so often incited conflicts between them during the recent centuries, have now at last found each other, and from now on will march together as brothers along the path of democracy toward socialism. Hence this day, too, is a feast of joy. It should serve as an example. We should remember it with enthusiasm.

It behooved me to answer. Nezval himself took my arm and led me to the podium, prodding me in French (the language we had conversed in) not to demur and say at least a few words.

Relations between the Czech and the Hungarian people had indeed been almost brotherly in the more distant past. We had had rulers in common, religious movements in common. Yet, to speak of fraternity, or even of friendship between us, would be at this junction of history wishful thinking rather than a statement of facts. This was what I said in reply to the speakers before me. And I added: whoever is sincere about such a friendly wish, must also speak sincerely: is it possible for the wish to come true—and if so, when? And even though we cannot become loving brothers right away, can we at some time in the future become at least good neighbors? In all sincerity, I went on, I can be no bearer of good news for the time being. Hungary's relations with all her neighbors are marked for over a hundred years not by friendship, but by suspicion and by ever more tragic consequences of hostility. No different are Czechoslovakia's relationships with almost all of her neighbors. Considering the psychology of history, it may take at least another hundred years to dissolve the accumulated bad feelings. It takes a long time for nations to recover from wounds of the mind. We should face these facts of life squarely. Thus at least we can prepare ourselves, if only for a discussion of our problems, for a discussion of what should be our role as intellectuals to bring about a humane atmosphere, so that we may live at least as human beings, in security and trust.

My words were polite, circumspect—more so, perhaps than I have recorded them here. Yet the audience was shocked. And while I spoke the shock turned into chaos. Some people started to loudly exchange their opinions. Nezval intervened, came up to the podium, stood next to me and interpreted, explaining in Czech my French sentences.

He wanted to address the audience. With frowns on his brow, with a stiff expression on his face, he sought the right words. Then, as if to compress all his thoughts into one action, he shook my hands hard, and embraced me tightly. It was dramatic, stage-like, but moving nevertheless. Romantic historical plays are made of such gestures, and they can be moving too.

The tension was relieved. The soirée wound up in a gay mood, with frequent toasts during the reception. Could it be that all of us there were ignorant—hosts and guests alike—of events that happened right that evening which rendered any yearning for friendship between us hopeless, perhaps for even longer than a hundred years to come? Even those who did know of the expulsions and deportations of Hungarians taking place in Czechoslovakia at that time, and of the atmosphere of Inquisition created by these events, probably ascribed these happenings only to bourgeois political shortsightedness, dismissing them, hopefully, as a last lawless act of the era of bourgeois politics.

Everyone called me "comrade." Great portraits hung on the walls, of Marx and Engels, and of the more recent pioneer fighters for international socialism, now at last triumphant.

My elaborately prepared visit included a tour of the country, and in the spirit of exuberant hospitality, we were accompanied by an interpreter and a guide. But in Slovakia, in bi-lingual Slovak-Hungarian areas, or in those regions where Hungarians were still the majority, we needed no guide or interpreter. My wife and I walked the streets of towns, and small towns which we would have known sight unseen from the pages of our Hungarian history and literature.

One morning, we walked in one of the legendary small towns of the "Kuruc" period (when Slovaks and Hungarians fought together against the Habsburgs in the 17th and 18th centuries). It was early, before noon, there were few people on the streets. Suddenly, out of one of the arcaded gates of a house a loudly yet kindly scolding, kerchiefed older woman dragged onto the street a stubborn little boy, probably her grandson. She did not mince words. It was the harsh vernacular of the Hungarian folklore, mixing grandmotherly sternness with almost sweet kindness: "You stinker, I wish the flames of hell would consume you!" "Do you want me to tie your heels behind you right now?"

I too had heard these incredible threats (that I will have my heels tied behind me) once upon a time as a little boy, but never since. My curiousity was aroused, I turned around, as if into the past, expecting what other familiar phrases from my childhood may reach my ears.

But as she noticed me, the grandmother instantly switched from Hungarian to Slovak, without changing the passion of her speech. Moreover, as if the pitch of her voice had even risen a bit (for me, the suspicious stranger, to hear more clearly that she was speaking Slovak—and not Hungarian).

I moved on, without turning around again, out of the old woman's and the little boy's hearing range—or, as they might have felt, firing range. I felt oppressed. Somehow the incident evoked literally the notion of firing range in me. These simple people (the young one still stumbling and the old one already shuffling along), had evidently been frightened by my presence. My wife tarried a while longer around them, then joined me saying that the dialogue between generations resumed in muffled Hungarian, with unabated passion, much less loudly.

This grotesque yet terribly sad episode, revealing repressed layers of everyday existence under terror, was a memorable experience of my study tour, a kind of "live history" lesson. Many more were to follow, on-the-spot personal experiences which, in sufficient numbers, can amount to reliable data, more authentic than statistics. Writers, men of letters and of spirit, collect such data, willy-nilly.

The episodes and data have multipled over the years. Living with a sensitive mind in the region of the Danube River, and of the Carpathian Mountains, one is bound to feel their impact. And the impact was upsetting—for all the people of that region speaking so many different languages.

Experience and data: they rarely meet in our understanding of the real world. They are prone to race against each other; and sentiments sometimes overtake logic, or the other way round.

One of the great merits of Kálmán Janics' book is that he lines up his data and then reaches his conclusions invariably by rules of a logical order. Hence, the book can expect to elicit the right reactions, regardless of the readers' partisan feelings. Dr. Janics strives to show us the truth for the benefit of all of us. His first and last words are inspired by the spirit of reconciliation. As if he would say: we all belong to the same world. Indeed, the future of mankind depends on it whether we realize soon enough the meaning of this simple truth. Dr. Janics, a greatly respected professional, is the kind of social scientist whose background is in the natural sciences. Along with his work in sociology, he is a physician. This has a lot to do with both his mastery of the subject and the independence of his judgment. He can delve as penetratingly into centuries-old archival materials as into the everyday present. The doctor's sentences suggest that he keeps his writing instruments clean too. He feels his responsibility when he opens the outer skin. He pays attention—and he expects patience from his patient even when he touches the quick. And he has confidence in curability. Does he recklessly tear up wounds? Not at all. After carefully treating them with antiseptics, he cuts the wounds and cleans them.

The author invites us to share with him his responsibility. He invites us to work with him, to follow his example, to make the voice of sincerity reach farther and farther, to make it sound loud and full.

Too much bad news about Hungarians living in Rumania has for too long diverted our attention from the Hungarians' plight in Czechoslovakia. Of course, to spread information on the Hungarians' situation in Transylvania in itself was an arduous and risky task, with Hungarian conditions in our own country being what they were. But hard as it was for us, it was a matter of conscience. Also, it was a task requiring a great deal of tact.

We, the "outs" in Hungary, were pitted against the "ins," the powerless against the powerful, and our task was to convice them of the rightness of our cause. It was a battle of principles in which truth was our sole weapon. At the beginning, only a few Hungarian intellectuals joined us in our struggle, and even they were blamed or scolded by many of their colleagues. Why to make waves, they argued, in the relatively calm waters? Under such conditions in our own country, no wonder that whenever urgent action on behalf of the Hungarians in Czechoslovakia was deemed necessary, even men of good will became worried and asked: why to increase tensions? Why to open a second front in our own bitter intellectual struggles at home?

Our own controversies strengthened in me the conviction that multi-sided problems call for multi-sided examinations. Let's see first the details. (I prefer *not* to say "front." I do now wish to use here this fashionable expression of ours, not even as a metaphor.) Then let's find out the connections between the details. Thus we may be able to get to the roots, to the base, of our problems. Thus we may be able to start building a system of ideas in the light of which solutions can be sought—solutions that are based on calm thinking and can lead us to lasting peace. Only a just order thus arrived at in the realm of ideas may guarantee a climate of good spirit and the peace of the mind. We writers are foremost responsible for creating such a peaceful atmosphere. And we Hungarians, wherever in the world we may live, because of our own very grave problems, are particularly called upon to work for peace. Not only as Hungarians, but also as Europeans. And while serving our own people, we serve humanity. This is our creed. And since our concern is justice, we are both justified and obliged to call the world's attention to the fate of our people. We make our case into an affair of the world, and we appeal to the world for its judgment, for its decision.

The world of today, uninformed as it is about us, may be shocked to learn about our case that the Hungarians are the most dispersed ethnic unit in Central Europe, both in absolute and relative figures.

The facts are as follows: According to the last prewar Hungarian census, the peace treaties after World War I transferred 1,660,000 Hungarians to Rumania, 896,000 Hungarians to Czechoslovakia, and 577,000 Hungarians to Yugoslavia. Altogether three million people, almost one-third of all Hungarains then living in the Danube region. It was done by a dictate, not by true treaties of peace respecting the rights of the people. There were no plebiscites.

What is the number of these so-called Hungarian minorities today? Was there any natural increase in Hungarian minority population? Why is their growth not proportionate to the increase of the majority populations? These are tricky questions, "many-sided" problems, for a variety of reasons.

The census became unreliable. Simply because it cannot be carried out properly. The available statistics beg for more data.

It becomes ever more difficult to determine how many Hungarians live beyond the borders of Hungary proper today. In places where national affiliation entails advantages and disadvantages, demography no longer belongs among the objective sciences. Current estimates based on data other than the census would bring the number of minority Hungarians closer to four million (which in itself is far from the proportionate increase of the majorities), but the data of the bureaucrats still speak of only three million, the same as well over half a century ago.

And would it alleviate at all the pain of millions of people involved in this battle of figures if statistics were scrupulously correct? To spell out the logical conclusion of our line of thought: Is it possible to measure human feelings with some sort of arithmetics of morality? Is it possible to measure statistically individual suffering?

The problem of Hungarians treated as second-class citizens because of their mother tongue is becoming an evermore burning issue. Not only for the Hungarian minorities, but for all Hungarians. There are about fifteen million Hungarians in the world today, and they are bound together by lively family ties as well as by close historical and cultural ties. Thus the number of suffering Hungarians is immeasurably greater than the minority statistics of bureaucrats would indicate. The human body jerks at the pricking of the smallest needle. So does the healthy body of a nation when subjected to humiliation, no matter how small is the tissue that ties the members together. In Central and Eastern Europe, ever since the beginning of the last century, the mother tongue has been reacting as the most sensitive skin does. And by now, it is a skin in a state of permanent inflammation. It reacts with utmost sensitivity even to pricks which would have once remained unnoticed.

Ever since their humiliation after World War I, the ethnic community of Hungarians was in an inflamed state of protest. They wanted at the very least to loosen their shackles. Their struggle from the very beginning was in defense of their natural rights as human beings. This is clearly demonstrated by their first rise in protest against their humiliation. It drove them into the camp of extreme internationalism: Communist Hungary's war in the spring and summer of 1919, fought on two fronts (against Czechoslovakia and Rumania) is cited in all Marxist history books as a manifestation of revolutionary patriotism.

A pure cause can become, alas, the victim of dirty political games. Relying on the power of the big imperialisms of Western Europe, the smaller imperialisms of Central and Eastern Europe drew up a *cordon sanitaire* around the Hungarians. They meant to cripple, and eventually to annihilate their Hungarian rivals. The counterrevolution led by Miklós Horthy, was Hungary's ugly response. The Horthy regime installed its own imperialism in the shadow of neighboring small imperialisms. It also tried (in vain) to reach an understanding with the big imperialisms which supported Hungary's rival neighbors in the economically crippled *cordon sanitaire.* Finally, Hungary's counterrevolutionary regime joined up with the Fascist imperialist powers poised against the rival small and big imperialistic powers. Thus the justice of the Hungarian people became discredited by the policies of the Hungarian ruling classes.

The course counterrevolutionary Hungary had taken was a fatal error. Yet there was another Hungary whose mind had been conditioned by the ideas of our great poets such as Petőfi and Ady. Those Hungarians who stood for reconciliation with the neighboring Danubian people often clashed openly with the official Hungarian nationalism, which responded to the neighbors' anti-Hungarian agitation in the same mean spirit. The popular aim of national policy was thought to be the peaceful protection of the Hungarian ethnic territories. However, slogans of official nationalism, such as "Crippled Hungary is no country—Integral Hungary is heavenly!" only exasperated our neighbors who believed that old Hungary of the prewar Dual Monarchy of the Habsburgs was nothing but hell ever since the national liberation movements began. Well, precision scales are needed to mete out justice to any suing party, but especially when nations are the suitors.

Hungarian feudalism and capitalism, helped into existence after 1919 by the policies of the Big and Little Ententes, was one of the most oppressive and also one of the most short-sighted anti-social associations of bloodsuckers in Europe. Instinctively, they followed their own class interests when they got on the bandwagon of chauvinism. They simply joined the same club where the bourgeois men of power of Hungary's neighbors had already been accepted as members.

It took a while to discover that the "justice" of the upper classes is not the justice of the people, not the justice of the masses. Once it was discovered it took yet another while to make it into common knowledge, not just in Hungary, but everywhere. So that the masses, the "man in the street," and also the intellectuals wherever they live, should become aware of how long, and to what ends, they have been manipulated, brainwashed. Perhaps we still have not been fully awakened on both sides of national borders to reality. That is exactly why Dr. Janics's book, paying no regard to established prestige and power, is more than just another historical monography.

The contagious disease of falsehood, which the authoritarian regimes by means of their total power rendered world-wide in mankind's mind, has still not been brought under control—not within our own borders either. The chemical formula of demagoguery is still with us: mix enough truth into a pack of lies so that those who thirst for justice should swallow it as a refreshing beverage. However, just because sycophants of some mad tyrant, bent on oppressing the people—in our time, mainly those of Hitler's—injected some of the people's real problems into their dirty tricks, should those problems now be taken for non-existing? Should not, rather, all care be taken that those problems will never be used again for ignominious ends?

The First World War was set off and prolonged to its well-known bitter end by the combustible problems of nationality which could never be contained by paper documents called treaties. A Serbian student shot the Habsburg heir who frivolously flouted South Slav national feelings. Hitler and company unleashed the Second World War by demagogically inciting the problems of nationalities, rendering any sensible discussion of these problems well-nigh impossible for decades to come.

I believe that those of us who have fought this demagoguery from the very beginning have the right to spell out the truth: it is not the worthy principle that becomes unworthy when it passes through unworthy mouths. Thus the just cause of nationality, too, has been abused in the dishonest chess games of politics.

In Hungary after the Second World War, the false belief has been forcibly spread that no pure soul may raise ever again national problems, no matter how just they are, although in the meantime these problems have grown two-fold bigger. Thus, on the one hand, we had to clear the real issues once and for all of the filth of the past and while, on the other, we had to approach their solution with a sense of responsibility so that everything we do should serve, in all its details, and for all times to come, true peace and lasting reconciliation.

Dr. Janics's book is profoundly concerned with providing a suitable basis for such a two-fold endeavor concerning the past and the future. Hence, it would be desirable that it be read first of all by those "who wield power." The book is objective. As such it deserves a wide audience and objective discussion. It should not be overlooked that the book deals with an area of Europe from which the devastating fires of both World Wars were ignited. If we want fire regulations, we should first think of preventative measures.

The long suffering people of the Danube Valley still expect of their writers and poets the kind of public role most poets of the preceding century have willingly taken upon themselves; the last one in the West to do this was Victor Hugo. Among the Czechoslovak poets of this type, in addition to the Czech Nezval, in whom I have taken the greatest interest, is the Slovak Ján Poničan. I had translated some of Poničan's early work; among them his first great poem in which he announces to the world his creed in the poet's mission:

> I came to conquer the world to watch
> That no more disgrace may touch it again
> For it has been violated for too long—
> The ancient birthright of our forebears!

It is precisely this birthright that has been violated in our case. The Hungarian case, too! This is the shocking realization with which the reader, enlightened by Dr. Janics's reliable and verifiable facts, puts down this book. The official census in Slovakia today knows only of about half of the once close to one million people of Hungarian mother tongue. Their situation in some respects is even worse than that of the Hungarians in Rumania. Geographically, they do not form a compact whole; they have no city that might serve as a cultural center of their land. Knowledge and defense of their mother tongue is disintegrating.

Just while these lines were written, I once again became involved in this touchy matter of Hungarian minorities, which is a matter of conscience with me. I had to answer (for a non-Hungarian audience) questions regarding the fate of millions of Hungarians suffering grave discrimination on account of their Hungarian mother tongue. It so happened that among the points of the questionnaire was the *good*-neighborly relations between

Slovaks and Hungarians. Point by point, in a rather lengthy interview, my answers in essence were as follows: 1) The issue is not how to further "improve" *good* relations but, rather, how to prevent or at least how to slow down, their futher deterioration. 2) What should be done for such "improvement" and by whom? Obviously, only those who are in positions of power to act can do something about the situation. 3) Speaking of past experiences? For many decades, we had no part in anything that was happening across the border; except, a little perhaps, intellectually. 4) As for literary activity? It should be twofold: to acquaint with our situation the outside world, and to educate our own people for setting an example by our virtues as Europeans and thus to *radiate* hope. 5) How to encourage our friends on the other side of the borders? By telling them that, whichever of us should be "up" or "down," we both should do better in the future as far as our radiations go. 6) Finally, we should bury the ugly past.

Unfortunately, and Dr. Janics's book is a confirmation of it, the ugly past is still very much with us. In many towns of Slovakia, once creative nests radiating Hungarian culture, the Hungarian language itself is banned. Even conversation of the simple folk in the mother tongue is driven underground. The episode of the grandmother and granson recorded above is a small lyric sample of the situation. But the lyric is only one of several interests of this poet's lyre. I have attacked on my lyre the symptoms of tyranny. And to me, no form of tyranny is more devastating—and more laughable at the same time—than the petty tyranny of mini-tyrants, of those despicable underlings, showing off their bravery in safe shelters. This is what tyranny breeds; instead of mutual understanding—so very timely!—instead of cleaning of wounds and cleansing of brains—so badly needed!

Throughout history, so many proposed remedies have failed to cure our poisonous and burning problems that every well-intentioned new proposal which appeals to reason is instantly silenced. Thus we yield only more ground to stupid skepticism—and even to tragedy.

Yet, quite a few solutions supported by reason and a sense of justice have in fact succeeded—but they get no publicity.

For instance: there are almost as many Germans in Denmark as there are Danes in Germany, and anybody on either side of the frontier, after graduating from high school or university, can be trained or licensed in either of the two countries. Or, another example: at the University of

Zürich, German literature is taught primarily and Swiss literature only as a supplement; in Geneva, on the other hand, French language and literature are taught primarily and its Swiss offshoot only as a second. Language and humane literature can indeed become bridges between *peoples,* even if as *nations* they might occasionally be swept by conflict against each other, as it happened several times to the French and the Germans in the course of their history.

There are other little known projects among several European countries under way. For instance, the mutual supervision of their textbooks, their joint production, that is, with the aim to mutually correct errors in a polite manner. There are projects, already in the process of realization, to accept each others' diplomas on a footing of equality; to guarantee the training of minority intellectuals at an appropriate level and in convenient locations; to open the way for a true confluence of intellectual life.

It is encouraging to know that there are places in the world where bridgeheads are being built in such a comforting direction. As the peoples of the globe are becoming economically increasingly interdependent, so grows stronger their urge to preserve, even to enhance their linguistic and ethnic characteristics. Even the world's tiniest minorities are striving today for the greatest possible independence—as further proof that liberty of the people is truly one and indivisible for all, and must spread uniformly, both upwards and downwards.

This peaceful road to collective consciousness and individual spiritual liberation is called in Western Europe "cantonization," in recognition of the Swiss model of cantonal self-government. In countries which follow the Leninist ideas, it is called "national autonomy." Not only national units counting millions of people, but even ethnic groups numbering barely ten thousand have demanded and were granted complete ethnic independence, and the logical follow-up thereof: spiritual liberation and self-government. Furthermore, the frontiers that have caused so much suffering are crumbling. (How outdated they are!) Or, they are crumbling at least in theory, until the great prophecy of both the utopian and scientific socialists, the withering away of the states, if fulfilled. There is ample literature on these subjects, especially with reference to its ramifications in Eastern Europe and the Balkans.

Among the serious problems that are bound to arise, one in particular ought to be mentioned here: what happens when a clear-cult line dividing ethnic groups cannot be drawn? When the mother tongues of the groups are spread out like pieces of a mosaic (*en puzzle,* as the French experts would say it) on both sides of any conceivable line of division? The specialists do have recommendations on how to solve the problems: let us balance the size of ethnic groups on both sides of the national border—like on two arms of a scale—and thus guarantee their decent treatment on either side. And let the indicator of the scale be visible to the eyes of mankind! For to let mankind watch what we are doing is a further guarantee of humane treatment. Mankind after all *is* the same as humanity! This book provides us with real food for thought on how to make our metaphor, the arms of a scale, work properly. The author's belief in peace through reconciliation is so strong that he occasionally may appear aggressive in the pursuit of his objectives. But we ought to be ashamed of ourselves, and doubly so because of our socialist-humanist convictions, if we dismissed the objectives of his book as hopeless, or, perhaps, as premature.

If ideas are no instant success, it does not follow that they have no influence; therefore, we shouldn't discount them, least of all when circumstances are unfavorable to them. The whole idea of public affairs (the *res publica*) is a two-wheel affair like the Roman chariot: one wheel is *political life,* the other is *intellectual* life. They do not run along the same course. Who could grasp the nature of the world's *political* confusion as thoroughly as to be able to predict its shape for as little as six months ahead? By contrast, every moment of the world of the *intellect* is stable. It is not changeable like the endless combinations of mathematics.

The measure of the intellect is ethics. And for the writer, no matter what his faith or ideology, there is only one ethical norm—that of the substance of the written word. If there is no lasting element in the written word, if the words do not have wings to fly in search for lasting influence —if *scripta non volent!*—they do not deserve the paper on which they are written.

Two models of how to deal with national minorities stand out in the more recent past. One is Lenin's, the other is Beneš's. The first model enacts not only complete equality of rights for the minority but prescribes courtesies and favors reserved, so to speak, for the treatment of a younger sibling. The formula is spelled out in Lenin's writings. Beneš's model and its consequences are discussed in this book. It is a formula for the liquidation by whatever means of the national minorities, their extermination, that is. It has been accepted as an official government program, and included even among the philosophical principles of international peace-making after the Second World War.

It seems as if the very course of contemporary history had taken a turn against the existence of national minorities. Industrialization centralizes, it inflates or even creates cities which, in turn, become centers of assimilation, favoring the language of the state, the language of the bureaucracy. It requires little planning on the part of forces bent on national oppression to disperse the homogeneous national minority areas by deliberate placement of factories and by purposeful relocation of populations.

Yet this is not the "peaceful assimilation" recent apostles of "necessity" like to speak of. There are historical precedents of such planned alienations, forcible population movements. When "necessity" no longer exists, the violation of the people's rights remains—like a disease which continues to spread its deadly poison after the source of contagion disappears. Thus, if we follow the ethical logic of moral protest, it would be criminal to accept something as "necessary" simply because it was the product of history. Did our ancestors accept the plague?

Wasn't there struggles against burning of witches and heretics, against the crazy accusations of ritual murder? Isn't there a world-wide front against the crimes of apartheid? "Historical necessity" is no excuse for the surrender of a people's human rights! It's treason, no matter what the motivation. It's treason, not only against the fatherland and nation but the future as well. Such a traitor is a Coriolanus of humanity.

The unexpected fury and world-wide spread of twentieth century nationalism is almost like the plague of the Middle Ages. It ravages the human mind. It is a *political* epidemic. To let it rage out of control is, to put it mildly, an omission—no matter whether the threat is just to our neighborhood across the street or to continents. Communities, of course, are sensitive to outside interference, in particular in *political* matters. Even the thought of interference in their affairs disturbs them. They jealously guard their ideological boundaries, believing in permanency and immutability on this earth.

The *intellectual* world, however, the world of ideas, that is, knows no boundaries—the higher the sky, the larger the horizon. The intellectual creates a community of its own which transcends the nation. The dimensions are boundless, and so-called boundary violations unknown. What is commonly known as interference becomes "aid and assistance," to use a favorite phrase of our century. In the world of the intellect, the person who defends himself necessarily defends his fellow man as well.

Spiritual culture and technological civilization alike have already discovered, and made it ambitiously known to mankind, that the home of humanity is the planet earth (and tomorrow perhaps the constellations of the universe). What is but a part of the whole must become more perfect in order to fit peacefully into the future whole. In this process, the national languages, even the "minority" languages, are parts of the whole waiting for peaceful signals—also in the realm of *political* cooperation—in order to be fitted into the future whole.

Dr. Janics's book sheds a ray of light in the direction of the above described historical process. Namely, that the whole world is ever more becoming a *res publica,* a global matter of public affairs. It's message is this: just as peace is one and indivisible, so is truth, which is the sole conceivable basis of true peace. And truth has but one opponent: the front of falsehood.

People of good intentions and of good eyes—perceptive people, that is—may become better world citizens after reading this book. Yet some readers may also raise their eyebrows, smile incredulously, or even condescendingly, and wonder: who are these two little people, the Slovaks and Hungarians of Czechoslovakia, bad neighbors as they seem to be, quarreling with each other? Let me explain. My own way. The poet's way.

The greatest Hungarian poet, Sándor Petőfi, was born bearing a Slovak name, Petrovič. And the greatest Slovak poet, Hviezdoslav, was born with a Hungarian name, Pál Országh. The name of Kossuth, the world's best known Hungarian in modern times, reveals Czech origins. And the world-renowned figure of the Czech spiritual rebirth, Komenský (or Comenius), when signing his last writings, recorded with a shaking hand the name of his Hungarian ancestors: Szeges. Is my explanation clear? Alas, in our time, not even the genius of immortals has been able to bring light into the darkened nationalist minds!

This book, I hope, will be published in the so-called world languages. I would recommend it above all to the attention of Czech and Slovak readers. But also to the attention of all people of the world with a long history of setbacks in the struggle for international brotherhood. I do that with some measure of hope. I am still moved by the memory of the moment recalled earlier, when a Czech poet, Vitězslav Nezval, stepped up next to me on the podium in Prague, to embrace me and me to embrace him. I have never met the Slovak poet Ján Poničan, whose poems, as I mentioned, I translated into Hungarian. But I did experience still another handshake with a poet-neighbor that warmed up into an embrace. The scene was my house of the shores of Lake Balaton. It happened between me and the greatest Rumanian poet of that time, the elderly Tudor Arghezi, following my reading of two of his most beautiful poems in my translation to him. So after all, the intellect, reason, humane manners, do have a way to prevail over political emotions and everyday passions, haven't they?

This book raises doubts but also hopes—exactly because it honestly acknowledges the reasons for doubt.

What fate the future holds for the minorities is unclear. Nevertheless, one or two harsh lessons can clearly be drawn from past experiences: if a country cannot treat its "minorities" the same way it treats its "majority," it is not worthy of keeping such minorities under its rule. In such cases of trouble, civilized mankind (itself seasoned by troubles) in its own interest must defend the minorities in order to forestall the easy recurrence of barbarism. For barbarism is mankind's plague whose symptoms nowhere appear more terrifyingly than in the treatment of the weaker, of the defenseless—of the minorities.

In his conclusions, looking at the situation from his side of the fence, the Czechoslovak side, that is, Dr. Janics is no preacher of facile optimism regarding Czechoslovak-Hungarian relations; his last sentences speak of no change in Czechoslovakia.

On the other hand, the situation did change considerably over here, in Hungary, for the better—though for a while in a rather upsetting manner. By an astonishing *political* metathesis, shortly after the Second World War, the official point of view in Hungary became critical of the nationalism of the *oppressed* Hungarians rather than of the nationalism of their *oppressors.* Callous to those suffering national oppression, this curious official Hungarian point of view provoked only predictable reckless reactions of "sympathy with the oppressed" on the part of those nationalist types who in their Fascist zeal are capable of condoning even genocide

against their foes. But our resurrected *intellectual* life has by now definitely evicted these ugly postwar phenomena from our society.

The most frightening fast rise of ethnic groups to national independence is one of the great surprises of our century. But so is, too, the astonishing fury of nationalism, reaching its most frightening climax in Fascism.
Not to distinguish between the two is sheer ignorance, confusing causes
and effects. The two phenomena (striving for independence on the one
hand, and Fascism on the other) are in fact as different as fire and water.
One sharply excludes the other, they are enemies of each other. Yet, surprisingly, intellectuals, of all people, had a hard time understanding the
distinction between the two. In this respect, Hungary is a case in point.
For years, it had been public policy to defend the thesis that oppression
of people's drive for freedom may serve progress towards freedom. An
uproar of national proportions finally stopped this risky nonsense. The
view of those blind to the sufferings of the oppressed was ejected from
Hungarian intellectual life. I have played some part in this process.

When it sounded almost like a stigma, I had been spoken of as the
last *national* poet. Why? Because consistently—and true to a tradition—
I have stressed the human rights of *all* people. Thus did I, rightly, I guess,
come to the realization that, perhaps, I may very well be my country's
first *international* lyricist after all. Of the kind, that is, who believes that
one's own nation, too, is entitled to rights, no matter whence the winds
blow and no matter who are the nations sitting in judgment over us. I
am bound to this tradition, both classical and modern, of our literature,
whose neon lights to the world are the names of Petőfi and Ady.

Our resurrected intellectual life today is rooted in the world of our
peasants and workers—our "two-handed" laborers, as our Hungarian
phrase would call them. The feet of our reborn life are planted in the
world of reality. Yet its stand, and its ability to withstand trials, does
not depend on itself alone. Its strength may give cause for worry to the
extent that strength in every historical situation is measured by the force
of the "challenge." Hungarian intellectual life—the national consciousness, that is, of the people laboring with their hands and minds—is fated
to be tied to the intellectual lives of its neighbors, to the "impacts" orig-
inating from there.

Dr. Janics's book, "The Homeless Years," does not give rise to instant
hopes. He is reporting a catastrophe one wishes no one should be stricken

by, not even those who caused it, and exploited it. Yet the author lifts his eyes towards the future. His book extends a hand. For a hard handshake, a manly one. It proposes friendship by its very honesty.

This book is the fruit of enormous labor. For our own Hungarian intellectual life, Kálmán Janics has produced a pioneering work. May similar situation reports spring up from all lands under oppression whose mother tongue is Hungarian! To inform the world—and to arouse its conscience.

INTRODUCTION

THE ACCUSED SPEAKS

The flow of human history is determined by much larger units of people than fragments of a nation. We are not used to reading monographs on the history of such fragments in the larger context of human events. But there are exceptional cases, when a historical drama with relatively narrow geographical limits produces explosive decisions which, in turn, give rise to human problems whose impact is felt far beyond the limits of time and space and their occurrence.

At the conclusion of the Second World War, the dramatic events that shook the Hungarian national minority in Czechoslovakia, if properly understood, are of such historical significance. That minority's right to very existence was being questioned. Over a half a million people fell victims to a historical conjuncture in which international law itself condemned national minorities to extinction in the alleged interest of domestic peace and international order. A small group of people of a small land of no particular importance in Central Europe—the Hungarian minority of Slovakia—was condemned to the same fate as the large German minority of Bohemia. The Czechoslovak policy of expelling the Hungarian minority has ultimately failed. Yet the struggle for their liquidation lasted for four years, leaving human ruins behind, the traumatic memories of four lawless, homeless years.

This four-year crisis and its vicissitudes were explained in many ways. But the basic question: the attempt to readicate an ethnic group, is mentioned only superficially. In postwar historiography in general, the fate of the Hungarian minority in Czechoslovakia is barely touched, if at all. Moreover, although the scene of events since the Second World War is within the Soivet orbit of power, an analysis according to the Marxist interpretation of class struggle is entirely missing. What is available are

28

largely subjective and extremely nationalistic explanations pieced together from distorted fragments of documentation. Surely, after three decades, the time has come to rectify the most crying mistakes, and to reject or correct the most exaggerated accusations levelled against the Hungarian minority of Czechoslovakia.

Some of the archival material is still inaccessible. But the contemporary press, the published documents and some historical works, and—last but not least—the eye-witness reports of survivors may offer a fairly faithful account of what has actually happened. Also, some of the missing links in this case can easily be filled in from the broader context of known facts.

In the aftermath of the Second World War, the Hungarian minority in Slovakia was shocked to learn that in order to ensure the future security of the Czechoslovak state, the Slav *ethnic* boundaries would have to be extended to the *political* boundaries of the state—in other words, that the non-Slav Hungarian population, living mostly along Slovakia's southern borders, would have to be expelled from Czechoslovakia.

Two favorable circumstances accounted for the Czechoslovak policy to liquidate the Hungarian minority. One was the unprecedented triumph of the Slav nations in World War II. The other, the wartime plans supported by spurious moral theories of the exiles, making the new migration of nations through expulsion of national minorities into a politically and morally acceptable principle of postwar international law. This new *raison d'état* conceived by Edvard Beneš, President-in-exile of Czechoslovakia, originally designed during the war against the large German minority of Czechoslovakia, has been extended after the war against the small Hungarian minority as well. The Hungarian extension did not work automatically on the international level. Nevertheless, after the war, Czechoslovak policy declared the Hungarian minority collectively guilty against the state and launched a massive campaign for its liquidation. The policy failed to win the hoped for approval. It was not endorsed by all the Great Powers, neither during the Nuremberg Trial of war criminals, nor by the Paris Peace Conference of 1946. Yet the anti-Hungarian campaign was effective enough to create inside Czechoslovakia an atmosphere of unprecedented hostility against the Hungarians—not only for the four years of lawlessness from 1945 through 1948, but for decades thereafter, in the form of rigid anti-Hungarian nationalist ideology, still pressing for uncritical recognition.

To counter these deplorable effects of Czechoslovak policy against the Hungarian minority, new ways must be found for a reexamination of the totalitarian theory of collective national guilt. First of all, it is necessary to prove that the anti-Hungarian atmosphere in Slovakia after the Second World War was not, as claimed, a revolutionary mass movement—not even a part of the postwar national revolution—but, rather, a nationalistic doctrine imposed from above on a national and democratic revolutionary situation. This way, it was made into a mass movement, turned into a seemingly organic part of "anti-Fascism," the all-powerful, sweeping nationalist program of the postwar era.

It should be noted that the press of the victorious Great Powers, too, both during and after the Second World War, readily aroused world public opinion against the national minorities. Reiterating as it did relentlessly the thesis, authored by President Beneš, that the war had been caused by the national minorities, the world press popularized the idea that the minorities must either be promptly liquidated by expulsion or left to their destiny and assimilated by the majority, with no protection of their minority rights as nationalities.

Slav nations, victors of the Second World War—who themselves had been national minorities before the First World War, who themselves fought for their liberty, in some cases for centuries, Poles, Czechs, Slovaks, Croatians—have unleashed a furious campaign against all national minorities. Most of them, Slavs and others, ganged up against the Hungarians. Thus, while peacemaking after the *First* World War had endorsed the idea that the national minorities should be liberated, the new order after the *Second* World War has been installed in an atmosphere of utmost hostility against the national minorities.

At the beginning, the postwar measures aimed at the liquidation of the Hungarians of Slovakia appeared to be realistic. The general anti-minority international atmosphere seemed to support the Czechoslovak policy against the Hungarian minority as well. Such a policy contradicted in a frightening manner the earlier Central European traditions of peaceful coexistence among the Danubian nationalities. But this was not the reason why it failed. Why the Czechoslovak policy for the total liquidation of the Hungarian minority had finally ended in failure was due to the fact that it could not enlist the unanimous support of the Great Powers—and, to no small extent, also due to pure chance.

During the four-year crisis, the Hungarian minority itself, accused of gruesome crimes with no foundation in reality, was a passive, helpless mass, shorn of all rights of protest, deprived of all means of self-defense. The collective voice of the people was silenced—not even the voice of individuals was allowed to be heard. Zoltán Fábry, a respected Hungarian Communist writer in Czechoslovakia, wrote an appeal in defense of the Hungarian minority, entitled "The Accused Speaks Out." The Czecho-slovak Writers' Union to which he addressed his appeal did not bother even to acknowledge its receipt. Such was the state of nothingness into which the once lively political body known as the Hungarian national minority had been reduced to in Czechoslovakia.[1]

Now that the accused looks back from a distance of three decades, he wishes to say everything that may help to extricate the truth from the fossilized mass of false accusations. In his search for truth, he invites friend and foe to face the facts—fully aware that myths may still block the road to truth which is full of obstacles under any circumstances.

CHAPTER 1

THE ACCUSED AND THE ACCUSER

As the Second World War was drawing to a close, Hungarian public opinion was imbued by an altogether mistaken notion about the future of Hungary's northern boundaries drawn by the Vienna Award of 1938. Since Tiso's Slovakia too, not unlike Hungary, was an ally of Hitler, the overwhelming majority of Hungarians believed that the Slovaks will be in no position to raise revisionist claims against the boundaries of the Vienna Award.

This mistaken simplification followed logically from the general misconception with which the Hungarians have viewed the course of the war. There was hardly anybody in Hungary who fully comprehended the background of Allied wartime diplomatic accords. In particular, Hungarian public opinion did not realize that, following the Soviet recognition of Czechoslovakia's prewar boundaries, everything that happened in Slovakia since the summer of 1941 (when Hitler invaded Russia), would be treated merely as misdeeds of a small clique of traitors who usurped power in that part of Czechoslovakia. Thus, the accomplished facts of wartime diplomacy came as a surprise not merely to the Hungarian ruling class, but to the uninformed and optimistic Hungarian public in general, to the intellectuals no less than to the peasants, and to the overwhelming majority of the workers as well. The renewed loss of the recently "repossessed" territories in fact became no less a shock after the Second World War than the dismemberment of Hungary has been after the First World War.

The mass of charges collected by the Hungarians against Slovak Fascism, and thought to become effective when the war ends, proved to be, of course, totally ineffective. The internationally recognized principle of Czechoslovakia's legal continuity absolved the Slovaks as a nation of any guilt for its Fascist crimes. The Hungarians of Southern Slovakia, returned after the war under Czechoslovak rule, learned to their surprise that Slovakia, since the summer of 1941, according to international law, existed only as a geographical term. Slovakia was treated as a territory under German yoke no less than the lands of the Czech Protectorate, consequently the Allies saw no cause even to declare war against the Slovak State of Tiso.

The wartime notion entertained by the majority of Hungarians of Southern Slovakia was that Slovak and Hungarian Fascism were identical phenomena. Or, if they were not exactly the same, as Fascist systems they shared equal responsibilities for their Fascist crimes. Furthermore, as the Hungarians saw it: Slovakia was Hitler's first satellite, having taken part, unlike Hungary, already in the war against Poland. Also, the Slovaks had preceded Hungary in racial persecution of the Jews. And in general, in repressing democratic freedoms, Slovakia's record certainly was worse than that of Hungary's. Naive as these views have turned out to be, the Hungarians seemed to forget one of the basic lessons of history: Losers cannot argue against victors, let alone against the interests of Great Powers and the accomplished facts of diplomacy.

Credit for achieving international recognition of the principle of Czechoslovakia's legal continuity goes to Edvard Beneš. Already in the early stages of the war, through international agreements and treaties, Beneš has succeeded in safeguarding the fundamental interests of the Czechoslovak State as he saw them fit. The significance of these accomplishments is not diminished by the fact that subsequent events—above all the Slovak national uprising of 1944—swept away the concept of a unitary "Czechoslovak nation," so dear to Beneš's centralist thinking.

During the war, anti-Fascism was Beneš's ideological platform upon which he built his theories of Czechoslovakia's legal restoration. However, with the war over, Beneš shifted his ideological emphasis from anti-Fascism to the principle of a homogeneous Slav nation-state free of national minorities. To justify the liquidation of minorities, he stressed the ideology of national self-defense. He declared in fact the homogeneous nation-state a prime necessity of national self-defense. In addition, the expulsion of national minorities from Czechoslovakia was declared a just punishment for their "mass betrayal" of the Czechoslovak State. The principles of this extreme nationalist ideology were laid down in the Government program of Košice in 1945.

The principle of "just self-defense," of course, is nothing new. Nor are the excesses that spring from a willful expansion of this principle. It is a

flimsy principle. For what passes for just self-defense at one time is rejected as such at another time. Also, history abounds in examples of how bel-
licosity in the pursuit of security leads to loss of self-control. Thus, already
the Romans "had fought in self-defense until they gradually forced the
entire then known world under their yoke."[1] Countless wars had been
fought in rightful self-defense through the ages. In our time, Nazism too
has made use of this dubious principle, when it claimed that "anti-Semitism was purely a defensive movement."[2] Where are then the limits of
rightful self-defense? Apologies for the policies of the Slovak Fascist
State vividly demonstrate the inherent dangers of this slippery principle.
For instance, we are told that anti-Semitism in Tiso's Slovakia, too, was
initially a defensive measure: "In the beginning not every anti-Semitic
measure was justified by biological or racial arguments but, rather, they
were termed measures serving the protection of the Slovak nation."[3]

Following the defeat of Slovak Fascism, anti-Semitic passions in Slovakia were turned into hatred against the Hungarians. This could be done
all the more easily since the events of 1938 (the loss of territories to Hungary) had left strong anti-Hungarian resentments behind in Slovakia. It
should be noted, however, that the post-1945 anti-Hungarian campaign,
in which the Hungarians took the place of the Jews as targets of public
hatred, was not spontaneous. It was the result of a massive manipulation
from above, it was an integral part of an ultra-nationalistic hate propaganda. It was built around the slogan of the Hungarians' collective "Fascist" guilt and was conducted in a spirit of absolute self-righteousness to
serve Slovak national interests.

The Hungarian minority was declared collectively guilty on the grounds
of betraying the Czechoslovak State in 1938. In order to justify this
charge against the Hungarians, the prewar treatment of minorities in
Czechoslovakia was described in glowing terms and considerably embel-
lished. It is true that the minority policy of Czechoslovakia was far more
democratic than those of Hungary, Rumania, Poland or Yugoslavia. Yet,
the Hungarian minority in Czechoslovakia could never feel entirely free
of discrimination. It was primarily in the economic field that the status
of second-class citizenship has been felt at every step. This was admitted
even by those so-called "activist" minority politicians who supported the
Republic and defended it against hostile attacks from both inside and
outside. For instance, in Piešt'any, on September 7, 1936, István Csomor,

a Hungarian member of the Czechoslovak Agrarian Party, presented Prime Minister Milan Hodža a memorandum detailing the grievances of the Hungarian minority. It read in part:

> We have wounds and we are waiting for the curing balm. Grievances have accumulated and these have to be redressed. The Hungarian minority has a new home, but that home has no roof yet. A lot remains to be done for the benefit of the Hungarian minority. . . . Let's see to it that every Hungarian of Czechoslovakia feels at home in his new homeland, that they are free citizens of a free state, the Republic of Czechoslovakia. We have put into writing the grievances of the Hungarian minority, its cultural and economic demands. We request that these be given serious consideration. Listen to the words and fulfill our wishes.[4]

However, during the Second World War, and even more so after 1945, including at the peace conference, the principal charge against the Hungarian minoritys was it's lack of appreciation of its privileges. It was said that, despite *complete* equality in the bourgeois republic, they almost unanimously betrayed the common fatherland during its crisis in 1938.

The political climate in the aftermath of war was unfavorable to revealing the facts about the prewar minority situation. And ever since, Slovak historiography has failed to evaluate the facts with professional objectivity. On the other hand, several works of progressive Hungarians have pointed out the homeless feelings in prewar Czechoslovakia. For instance, Edgár Balogh, a well-known Hungarian Communist in interwar Czechoslovakia, now living in Transylvania, wrote: "The crux of the problem was that this state [Czechoslovakia] was unable to become our fatherland."[5] " . . . we were facing chauvinistic ambitions of the same kind with which, in former times, the Hungarian imperialists have persecuted their minorities."[6] Imre Forbáth, another Hungarian Communist writer of the same background, bids goodbye to Czechoslovakia with the same bitter sincerity:

> Even the minority policy of a most democratic bourgeois system [such as prewar Czechoslovakia's] is not free of the ruling class ambition to maintain the hegemony of the ruling nation, to hide the social antagonism of classes behind artificially nurtured racial,

national, and other conflicts. The tragic disintegration of the Czechoslovak Republic—albeit its principal cause was certainly the attack of
Fascism and the surrender of the bourgeoisie—was also the consequence of its minority policies. . . . After decades of neglect, not
even in the moment of extreme danger, could a greedy and short-
sighted ruling clique bring itself to correcting the situation by a rapid
and earnest reform. Thus, not even honest effort of the best people
was able to save the fatherland from the consequences of a mass of
crimes. . . . In the decisive moment, the large majority of Czechoslovakia's minorities had left the country in the lurch.[7]

It is almost impossible to unravel the true historical forces affecting
events of almost four decades ago, to describe and evaluate, according to
its true value, the will of the masses. The perception of events of the past
have been distorted above all by nationalist prejudices. Hence, in all our
search for the truth, we must arm ourselves not only with scientific arguments supported by information from reliable sources, but also with
memories of contemporaries and eyewitnesses.

In the twenty years of the Czechoslovak bourgeois republic, it was plain
for everyone to see that one of the most important foreign policy objectives of the post-First World War era was the isolation of Hungary. Political
thinking was determined by the anti-Hungarian ideology of the Little
Entente. The postwar German danger was discovered only when Hitler
began to threaten the Republic. But a change of policy toward Hungary
was still not being considered, although well before Munich an English
friend of Czechoslovakia had warned: "It was rumored since the end of
1936 that a German attack was imminent against Czechoslovakia. An improvement of the Hungarian minority's situation is highly desirable, either
on the basis of satisfying Hungarian demands, or simply for the sake of
justice. If the Czechoslovak government were farsighted, it would not try
to extract a high price for the fulfillment of such concessions."[8]

R. W. Seton-Watson (alias Scotus Viator) has actually noticed already
in the aftermath of the First World War that not everything was right with
the "solution" of the Hungarian question. He was astounded by the nationalist land-reform Hungary's rival neighbors have carried out on Hungarian ethnic territories at the expense of the Hungarian populations.[9]
Indeed, many things were not right as far as Czechoslovakia's Hungarians

were concerned. Hence there was enough cause for bitter feelings in 1938. Who could anybody expect the Hungarian minority to forget its national grievances and adjust its feelings to the anti-Fascist interests of the European balance of power?

The pro-Czechoslovak stand taken by the Hungarian anti-Fascist left in 1938 could hardly have affected the sentiments of the Hungarian minoirty as a whole. The leftists could stage a few successful demonstrations. But the leftists themselves, in particular the Communists, were in disarray in 1938, not to speak of the many disappointments that weakened their influence already well before 1938 among the masses. We cannot place the blame for the lack of an anti-Fascist mood on the Hungarian masses alone, or on their leaders. Above all, the Czechoslovak regime's ruling classes, their narrow-minded, anachronistic nationality policy are to be blamed.

No wonder that, in spite of the not particularly attractive traits of the Horthy regime, South Slovakia's Hungarian population was in favor of return to Hungary. This mood was noticeable already at the time of the communal elections in May 1938. By late summer, and certainly by early fall, open irredentism became quite obvious. Moreover, Sándor Balogh rightly summed up the "choices" when he wrote in retrospect: At that time [in 1938], the Hungarian national minority in Czechoslovakia could no longer choose between the bourgeois democratic Czechoslovakia and the Fascist Horthy regime in Hungary, but only between an autonomous Slovakia under the totalitarian Fascist regime of Tiso, and the Hungary of Horthy."[10]

It is hypocritical to ask: why didn't the overwhelming majority of the Hungarian minority in Czechoslovakia demonstrate its patriotic loyalty to the Republic during the crisis of 1938? Everybody knows that such a patriotism did not exist and could not have existed. The ruling class of the ruling nation itself did not want it to exist.

No less hypocritical was the charge of betrayal. For where there is no genuine loyalty there can be no real betrayal either. The Czechoslovak majority itself was not sure how to sort out the so-called traitors. In the first years after the war, the national minorities as a whole were charged with treason. After 1948 for a while, under Communist rule, a certain measure of Marxist objectivity has been practiced by judging individual cases from a class point of view. However, after the mid-1960s, a relapse into nationalist prejudices has gained ground again, and, in the 1970s, Slovak historiography returned all the way to the indiscriminately biased points of view of 1945, with Samuel Cambel's work on the postwar agrarian question in Slovakia in the lead.[11]

Paradoxically, right after the war, occasionally the historical truth came to light more sharply on certain occasions than in the works of Slovak historians. For instance, General Bohuslav Ečer, head of the Czechoslovak delegation to the Nuremberg trials truthfully admitted: "In our country the role of the fifth column was played by the Sudeten Germans and Tiso's [Slovak] L'udáks."[12] In the judicial commentary on Tiso's death sentence, too, a listing of real forces that contributed to the destruction of the Republic, no mention was made of the Hungarians: "The cause of the destruction of the Czechoslovak Republic was not its incapacity to defend itself, but inner political disintegration precipitated by the [Slovak] Hlinka party and its cooperation with the Germans."[13] Also, Igor Daxer, president of the National Court of Bratislava, has termed the Hlinka party's cooperation with the Sudeten Germans as crucial in Czechoslovakia's destruction. He wrote in his memoirs: "The first step was taken by the lifetime leader of the People's Party, Ondrej Hlinka, on February 8, 1938, at Ružomberok, a month before the [Austrian] *Anschluss,* when he reached an agreement with K. H. Frank, Kundt, and Karmasin—representatives of Konrad Henlein—on all essential aspects of the struggle for autonomy . . . .[14]

However, as time went on, the destructive role of the Hlinka party came to be described in an ever more muted tone in the works of Slovak historians.

In the course of the postwar anti-Hungarian hate campaign much was said about the destructive anti-State activities of János Esterházy, political leader of the Hungarian minority. Listed among his crimes was his "siding" with the struggle for Slovak autonomy in cooperation with the Sudeten Germans. Curiously, the autonomist Hlinka Party's struggle, and its collaboration with the Germans, is no more regarded as too much of a crime by Slovak historiography; nor is it remembered that, in addition to the Hungarian and Sudeten German political leadership, a Slav family member, the Ukrainian Pieščák, too, was "siding" with the Slovak autonomists.[15]

In particular, Esterházy's meeting with Henlein's lieutenant, K. H. Frank, in the summer of 1938, has been treated since 1945 as a capital

Hungarian crime.[16] Frank, appointed Bohemia's Reich Protector by Hitler in 1942, following the Heydrich assassination, came to be known as "the executioner" of the Czech nation. On the ground of Esterházy's single meeting with Frank four years *before* Frank's appointment as Bohemia's Reich Protector, the postwar hate campaign declared the Hungarian minority collectively guilty of complicity in the Lidice and Ležáky mass murders organized by Frank! This absurd charge against the Hungarian minority was brought up even at the Paris peace conference in 1946.[17]

The identification of Hungarians with the Fascist mentality was not limited to the Hungarian minority of Southern Slovakia. The postwar anti-Hungarain propaganda in Czechoslovakia denounced the entire Hungarian nation as the outstanding European representative of Fascist anti-Semitism and national oppression. An image has thus been created of the Hungarians as inferior people. And to top national humiliation: Communist-sponsored so-called "national self-criticism" in postwar Hungary encouraged views similar to those of the Czechoslovak anti-Hungarian propaganda.

This was the postwar state of official opinion propagated in the Danube region in matters pertaining to the Hungarians. In closed scientific circles, however, the truth has slowly been brought to light even in Czechoslovakia. For instance, at a scientific conference on prewar minorities, held in 1974, the Czech Jozef Kolejka no longer placed the Hungarians in the forefront of anti-Semitism and national oppression. In his words: "The Jews were exposed to repression to varying degrees, most strongly in Poland and Rumania, somewhat less in Czechoslovakia and Hungary.... National oppression was most pronounced in Rumania and Poland."[18]

To set the record straight as to the policy of the Hungarian United Party in prewar Czechoslovakia (of which János Esterházy was one of the leaders): before Munich, in 1938, the Hungarian political leadership in Czechoslovakia had no clear idea of the future. They were hesitant of cooperation with the Sudeten Germans. For instance, Kunzel, a Sudeten German member of the Czechoslovak Parliament, expressed his concern over the lack of cooperation with the Hungarian minority. In an interview with István Bethlen, the well-known Hungarian statesman, Kunzel expressed the wish of the Sudeten German leadership that "pressure should be exerted from Hungary on the leaders of the Hungarian minority in Czechoslovakia, in order to encourage cooperation with the Sudeten Germans in joint actions against the Czechoslovak state ideology."[19] In the 1930s, during the appeasement period, Hungarian anti-state activism in Czechoslovakia was launched hesitatingly, and did not become a mass movement until September 1938.

As for the Slovaks of Czechoslovakia, the situation was quite different. The truth comes to light even from published Slovak sources. The conservative Slovak bourgeois movement lead by Ondrej Hlinka following World War I grew step by step into a Fascist movement. It adjusted itself readily to the Hitler era in the appeasement of the 1930s. Yet, even observers with some sense of objectivity are ready to blame the "irredentist minorities" for the Hlinka Party's total "fascization." Thus, we read in a postwar analysis of the Slovak antonomist movement by L. Lipscher: "In the spring of 1938, the process of fascization developed into a nationalist aggressivity through steady cooperation with the irredentist minorities."[20]

Slovak historical writers (Cambel, Vietor, Purgat, and others) treat the political party of the Hungarian minority simply as a Fascist party; they have to, in order to justify the postwar anti-Hungarian reprisals. But there are a few exceptions to this willful interpretation. According to L. Lipscher: "The truth regarding the times of the first Republic is that the only representative of Fascist movement in Slovakia would be the Hlinka Party . . . ."[21] Lipscher dates the Fascist orientation of Hlinka's Slovak People's Party from 1936, the date of the Party congress at Piešt'any. According to Lipscher, Hlinka's party became "Fascist" in 1936 because it accepted the totalitarian principles of "one nation, one party, one leader." One may add to Lipscher's story of "fascization" that anti-Semitic propaganda appeared regularly in the Slovák, the Hlinka party's daily, since the 1930s.

The impact of Munich completed the fascization of the Slovak People's Party. A week after Munich, a decisive step was the fusion of all Slovak political parties carried out by the Žilina agreement of October 6, 1938. This marked the end of the quite significant role the Czechoslovak Social Democratic and Agrarian parties had played for twenty years in Slovakia. The new united Slovak political leadership ignored the draft-constitution of post-Munich hyphenated Czecho-Slovakia, a work of the Agrarian and Social Democratic parties, although the draft endorsed the program of the Slovak autnomists. Published after the war by Ivan Dérer, a Slovak

Social Democrat, the draft-constitution's leading principle, revising the relationship between Czechs and Slovaks, was the consolidation of Slovak autonomy.[22] On the other hand, the draft took no notice of Slovakia's Hungarian minority, because it took for granted that Slovakia will loose the Hungarian inhabited southern borderlands. Or was the omission perhaps a premature first step toward the postwar concept of a homogeneous Slovak nation-state with no Hungarian minority? Certainly, after the Second World War, the Socialist-Nationalist Ivan Dérer became one of the most determined spokesman for southern Slovakia's "de-Magyarization."

The United Hungarian Party (as the bourgeois-conservative nationalist party of the Hungarian minority was called since 1936) is described by Slovak historians as a "separatist irredentist" party. This is a label arrived at by *a posteriori* oversimplification. Even though by 1938, the party did have separatist aspirations, and Hungarian revisionist propaganda always had an impact on the Hungarian minorities, the party had its own legally approved program, and was functioning accordingly. Anyway, there was no realism in irredentism before 1938, and the Hungarian political leadership knew it. Irredentist movements would have been promptly liquidated by the Czechoslovak authorities—the well-known Tuka incident of 1929 is a case in point.

Certainly, indulging as it did, in politics of grievances against Czechoslovakia, the Hungarian party never developed a positive ideology. Its press, while never criticizing the Horthy regime, openly sided in times of international conflicts with Hungary. The assertion, however, that the Hungarian party's press in Czechoslovakia propagated "Fascist" ideas between the two wars in simply not true. Published in Prague, the party's daily, *Prágai Magyar Hirlap,* openly criticized, in fact, the Nazi ideology. Several of its staff members were of Jewish extraction and never, since its founding in 1925, did the paper publish any anti-Semitic pronouncements. After the Vienna Award in 1938, the paper moved to Budapest and was renamed *Felvidéki Magyar Hirlap* ("Felvidék"-Highlands—being the ancient name of Hungary's northern provinces). And, during a press debate on the Jewish question, the paper declared in an editorial statement: "From 1925 all the way to 1938, the year of return [to Hungary], we have consistently avoided any tone which might have hurt the sensitivity of Jews who remained faithful to us [to the Hungarian minority, that is]."[23]

In 1938, the Hungarian party had realized that, while it had voters (by then it had won the support of 80 percent of the Hungarian voters), nevertheless, the party was no mass organization and hence not suitable for the kind of activities the Sudeten German party led by Henlein came to be engaged in. Consequently, no significant, irredentist demonstration had ever taken place in Slovakia's Hungarian populated regions. This was noticed by both the Budapest Government and the Sudeten German Party, whose representative, Kunzel, had this to report to the German Foreign Office in Berlin on his interview with Kálmán Darányi, the Hungarian Premier, in the spring of 1938: ". . . it is necessary to built up the real political strength of the Hungarain minority of Czechoslovakia, as well as its own economic organization. For that purpose, Darányi requested that we should help the Hungarian minority with out advice and actions. . . ."[24] Indeed, in the spring of 1938, the Hungarian Party's capacity for action was limited to politics as usual; it was not fit, either morally or organizationally, for the provocation of incidents, let alone terrorist acts on the Sudeten German model.[25]

Following the Vienna Award of November 2, 1938, about 70,000 Hungarians remained in Slovakia, while an estimated 300,000 Slovaks were attached to Hungary along with 700,000 Hungarians. Of the Slovaks, about 50,000 had left voluntarily. Of the remaining 250,000, according to the Hungarian census of December 1938, only 121,000 declared themselves as Slovaks. The difference of about 130,000 can be explained by the flexible attitude of the so-called "bilinguals"—mainly inhabitants of towns—who spoke Hungarian and Slovak equally well.

The political evolution of the Hungarians who returned to Horthy's Hungary differed, of course, from that of the minority Hungarians who remained in Tiso's Slovakia. The population reattached to Hungary became the target of various Hungarian political parties; the workers movement was liquidated; disaffection of the masses was exploited by extreme right-wing movements with a varying degree of success. In Tiso's Slovakia, on the other hand, the Hungarian Party had to organize itself for self-defense. It was a party in opposition, often voicing openly anti-Fascist opinions.

Wholesale racial persecution started in Tiso's Slovakia already in 1942. That year, at Slovak initiative, 65,000 Jews were handed over to the Germans. The Slovak historian, Daxner, describes the situation as follows:

"The whole persecution was carried out, until May 18, 1942, without any legal grounds. The Fascist elements, however, wanted to equip their action with the semblance of legality. Therefore they adopted the constitutional law 68/1942 which legalized the deportation of persons of Jewish extraction into death camps."[26]

A memorable episode involving the Hungarian minority had occurred on the occasion of the adoption of the law regarding the deportation of Jews. A Slovak eyewitness, Ivan Kamenec, described the episode as follows: "The Slovak National Assembly voted by acclamation, by show of hands. It was easy to note that the only representative who did not raise his hand was the representative of the Hungarian National Party, János Esterházy. Consequently, he came instantly under the attack of the [German] *Grenzbote* and the [Slovak] *Gardista* as well."[27] Kamenec added, however, that in the preceding years Esterházy had made anti-Semitic statements in the Slovak Parliament, "approving the isolation of Jews and the discrimination against them."[28] Kamenec's effort to incriminate Esterházy does not alter the fact that the only member of the Slovak Fascist National Assembly condemned to death after the war was the Hungarian Esterházy, who alone voted against the deportation of Jews.[29]

Esterházy's vote duly expressed the Hungarian public opinion against Slovakia's total barbarization. The temper of the Hungarian minority had turned against the Fascist regime, a trend so well expressed by the well-known Hungarian anti-Fascist, Zoltán Fábry, in his postwar dramatic appeal quoted in our Introduction.[30] Other documents and facts, too, which have come to light only recently are proofs of the Hungarian minority's anti-fascist attitude. Foremost among these is a situation report of the Central Committee of the illegal Slovak Communist Party, carried to Moscow in July 1944, by K. Šmidke. This report convincingly contradicts the postwar theories regarding the "Fascist" Hungarian nation. It says: "It can be said that the Hungarians, unlike the Germans, behaved decently in Slovakia, the majority of them were democratic, and many among them of left-wing tendency . . .in general it can be said that, with the exception of the Germans, all national minorities are against the regime."[31]

Incidentally, the text of the July 1944 Communist report had been known to Slovak historians for a quarter of a century. Yet is was published only in 1969. It had to be suppressed because it did not fit into the justification of the anti-Hungarian article VIII of the Košice program of 1945.

To understand the objective tone of the Communist report, it should be kept in mind that, in July 1944, the mode of "solving" the Hungarian problem had not yet been synchronized between the illegal Communist Party at home and the Moscow emigration led by Klement Gottwald. (The story of synchronization will be told in Chapter 3.) At that time, the Communists at home could still report objectively on the democratic attitudes of the Hungarians. They did not know that the emigrés in Moscow, in agreement with the Beneš-led exiles in London, decided to brand the Hungarians collectively guilty as "Fascists" and solve the Hungarian minority problem by total expulsion.

The tone of postwar nationalist Slovak historiography condemning the Hungarians is pregnant with hatred and prejudice. For instance, this is how historian M. Vietor describes the attitude of the Hungarians at the time of the deportation of German-occupied Hungary's Jews in 1944: ". . . they looked on apathetically and without feeling while the gendarmes and the SS carried out their bloodthirsty doings. The servility inculcated during centuries by means of the whip, twenty years of official anti-Semitic propaganda, the Hungarist official nationalism and anti-Bolshevism had blinded the overwhelming majority of the population, while it drove large strata of the ruling circles and exploiters into a hysterical, irresponsible, cruel, immoral, and cowardly rage."[32]

Should we remind Vietor that in Slovakia, in 1942, the roundup of Jews for deportation to the Nazi death camps was carried out by the Slovaks themselves, and—unlike in German-occupied Hungary in 1944—without the presence or assistance of the German SS, yet the Slovak population made no attempt to save the Jews? According to Vietor's distorted "comparative analysis": In Slovakia it was only the ruling minority that was Fascist. But in Hungary—and in the community of Slovakia's Hungarian minority as well—the society as a whole was Fascist. Also, Vietor emphasizes the "Czechoslovak traditions" and the "strength of the Communists" in Slovakia.[33] But he takes no notice of the fact that the Hungarians of South Slovakia, too, lived, until 1938, under Czechoslovak democracy and gave twice as many votes for the Czechoslovak Communist Party as the people in the Slovak regions.[34]

More will be said about Hungarian Fascism in a later analysis of Hungarian conditions. Here it should be pointed out only that the Fascsist

"seizure of power" in October 1944—a favorite evidence in Slovak denunciations of Hungary as a "Fascist nation"—is no proof of Fascist
strength. The Fascist Arrow Cross movement was actually in total disarray in Hungary toward the end of the war. Whatever mass appeal Fascism
ever had in Hungary, it rapidly declined after the German defeat at Stalingrad. Rather than "seizing" power in 1944, the Arrow Cross "leader"
Ferenc Szálasi was a Nazi puppet, maintained in "power" by the German
armed forces in Nazi-occupied Hungary.

In contrast to the biased nationalist Slovak interpretation, there are a
few scattered objective opinions from other sources dealing with the history of the Hungarian minority in Czechoslovakia before and during the
Second World War. For instance, the Czech historian R. Hoffman argues
forcefully against the theory of a Hungarian "Fascist nation." In his opinion: "Except for the most extreme periods of the Horthy era (in 1919-
1920 and 1944-1945), the advocates of a totalitarian Fascist system
never obtained key posts in Hungarian political life. And, with the exception of the radicalized petit-bourgeoisie, the Fascists were unable to
find a mass basis either among the workers, or among the peasants."[35]

Indeed, the Slovak view of seeing the Hungarians as a "Fascist nation"
does not fit the facts. Here is an oft-quoted example which proves the
very opposite of what the haughty Slovak theory, spreading contempt
of the Hungarians, is advocating: The Slovak daily, *Slovenská Jednota,*
published in Hungary during the war, was a much sought after parper
in Slovakia during the war. It was called the "free-est Slovak paper of the
times, the one in which it was easiest to read between the lines."[36] This
is not an isolated opinion. In a collection of documents, edited by the
Slovak historian V. Prečan, a letter dealing with the life of Slovaks in Hungary says: ". . .*Slovenská Jednota* is the most widely read paper in Slovakia, because it provides information with greater freedom and flexibil-
ity on politics and on the war."[37] According to another opinion: ". . . the
Slovak readers considered the Slovak daily of [the Slovak minority in]
Hungary a progressive organ; within limits of course . . . [but] in Hungary
it was possible to write more openly about certain things."[38] The political
significance of this fact was not overlooked by objective observers: "The
Slovenská Jednota cleverly took advantage of the possibilities afforded by
Hungarian constitutionalism, and became the interpreter of anti-Fascist
thought, not only among the Slovak minority of Hungary, but in Slovakia
under the Slovak People's Party rule as well."[39]

The case of the *Slovenská Jednota* is not the only proof that refutes the Slovak theory of the Hungarian "Fascist nation." More recently, Hungarian historians have dealt with several aspects of Hungary's anti-Nazi wartime record. The treatment of Polish refugees and of Allied prisoners of war who found refuge in Hungary is by now a particularly well-researched topic. "National self-criticism" preached by Hungary's Communists (unique of its kind in the postwar Soviet orbit), opposed the publication of such works when they were most needed. But it is still timely to quote some of these Hungarian views in opposition to the Slovak views, because the Slovak theory of the Hungarian "Fascist nation" is still around.

Thus, Ferenc Z. Nagy, writing about the Polish refugees, says: ". . . the force of public opinion was such that [Prime Minister Pál] Teleki was able to maintain the care and decent treatment of the refugees. Nor, after his death, were his successors able to change this policy."[40] Endre Kovács draws the moral implications of this policy out of oblivion: "The number of those who arrived in Hungary amounted to about one hundred thousand . . . . Both the authorities and the population showed warm sympathy towards them. In their camps, under humane supervision, the Poles could carry on the national culture; they had their schools, organizations, newspapers . . . ."[41] It is characteristic of the postwar hate campaign of Slav nations against the Hungarians—in which Beneš's Czechoslovakia took the lead—that after the war the Hungarians have so belatedly been given credit publicly for their friendly treatment of the Polish refugees. Even in Poland, only very recently has the subject been broached (in a book by J. R. Nowak). It should be sadly noted, too, that during the 1946 Paris Peace Conference, victorious Poland supported victorious Czechoslovakia's demands against Hungary, dictated by hateful vengeance.

Hungarian communist regime-historians have inadvertently refuted the hatefully propagated image of Hungarians as a "Fascist nation" while studying the fate of Allied prisoners of war who found refuge in Hungary. Thus, for instance, Zsuzsa Boros, has come to the conclusion that ". . . offical measures taken concerning French prisoners, as well as their treatment in general, was rather humane . . . . Unlike Germany's other allies and in the defeated countries, depite strong Fascist influence, Hungary's political life was not completely *gleichgeschaltet* [streamlined the Nazi way]. Although their freedom of action reduced, the opposition parties, including the Social Democrats, were allowed to function; and, although its freedom curtailed by censorship, the Hungarian press had more than one color."[42]

And, since we are dealing with the Slovak-concocted charges against Hungary as a "Fascist nation," let's remember (as did a Hungarian periodical recently) the difference between Slovakia's and Hungary's attitude the day after the outbreak of the Second World War: " . . . the Hungarian Government sharply rejected a demand Slovakia's vassal Government made, in conjunction with a similar German demand, to allow their troops to cross Hungarian territory against Poland, declaring that any such attemp would be regarded as an aggression."[43]

All this is relevant to the postwar history of the Hungarian minority in Slovakia, because all reprisals against the Hungarians were explicitly taken as a punishment of the Hungarian "Fascist nation" as a whole, not just on the basis of charges of the Hungarian minority's betrayal of Czecho-Slovakia. The Slovaks, on the other hand, in line with a Panslav dogma, were treated a members of the democratic peace-loving Slav family of nations. This was, so to speak, the ideological justification of the double standards in punishing the "Fascist" Hungarians. And what were those "Fascist" crimes committed by the Hungarians?

The foremost Slovak charge is that the Hungarians expelled masses of Slovaks who came under their rule as a result of the Vienna Award in 1938, expropriated their properties, and, in general, cruelly persecuted them in one way or another. The fact of the matter is that, after World War I, many Czechs and Slovaks were given land in the course of the Czechoslovak land reform in Hungarian-populated territories which came to be known as "Southern Slovakia." They were, not unnaturally, regarded as an alien body in a purely Hungarian ethnic territory. After 1938, a good part of the Czech and Slovak settlers left voluntarily. Another part survived undisturbed until the restitution of Czechoslovakia after World War II. Still another part was forced to leave under the threats or direct force. According to Loránt Tilkovszky, the number of families thus removed was altogether 674.[44] Also, former Czechoslovak civil servants were expelled. Their approximate number is not hard to determine. According to the Slovak State Statistical Office, in 1938, before the Hungarian authorities moved in, some 81,000 Czechs *and* Slovaks moved out voluntarily with the support of Czechoslovak authorities, who helped them remove their belongings.[45] It was estimated that 31,000 of the 81,000 were Czechs; thus the number of Slovaks must have been around 50,000. In addition, of the 1088 Slovak teachers working in Southern Slovakia in 1938, only a "small fraction," according to Slovak sources, heeded the order of the Slovak Ministry of Education to stay and to assume the fate of a Slovak minority under Hungarian rule.[46] Thus, the number of those who stayed could not have been more than a few hundred. (Lóránt Tilkovszky's statement that the Hungarian gendarmes "threw 900 Slovak teachers across the borders,"[47] must be termed unreal, since it is hardly possible to expell 900 from a "small fraction" of 1088.) Altogether, therefore, the forcible expulsion of some 1000 Slovak families (settlers and teachers) can be accepted as a historical fact.

Slovak nationalist propaganda and historiography, however, is consistently talking about "several tens of thousands," or (see Vietor), even about a "hundred thousand" of "rudely expelled" Slovaks. As for the manner of expulsion, I was one of the eyewitnesses in Komárno, in October 1938, and I can testify that the Slovak civil servants who feared Hungarian rule left peacefully, in good order, with the help of the authorities, using trucks provided by the state, and bade goodbye to their Hungarian friends and acquaintances.

The anti-Hungarian exaggerations and groundless accusations of some Slovak historians were never corrected, and authors kept quoting the invented stories from one another, such phrases as the "several tens of thousands of expelled," or the "terrible sufferings" under Hungarian rule. At the same time, many facts concerning the Slovak Fascist regime's doings were conveniently forgotten. For instance, nobody mentioned the roughly 120,000 Czechs who were expelled from Slovakia following the proclamation of Slovak independence in March 1939. In 1937, some 161,000 Czechs lived in Slovakia, whereas in 1950 only 40,000 remained.[48] Moreover, the departure of the Czechs from Slovakia did not take place under the most pleasant circumstances. According to historian Daxner: ". . . on March 14, 1939, the Minister of Interior promptly ordered that Czech nationals should be ruthlessly expelled from Slovakia as soon as possible, above all civil servants, while their property should be retained."[49] The Slovak order was no different from the Hungarian action taken against the Czech and Slovak settlers in Southern Slovakia annexed by Hungary in 1938. However, the number of people affected by these measures was far greater in Slovakia than in Hungary; assuredly, also the number of cruelties was greater in Slovakia: "The Hlinka gardists, appointed to carry out the order, arbitrarily and illegally took the money and the valuables of the expelled persons."[50]

After the war, only a few Slovaks were held responsible for the expulsion of the Czechs. On the other hand, the "Hungarian atrocities" in Southern Slovakia, publicized worldwide, have served in the spirit of *vae victis* as justification for the postwar charges of collective guilt levelled against the Hungarian minority in restored Czechoslovakia. Hungarian ruthlessness thus has been exaggerated out of proportion, while the 120,000 Czech victims at the hands of the Hlinka gardists were simply left unmentioned. Forgotten, too, were the words of Vladimir Clementis, condemning in his wartime broadcasts from London the Hlinka gardists' actions: "In morbid perversion, they threw themselves on the members of our brother nation [the Czechs] without whom the Slovaks would never have freed themselves from the Hungarian yoke [after World War I]"[51]

To sum up: The Hungarian minority in postwar Czechoslovakia was accused and found collectively guilty on two counts: 1. The Hungarians were guilty because they were members of the "Fascist" Hungarian nation. 2. The Hungarians were guilty because they "betrayed" Czechoslovakia. The aim of the Slovak accuser was to punish the Hungarians by liquidating them. Czechoslovak policy against the Hungarian minority was in accordance with the postwar aims of making Czechoslovakia into a purely Slav state of the Czechs and Slovaks.

Contemporary Slovak historiography approves the nationalist objectives of Czechoslovak policy against the minorities. In the 1960s, at the time of the "thaw" that led to the "Prague Spring" of 1968, some authors (Jablonicky, Zvara, Purgat) did raise some objections against certain "bourgeois nationalist" excesses. Discrimination against the Hungarian minority has thus been treated as a brainchild of the "bourgeois-nationalist" Beneš and his collaborators. It was taken for granted that in 1948, with the dictatorship of the proletariat, both Beneš and the policy of discrimination was swept away. Communist historiography in Hungary, too, treated the postwar Czechoslovak-Hungarian conflict in that sense.

The truth of the matter is that, although Beneš was swept away in 1948, his theory and policy that called for the persecution of the Hungarians has never come up for a truly critical examination, not even during the "liberalized" mid-1960s. The nationalist policy in general is being interpreted in terms of proletarian internationalism while keeping certain distance from the anti-humanitarian "bourgeois-nationalist" methods employed before 1948.[52] Even the small concessions to criticism of the mid-1960s have disappeared by the end of that decade. The pioneer in the new uncritical nationalist trend in Slovak historiography was Martin Vietor, followed by Samuel Cambel, who fully rehabilitated the anti-Hungarian atmosphere of 1945.[53]

Hungarian historiography in the meantime has critically reexamined the role Hungarian nationalism has played in the conflict between Slovaks and Hungarians. A similar reexamination, alas, is nowhere noticeable in Slovak historiography.

At the end of the Second World War, the Hungarian masses, too, were longing for peace, internationalism, democracy. They believed that the Hungarian-Slovak conflict would be finally solved. Czechoslovak policy toward the Hungarian minority shattered these hopes.

CHAPTER 2

PLANS IN EXILE AND THE MINORITIES

Right after Munich, in the fall and winter of 1938-1939, Czechoslovak exiles began to organize themselves. When war broke out in September 1939, they began to coordinate their plans with the policies of the Allies. The formulation of exile plans had met with some difficulties, mainly on account of conflicts between Czechs and Slovaks, both at home and abroad. On October 17, 1939, the Czechoslovak National Committee was formed in Paris, mostly by followers of former President Edvard Beneš. In February 1940, also in Paris, a Slovak National Committee was formed by Milan Hodža, former Czechoslovak Prime Minister. Before long, it was the group of exiles around Beneš that set the tone of exile politics and it was that group that founded the Czechoslovak government-in-exile in London in 1940.[1] After the fall of France in the spring of 1940, the London government led by President Beneš became the sole agent of exile politics. Even the Communists and a few Social Democrats who emigrated to Moscow recognized the London government in the summer of 1940, in order to further its international recognition.[2]

The rift between the followers of Beneš and Hodža was never healed. Hodža, who moved to Washington, never found his way to the London Czechoslovak government-in-exile, nor was he capable of forming his own exile organization of international prestige and influence among the exiles comparable to the Beneš achievement. The conflict between Hodža and Beneš was over the future structure of both Czechoslovakia and of Central Europe in general. Hodža in exile became an ardent advocate of a federal reorganization of Central Europe, and he opposed Beneš's centralist concept of a unitary Czechoslovak nation which denied the existence of a separate Slovak nation. Later on, they also disagreed on the exile government's foreign policy, with Hodža becoming ever more critical of Beneš's Soviet orientation. There was no way to bridge the gap between

51

the two antagonists. Conveniently for Beneš, Hodža died in 1944. While their conflict still caused inconveniences to Beneš, he referred to Hodža and his followers contemptuously as "autonomists," a bad word since it was associated in prewar Czechoslovak politics with Hlinka's followers who, in turn, became the Slovak fascists of the Hitler years. To Beneš's way of thinking, Hodža and his most distinguished follower, Štefan Osusky, former Czechoslovak Minister to Paris, betrayed Czechoslovak unity. As he contemptuously remarked at the time when his Slovak opponents-in-exile set up headquarters in the United States: "The trend toward [Czechoslovak] unity is more alive at home than among the meophyte [Slovak] autonomists, Messrs. Osuský and Hodža."[3]

The wartime activity of the Czechoslovak government-in-exile in London was dominated by the talents and prestige of President Beneš. In due course, his authority became dictatorial. He fought with great perseverance and consistency for his nationalist objectives. He waited patiently till the moment became suitable for action. He was an opportunist and a master of political maneuverings. He paid scant attention to momentary setbacks. He was self-centered, ruthless. He lacked a sense of solidarity even with his collaborators. He lacked, as one of his closest collaborators observed, "spiritual greatness." Above all, he was unscrupulous and clever in expoliting the opportunities for action. His characterization by Jaromir Smutny, head of the President's Chancellry, is the most fitting:

> Beneš is an excellent tactician and strategist, the great Machiavelli of our time, but he lacks the charisma to move the masses. . . . Beneš is our good fortune, without him we would devour each other in our personal struggles for power. We recognize Beneš, because he is high above us in intelligence, as well as in determination and capacity for work. . . . He is a machine, born to think and work, without any human feelings—which also accounts for his weaknesses.[4]

In both World Wars, his tactics were aimed at the creation of *faits accomplis*, which were attainable only under the chaotic conditions of the aftermath of a war. In the last few months of the First World War, he was successful with his *faits accomplis* policy in the matter of Czechoslovakia's frontiers. Toward the end of the Second World War his aim was to liquidate the national minorities within those frontiers before the pressure of world public opinion could intervene against his brutal objectives. His plans to expel the Hungarian minority entirely by a *fait accompli* did not succeed. Yet, in the postwar turmoil, he had some success in expelling the Hungarians, which could not have been achieved in peaceful times at all.

Allied public opinion paid no attention during the war to the question of Hungarian minority in Slovakia. There were other, more important matters to think about. Even for the Hungarian public, the future of minorities remained a moot issue until 1944. In the spring of 1944, however, rumors of a radical solution of the question of minorities began spreading. On the eve of Hungary's German occupation, in March 1944, a Hungarian publicist wrote:

> In his Moscow statement, following the signing of the Soviet-Czecho-slovak treaty [in December 1943], Beneš declared that Stalin hoped for a Czechoslovakia that would be as homogeneous as possible. And in his London speech, on February 2 [1944], Beneš emphasized that by Czechoslovakia he always meant Czechoslovakia before Munich. How is this compatible with a nationally homogeneous Czechoslovakia, which, presumably, Stalin wishes to see? In one way only, namely, by Beneš's plan of making Czechoslovakia into a homogeneous nation-state by means of mass expulsions. Items to this effect in fact have begun to appear for some time in the world press; reports are circulating that the Czechs are planning to expel most of the Sudeten-Germans.[5]

While the fate of the Sudeten Germans was a matter of guesswork, as for the future of the Hungarian minority, the Hungarian press did not even have guesses to offer. Hungarian public opinion had no inkling of what in exile circles had become a decided matter: Czechoslovakia would be restored as an ethnically pure nation-state, according to plans for the liquidation of both the Hungarian and the German minorities. How did the exiles reach this extreme decision?

Between Munich and the end of the war, the public statements of President Beneš and his collaborators regarding the national minorities have undergone changes according to the changing military-political situation. The toughest threats alternated with democratic promises. Yet, in retrospect, a systematic scheme is detectable in Beneš's pronouncements, revealing three phases of his policy for the liquidation of the minoriites.

The President's attitude from Munich to the end of August 1939 was threatening, militant, anti-minority. During this first phase, Beneš believed in a grand European coalition against Hitler and in a quick military defeat of Hitlerism. The anti-minority pronouncements suddenly came to a halt with the signing of the Soviet-German Non-Aggression Pact on August 23, 1939, and the subsequent outbreak of war in September.

Czechoslovak historiography since the war skips the second phase that lasted from September 1939 to Hitler's attack on Russia in June 1941. It is *de rigeur* today to maintain that exile policy consistenly condemned the collective betrayal of the minorities. Those who wish to keep alive the theory of the collective crime of the Hungarians as a justification of the reprisals taken against them, after the war, are fond of quoting Beneš's following words: "Already in November 1938 I said that the minorities will have to suffer for the war which inevitably had to break out."[6] No doubt, with no letdown, Beneš was filled with feelings of rage and revenge against the minorities. He was encouraged by the anti-German mood rising in Europe. He was hopeful that with a new world conflict, the forcible reduction of the large German minority within Czech historical boundaries would become possible, something for which the conditions after the First World War were not favorable. On November 12, 1938, Beneš confided to his close collaborator, Hubert Ripka: "There will be great changes in our country, both on socio-economic and political levels. New people with new ideas will come forward. Their methods in dealing with the Germans and with minorities in general will be completely different. . . ."[7] Also, in a letter he wrote to Kr. Rašín in November 1938, Beneš expressed his faith in Hitler's imminent defeat and in the subsequent radical settling of accounts with the minorities: "Of course, we must never forgive anyone for their betrayal. We shall never give away our rights, and our stolen territories."[8] He spoke with equal determination in Chicago on July 8, 1939: "We will not accept the Vienna Award by which Hungary violated Slovakia and Sub-Carpathia."[9] He struck a no less resolute tone in a letter he wrote on August 21, 1939 from London to his friends at home: "As regards our wishes, for the time being, we will speak with restraint but gradually will advance the maximum attainable demands."[10]

However, with the outbreak of war, Beneš was forced to face the new reality. Above all, he realized that he would have to count on a long war. He was aware that time changes the moods of the moment, and unforeseen circumstances may arise.

To what extent political morality is the product of circumstances and of the moment, this was demonstrated by the sudden change in Beneš's public attitude in the second phase of his policy toward the national minorities in the fall of 1939.

The Nazi-Soviet Pact and the outbreak of war changed the tone of Czechoslovak exile pronouncements. No longer are the minorities branded by collective betrayal. A spirit of reconciliation is sounded in the solemn declaration of the Czechoslovak National Committee on October 17, 1939, the day of its founding in Paris: "We enter the struggle in the spirit of Masaryk and Štefánik, in the name of our national heroes and martyrs. We do not recognize any differences of party, or class, or anything else. We are determined to fight for a free and democratic Czechoslovakia, for a republic which will be just towards all its nationalities. We want a socially just Czechoslovak Republic, built on equal rights and duties of all its citizens."[11] There is not a word about the minorities "base betrayal" which must be punished.

Cultivating the spirit of reconciliation, Beneš went even farther in one of his London speeches in the fall of 1939: "Now we may all be able to evaluate correctly what our Republic had meant to the Czechs, the Slovaks, the Germans, the Hungarians, the Ruthenes, to all its inhabitants. . . .We also declare that in the realm of social justice and nationality politics in particular we will eliminate the errors which existed in our Republic in the past."[12] These words are worlds apart from the charges that, despite perfect equality with the majority, the national minorities had been in 1938 the prime causes of Czechoslovakia's catastrophe.

The fate of Czechoslovakia's Hungarian minority after World War II was, in fact, not determined by their prewar behavior but, rather, by the vicissitudes of the international military or political situation. To state this truth has been treated as treason after the war. A whole set of myths, feeding on deep-seated prejudices and distortions, has sprouted and grown out of control ever since. And, as time passes, it becomes ever more difficult to argue against them.

A great success of exile policy was the British recognition of the provisional government formed from the Czechoslovak National Committee on July 24, 1940. At the same time, the British also recognized the continuity of Beneš's presidency. On that occasion, in his first message as restored president, Beneš was still paying tribute to past democratic principles, to be applicable in the future to the minorities as well: "I solemnly declare all these fundamental principles political and legal, and I emphasize that these principles are applicable to all citizens of our state, to all members of our nation, to Czechs, Slovaks, Germans, Ruthenians and others."[13]

Although the Hungarians were relegated to the "others," the pledge of democratic treatment must have applied to them too, if it did explicitly even to the Germans. All the more so, since the Western powers at that time still maintained diplomatic relations with Hungary. This was no time to speak of the minorities' collective guilt or of reprisals against them. The future was to be guided by Czechoslovak republican traditions of a common democratic past.

The "democratic" second phase regarding the treatment of the minorities in Beneš's policy did not end abruptly. And during the second phase, its guiding principle was tolerance—sandwiched between the sharp tone of the first phase, before the outbreak of the war, and the third phase, shortly after Hitler's invasion of Russia.

The change to the third phase had come gradually. Even after the Nazi attack on the Soviet Union, Beneš still struck a conciliatory note, he said on July 26, 1941: "The most significant thing, politically, diplomatically, and legally is that your President elected by the large majority of Czechs, Slovaks, Germans, Ruthenians according to our constitution prior to Munich has again been recognized and is functioning. . . ."[14] Once again, he omitted mentioning the Hungarians explicitly, which in this particular case, was not only forgetful on his part but ungrateful as well. After all, in 1935, the Hungarians too voted for Beneš to succeed Masaryk as president.

Significantly, during the second phase of the western exiles' tolerance toward the minorities, the illegal Communist party at home, too, knew nothing of the "betrayal" of the Hungarian minority. The Communists at that time advocated a program of a "Soviet Slovakia," and even rejected the idea of Czechoslovak continuity. From the Communist point of view, this seemed a popular course to take at that time. After all, until the Nazi attack on the Soviet Union, the USSR was represented by an ambassador in Bratislava, the capital of "independent" Slovakia.[15]

The London exile's tolerance toward the minorities came publicly to an end soon after Hitler's invasion of Russia. Moreover, even during that publicly "democratic" second phase, behind-the-scenes discussions had taken place on the subject of minorities which kept the continuity of intolerance alive. On the subject of minorities, for instance, Presidential Secretary Smutný recorded on March 9, 1940 a noteworthy discussion: "The view seems gradually prevailing is that the Sudeten German question has to be solved by a transfer of the Germans. Dr. Beneš remarked, however, that a certain number of Germans was bound to remain within the borders of the Republic, for it is not possible to expel three and a half million Germans. Nevertheless, he is in agreement with the principle of expulsion."[16]

Also, Secretary Smutný's notes imply that the principle of expulsion began to find support in certain British circles. According to a letter sent to Prague: "The first question politically influential Englishmen are asking us: What do we intend to do with our Germans?"[17] In contrast to what is being said about the Germans, the tone of discussions on the Hungarians is still remarkably conciliatory at that time. According to Smutný's notes, in the course of a confidential discussion, Beneš declared on April 5, 1940: "As for me, I believe that we will not quite regain our former boundaries in Slovakia. But it is not even in our interest to spoil again our relations with the Hungarians. Especially in view of the past and present behavior of the Slovaks."[18]

Beneš's remarks gain truly historical significance in view of the fact that after the war Slovakia's Hungarians were declared no less responsible than the Germans for destroying the Czechoslovak Republic. After the war, it was conveniently glossed over that at one time, President Beneš himself knew nothing of the "collective sin" of the "Fascist" Hungarian minority. Rather, he found the "behavior" of the Slovaks blameworthy. His anger against the Slovaks at that particular time might have been aroused by the expulsion of Czechs from Tiso's "independent" Slovakia.

British involvement in Beneš's expulsion plans against the Germans was taking shape rapidly, as recorded by this entry in one of the documents on early wartime exile policy: "We share with the British our views regarding the Sudetenland; it has to be part of the Republic once again. They [the British] want us to have as few Germans as possible. . . . They reckon with frontier rectifications. They talk seriously about the expulsion of Germans from the country's interior."[19]

In February 1940, while tension between the United States and Germany was growing day by day, Beneš felt the time had come to inform Roosevelt about his views. He asked the Czechoslovak ambassador in Washington, Vladimir Hurban, to relay his ideas to the President: "I emphasized the need of a unitary Czechoslovak state, [the need] of the revision of boundaries between Czechoslovakia and Hungarry [sic], of letting the Ruthenians decide for themselves; otherwise we insist on our rights; with minor boundary changes, the Sudeten Germans have to be returned [to Czechoslovakia]. In principle, we accept the idea of federation but we want to know in advance with whom and how we are to be united."[20] This text, prepared by Beneš for the sake of informing the President of the United States, is remarkable for its complete lack of any trace of hostility toward the Hungarians.

In dealing with the British, too, from the very beginning, distinction had been made between the German question and the Hungarian question. There was no British inclination shown to discuss the case of Czechoslovakia's Hungarians on the smae level with that of the Sudeten Germans. Also, the British were reluctant to discuss future boundary questions, always so dear to Beneš's heart. Minister of Foreign Affairs, Lord Halifax, informing Beneš of the recognition of the Czechoslovak Government-in-exile, stated in a letter in July 1940: "I wish it were clear that His Majesty's Government has no intention to commit itself, by this act of recognition, to any particular future solution of the boundary problem in Central Europe."[21]

In the spring of 1941, the Czechoslovak government-in-exile discussed the transfer of the Germans, but the positions taken were not unanimous. A member of the exile government, Jaroslav Stránsky, opposed Beneš's views on expulsions. As Smutný noted: "He does not like the expulsion of populations. This, he thinks, is a Nazi invention. He would understand if [spontaneous] expulsions would take place in the moment of victory;

but not by means of decrees; that would be cruel."[22] Yet, in due course, Stránsky too accepted the principle of population transfer, along with all the other members of the Czechoslovak government-in-exile.

When the time for exploiting victory was approaching, Beneš and his collaborators returned in full force to the post-Munich anti-minority accusations, namely, that the national minorities had been the prime cause of all of Czechoslovakia's and of Europe's disasters. Consequently, since they are a cancer of civilized society, the minorities have to disappear either by expulsion or by assimilation. Death to the minorities! The loose anti-minority slogans of the post-Munich Phase One became concrete policies of Phase Three by the end of the war. The battle cry against the minorities was no longer just a matter of abstract arguments. It was a policy of intended *faits accomplis*. And its target was not only the German minority, but the Hungarian minority as well.

An atmosphere of utmost hostility surrounded the minorities at the war's end. Unlike after World War I, no measures for the international protection of national minorities had been even considered after World War II. The peace conference after World War II regarded the national minorities as "sinful," and eager to condemn and punish them. The peace settlement surrendered the national minorities to the nationalist greed and vengeance of the victors. History's clock was turned back.

The attitude of the peacemakers after World War II in a way returned to the pre-World War I philosophy. It rehabilitated the long outdated principle that national minorities have no rights or, if at all, only as individual citizens. This "civil rights" approach, recognizing individual rights, as every nationality expert knows, in practice does not protect the national minorities; rather, it surrenders them to the arbitrary rule of the dominant majority. This is exactly the kind of approach the oppressed nationalities of Central Europe had fought against since World War I— and nobody knew the score better than Beneš, having been once himself a member of an oppressed nationality before World War I.

It was sheer hypocrisy on Beneš's part to assure the West during World War II that "the minorities will be guaranteed the rights of individuals and of citizens."[23] He knew very well that such "guarantees" are worthless. Anyway, by embracing later the principle of expulsion and assimilation as a "solution" of the minority problem, he openly admitted that he is for the liquidation rather than the protection of the minorities.

Beneš's triumph in his battle against minorities affected primarily the Hungarian minority of over three million people in the Danube region. After World War II, they became Europe's largest remaining minority. No effective guarantees have been drawn up for their protection either in the peace settlement, or ever since.

When during the Second World War, Beneš launched his campaign for the creation of an ethnically homogeneous Czechoslovak nation-state, he accused both the Germans and the Hungarian minorities of in-gratitude for the democratic rights they have enjoyed in interwar Czecho-slovakia. He failed to mention, however, that the status of the German minority was far more favorable than that of the Hungarian minority.

Before Hitler's rise to power, Czech-German relations in fact seemed to be moving toward a status of parity in Czechoslovakia, a favored treat-ment which the Hungarian minority has never been able to achieve. A much larger proportion of Germans than Hungarians entered the civil service or became officers in the army. Education in their own language was more readily available to the Germans than to the Hungarians. The Hungarians were never allowed a university of their own, whereas German higher education flourished. In general, the Germans were much better integrated into the state than the Hungarians.

In Slovakia, the home of the Hungarians, Slovak nationalism was given free reign to reduce the Hungarians from one-time status of majority to the status of a second-class minority. Consequently, all the customary minority grievances entrenched themselves much more deeply in Slovakia than in Bohemia, the home of the Germans. Prague in fact often kept referring to the satisfaction and loyalty of the Germans to rebuke the Hun-garians for their constant complaints—particularly during the Locarno era of the 1920s when Czechoslovakia's relations had greatly improved with Weimar Germany, but not at all with Horthy's Hungary.[24]

Common historical traditions between Czechs and Germans were apparently more conducive to appeasement in Bohemia between the two rival nationalities than between Slovaks and Hungarians in Slovakia. Both Germans and Czechs were developed national societies. The Slovaks, on the other hand, were struggling to create a national society of their own which they have never achieved before. Demographic data duly mir-rored the difference between the status of Germans and Hungarians in

Czechoslovakia. The Hungarian minority diminished under Czechoslovak rule, whereas the German minority increased.[25]

Although the Germans, not unlike the Hungarians, had been incorporated against their will into the newly founded state of Czechoslovakia after World War I, the Germans found a more secure place for themselves in the new Republic than did the Hungarians. As an impartial observer, the Swede A. Karlgren remarked:

> The Germans were forced to concede that the state organized by the Czechoslovaks without their help, was completely capable of surviving. . . . Around 1925, the German parties gave up one after the other the policy of boycotting the Czechoslovak state, and adopted a line usually referred to as activist, which consisted in collaborating with the Czechoslovaks, and defended their rights within the framework of the constitution. They accepted positions offered in the government. By 1930, all the significant German parties had become activist in this sense.[26]

Czech-German cooperation was jolted by the world economic crisis. More than half of Czechoslovakia's unemployed were Germans.[27] No wonder, when Hitler rose to power, Nazi propaganda found fertile ground in the Sudeten German regions of Czechoslovakia. Yet it should also be remembered, despite Nazi propaganda, that German Socialist workers remained to the very end in the vanguard of the democratic revolutionary struggle.

The entire peaceful historical record of Czech-German relations came to be forgotten during the Second World War. Only bitter memories were remembered. Retribution for defeat in the Battle of White Mountain in 1620 became the Czech exile's battle cry against the German minority. In the words of the leader of the Czech Communists, Klement Gottwald who, in his exile in Moscow joined Beneš in London to campaign for the expulsion of the Germans:

> You must prepare for the final retribution of White Mountain, for the return of the Czech lands to the Czech people. We will expel for good all descendants of the alien German nobility, the robbers who carried out their misdeeds after White Mountain.[28]

After the guns of the Second World War fell silent, deeds followed words. On June 23, 1945, a triumphant Gottwald declared: "Now we definitely compensate for White Mountain. . . . And not only that; now we reach even deeper into our nation's history. By confiscating the property of the Germans we will rectify the mistakes committed by the kings of the Přemysl dynasty who called in the German settlers. Now they will be expelled from our land once and for all."[29]

It is difficult to reconcile these words with the Marxist theory of class struggle and internationalism. Nobody at that time had even attempted to do so. But more recently, another Czech Communist, Karel Pomajzl, did come up with just that: "Intervention [of the Western imperialist powers] into the internal affairs of Czechoslovakia [after the war] was not excluded . . . [therefore], when the Socialist revolution began to evolve from a democratic national revolution and the workers launched their struggle against the bourgeoisie which had always used nationalism to paralyze the socialist revolution, the expulsion of the Germans was the best solution."[30] In other words, according to this Marxist interpretation, expulsion was a preventive measure against the threat of Western "imperialist intervention."

It took little effort on Beneš's part to have his German expulsion plans endorsed by the Allies "in the interest of peace and security." However, it was not so easy to force his demand for the expulsion of the Hungarians into the larger framework of "European peace and security." Nevertheless, since winning so easily both Western and European support for his German expulsion plans, it might have seemed to Beneš realistic to assume that the principle of population transfer may win approval sooner or later against the Hungarian minority as well. It did not. As far as the Hungarians were concerned, the Western Powers were not impressed by Beneš's arguments in favor of expulsion. His appeal to Czechoslovakia's right to self-defense, and to collective reprisals as a punishment for collective crimes was effective against the Germans, but he never succeeded in convincing the Western Powers that the Hungarian minority would jeopardize either the security of Czechoslovakia or the peace of Europe.

After the war, some Slovak nationalists thought the Czechoslovak leaders in exile did not press hard enough the issue of expulsion against the Hungarians. These charges were unfounded. Both Beneš in London and Gottwald in Moscow did everything they could to win support for the same punishment against both Germans and Hungarians. The Hungarian expulsion plans ultimately met with success in Moscow. But neither London nor Washington were willing to close ranks with Moscow regarding the expulsion of the Hungarians.

At the outset, the British commitment to population transfer was strictly a theoretical one. As Beneš recorded in his memoires: "We were told, via British Ambassador Nichols, (accredited to the Czechoslovak Government-in-exile), that the British Government discussed the questions of expulsion of minorities from the Republic in detail. In view of all that happened to us in 1938. . .the British will not object to the principle of transfer of minority populations, on the grounds that Czechoslovakia should become as nationally homogeneous as possible."[31] Several historians interpreted this as a British promise to support the expulsion of the Hungarians too. The truth of the matter is that Beneš never received such a promise, although he tried hard to get one.

Beneš commented in his memoires on his difficulties with the "solution" of the Hungarian problem: "This [the expulsion] solution is particularly applicable to our Hungarians, and I spend all my efforts to convince all our allies to that effect, thus ensuring final peace and Czechoslovak-Hungarian cooperation after the war."[32] He went on arguing with the Allies along these lines, claiming that the Hungarians can prove their acceptance of democracy only if they agreed to the expulsion of the Hungarian minority from Slovakia.

He was not so outspoken about his views when, during his visit to the United States in the spring of 1943, he met an old Hungarian friend of the Czechs and an arch enemy of Horthy's regime, Professor Rusztem Vámbéry. Beneš's Cabinet Secretary, Smutný, recorded the following on the Beneš-Vámbéry conversation: "As regards frontiers, Beneš explained that after the defeat of the enemy, it will be necessary to re-establish the old [pre-World War II] boundaries. On the other hand, after Hungary's democratic transformation. . .the new Hungary will find the Czechoslovak Republic sympathetic in this matter."[33] Beneš simply misled Vámbéry. He said nothing about his plans to expel the Hungarians. On the contrary, according to Smutný's notes: "As regards the exchange of populations Beneš explained to Vámbéry that his is primarily interested in Nazi war criminals, first of all the Sudeten German Nazis. He added:

No matter what the regime, we must expect that there will always be minorities."[34] The gullible Vámbéry believed Beneš's assurances that a democratic Hungary could count on a generous Czechoslovakia. Throughout the war, Vámbéry remained one of Beneš's staunchest public supporters in the United States.

Beneš's deception of Vámbéry took place at a time when he was fully engaged in his efforts to extend his expulsion plans to the Hungarians. As Smutný recorded, a few months later, a conversation between Beneš and Philip B. Nichols, British Minister accredited to the Czechoslovak Government-in-exile: ". . . [Beneš] insisted that the British Government give its explicit approval to the transfer. Nichols asked for a memorandum on how the transfer would be carried out. Dr. Beneš spoke of two million Germans and 400,000 Hungarians. . . . [But he] rejected the notion of a memorandum. First I want a decision regarding the principle, [he said], then I shall hand over a memorandum. Furthermore, it is possible that Roosevelt will need the vote of 400,000 Hungarians in the United States, and everything will collapse. Beneš laughed, and so did Nichols."[35]

Beneš's battle against the Hungarians was not yet won. And he admonished in March 1943 his Slovak followers: "I don't want to hide from you the fact that not everything is won for Slovakia yet, grave dangers lay still ahead."[36]

As World War II was drawing to a close, there was no time to lose. The world public opinion had to be made aware of the "necessity" to liquidate the national minorities. The world had to be persuaded that the existence of national minorities is harmful and dangerous, that their international protection should cease, that their elimination would serve world peace. Beneš's concept had finally won international approval. Nothing was heard of the principle of international protection of the national minorities at the peace conference, nor during the subsequent decades. Beneš's thesis that the question of national minorities was strictly a matter of internal affairs become unwritten international law.

The Beneš thesis on national minorities was the topic of a lecture at Oxford in November 1943 by one of Beneš's closest collaborators, Dr. Hubert Ripka, in which he said: "It does not seem likely that we shall return to the international protection of minorities. . . Germany and Hungary have used the national minorities as fifth columns. They had used them for aggressive and military purposes . . . hence it is just and right to oblige Germany and Hungary to bring home their compatriots. . . ."[37] The essential point in Ripka's lecture was to lump Germans and Hungarias together. This has been a maxim of the Beneš propaganda ever since the First World War. For the time being, however, Beneš's campaign, advocating the expulsion of minorities, scored success against the Germans only.

It was during his stay in the United States, in the spring of 1943, that Beneš received word of the Soviet consent to his transfer plans of the Germans: "Moscow communicated its agreement in principle via Ambassador Bogolomov [in London] to Dr. Ripka on June 5, 1943, who immediately forwarded the information to me in Washington; thus, I was able to discuss it with Roosevelt as well."[38] At that time, much as he tried, Beneš was unable to obtain Moscow's support to the transfer of the Hungarians. Nevertheless, in his negotiations with President Roosevelt, he made full use of the British and Soviet support of *the principle* of expulsion: "After I obtained the agreement of London and Moscow, I brought up the matter with Roosevelt, who immediately gave me his personal agreement, adding that anything that brought about a catastrophe such as Munich has to be eliminated once and for all."[39] Beneš then immediately informed the British Government of his discussions with Roosevelt: "He [Roosevelt] agrees with the plan that after this war the number of Germans in Czechoslovakia should be reduced to a minimum by means of resettlement. He asked no questions with regard to Slovakia."[40] The last sentence was a clever remark to keep the unresolved Hungarian problem alive with the British.

No breakthrough in the Hungarian problem had occurred, as Beneš hoped it might, during his visit to Moscow in December 1943. He signed a treaty of friendship, mutual aid, and postwar cooperation with the Soviet Union. He discussed with Stalin and Molotov both the German and Hungarian problems. They reconfirmed their agreement on the expulsion of Czechoslovakia's Germans, but Moscow did not consent yet explicitly to the transfer of the Hungarians. Nevertheless, Beneš did make enough headway that he could write to the Polish Premier Mikolajczyk in London: "Moscow accepted the notion of the transfer of our Germans. . . .We will have united or parallel policies toward Hungary."[41] There is no trace in Beneš's memoirs that Mikolajczyk would have ever objected to the expulsion of the Hungarian minority from Czechoslovakia. Such a friendly gesture—considering the friendly treatment of Polish refugees in Hungary during the war—would have been warranted both then and after the war.

In Moscow, in December 1943, Beneš conducted a series of negotiations with the leaders-in-exile of the Czechoslovak Communist Party. The published minutes of these discussions extensively mention the question of expulsions:

> Only the anti-Fascists, democrats, and Communists among the German population will be allowed to remain in our country, as well as those who participated in the anti-Hitler struggle abroad. Beneš emphasized that he obtained the agreement of the Soviet Union to the relocation of the Germans from the territory of the Republic, and he had likewise obtained ever earlier the written consent of the British and of Roosevelt. We will employ the same method against the Hungarians as we had against the Germans, a measure that will be facilitated by the exchange of the Slovak population of Hungary with the Hungarians of Slovakia.[42]

The Slovak-Hungarian population "exchange," which from then on became a corollary of Beneš's expulsion plans, was a rather lopsided affair. There were at best 200,000 Slovaks in Hungary, attracted by the fertile Hungarian South, an island of settlers, far removed from the mountainous home of the Slovaks in the North—whereas there were at least 600,000 Hungarians in Slovakia, most of them living along the northern rim of the large homogeneous Hungarian ethnic bloc of the mid-Danube region, and separated from the rest of Hungary only by the wilfull political boundary drawn after World War I.

Beneš counted mainly on Soviet and Czech Communist support against the Hungarians. In a note addressed to Václav Nosek and Vladimir Clementis, dated December 21, 1943, Klement Gottwald from Moscow informed the Communist exiles in London of his discussions with Beneš:

> The President of the Republic explained to us his population transfer plans. . . . Our reply was that the tactics of the measure have to

be modified. It would be more useful if the matter could be solved in the spirit of the anti-Fascist struggle within the framework of punishing the war criminals who committed crimes against Czechoslovakia. . . . The President stated in his response that his original plan can be realized with the application of our tactics. At the same time, he emphasized that, as a consequence of this cleansing action, the Czechoslovak Republic will be converted into a nation-state.[43]

Ever since the thesis of "anti-Fascist tactics" dominated both Communist and non-Communist Czechoslovak interpretations of the expulsion policy. The postwar persecution of the Hungarian minority, too has been described as an "anti-Fascist" activity.[44] Actually, ideological "tactics" did not matter. Naked force prevailed against the Hungarian minority.

The reconquest of the "lost Slovak lands" (inhabited mostly by Hungarians) became the battle cry of the Czechoslovak military units formed on Soviet territory: "Prepare for the struggle . . . to free our brothers and sisters pining under the yoke of Hungarian counts and gendarmes!"[45]

All anti-Fascist resistance movements in Europe called for liberation of the nation and the return of lost territories. The anti-Fascist Hungarian resistance alone was condemned to couple its struggle with surrender of purely Hungarian territories to vindictive neighbors. Well before the end of the war, the decision to restore the boundaries drawn up after World War I by the Treaty of Trianon was already an accomplished diplomatic fact. And, on top of that, Hungarian anti-Fascists were condemned to face the possibility that victory over the enemy might confront them with the threat of expulsion from their homelands.

Although during his visit to Moscow in December 1943, Beneš failed to get unqualified Soviet support to his plan to expel the Hungarian minority from Czechoslovakia, he did not lose faith in the final triumph of his policy. Dated January 19, 1944, the Foreign Ministry of the Czechoslovak Government-in-exile issued a circular signed by Hubert Ripka, informing the Allied Embassies in London of Beneš's negotiations in Moscow. The circular exuded confidence that it will be possible to lump together the German and Hungarian questions:

The Soviet Union is in agreement with us that, given our experience with the Sudeten-Germans (and with the Hungarians) it will be necessary to reduce their numbers to the lowest level, to a degree that will enable us to build a true Czechoslovak nation-state. The British and the United States governments also agree with our stand.[46]

Following the German occupation of Hungary, in March 1944, when a new Hungarian government was installed under Nazi auspices, the Czechoslovak emigré press in Moscow (*Československé Listy; Naše Vojsko v SSSR*) struck a strident tone against the Hungarians and made no secret of the expulsion plans. The Hungarian Communist exiles, however, remained strangely silent on the expulsion issue, and it is not known whether there has ever been any exchange of views between Czechoslovak and Hungarian Communist exiles in Moscow on the expulsion of the Hungarian minority from Czechoslovakia.[47] Anyway, Hungary's occupation in the spring of 1944 enabled the Czechoslovak propaganda to fully identify the Hungarians with the despised Nazi Germans. There was no longer any fear either of a Hungarian military or political force capable of resisting population expulsions. The stage seemed to be set for a *fait accompli* solution to the Hungarian problem.

Communist views regarding minority rights, once inspired by "class consideration," had completely disappeared by the spring of 1944. On May 11, 1944, Klement Gottwald stated in a broadcast over Radio Moscow: " . . . the moment is not far away when we will sweep our country clean of the dirty German and Hungarian traitors."[48]

The Czech Communist party paper in Moscow, *Československé Listy*, considered the Hungarian question as already settled. In its issue of August 1, 1944, the paper wrote: " . . . what applied to the Germans, applies to the Hungarians as well."[49] Not even the Jews were spared of nationalist hatred if they have anything to do with Germans or Hungarians. The Jews are being exterminated by the Nazis irrespective of their nationality, but the Communist Václav Koplecký, Gottwald's closest collaborator, declares:

Those Jews who feel as Germans or Hungarians must face the same measures that will be taken against the Germans and Hungarians in Czechoslovakia. The liquidation of anti-Semitism does not mean that we will grant the Jews special privileges if they feel as Germans or Hungarians. Nor will we allow those who feel as Germans or Hungarians to hide their true feelings behind the claim of Jewishness.

Liquidation of anti-Semitism cannot be allowed to cause harm to the national and Slav character of the future Czechoslovak Republic.[50]

By the summer of 1944, the Moscow Communist exiles had become as ultrachauvinist Czechoslovaks as the London bourgeois exiles. F. Hála, representing the London exiles, reported of his negotiations with the Moscow exiles: "Gottwald, Kopecký, and Šverma asserted unquivocally that we shall build a Slav state, where the Czechs, Slovaks and Ukrainians shall enjoy democratic rights, but not the Germans and the Hungarians."[51] It looked, in fact, as if the main driving force of Slav nationalist radicalism would now come from Moscow. At the time of fighting on the Czechoslovak border at Dukla, *Za svobodné Československo,* the Communist paper of the Czechoslovak military units formed on Soviet territory, wrote on October 6: ". . . we must clean Slovakia of all intruders and traitors. . . the traitors who have been severely punished will never betray us again! The cleansing of the Republic of all Germans, Hungarians, traitors has begun."[52]

Indeed, the military situation in October 1944 was such that it seemed likely that the Hungarian minority of Slovakia may flee before the advancing Soviet front the same way the German population had fled from the Baltic regions, from Poland and, also from Northern Slovakia. That the Hungarians, too, would flee, turned out to be a wrong assumption. South Slovakia's Hungarians, mostly peasants who lived there since time immemorial, never thought of fleeing. Moreover, the failure of the Soviet operations at Dukla, and the defeat of the Slovak national uprising, had changed the military situation. In the late fall of 1944, expulsion of the Hungarian minority from Czechoslovakia was no longer expected by purely military means by the Czechoslovaks themselves. Once again, diplomacy took over the initiative.

On November 23, 1944, the Czechoslovak government in London handed the three Great Powers a memorandum requesting that the measures approved against the Germans should be recognized as legitimate against the Hungarian minority also:

The presence of a Hungarian minority in Czechoslovakia constitutes no less of a danger as the German minority. The Czechoslovak government reserves the right to take the measures described in this memorandum against all those members of the Hungarian minority who have exhibited hostility towards the Republic. . . . It should be noted that the Czechoslovak government has the authority to decide which Germans and Hungarians may or may not remain within the Republic.[53]

The postwar interpretation of this memorandum maintained that the Czechoslovak government proposed all Germans and Hungarians to be deprived of their citizenship, not merely the compromised individuals and the Fascists.[54]

At any rate, reply of the three powers to the memorandum was negative. The Hungarian questions remained deadlocked. The expectations of "solving" it by military means had not been fulfilled. Also, politically, the Hungarian situation had changed toward the end of 1944. Regent Horthy's attempt in October to overthrow the pro-German government in German-occupied Hungary, and to sue for an armistice, had failed. However, the Hungarians soon improved somewhat their political status. In December, an anti-Fascist government was formed in Russian-occupied eastern Hungary and an armistice was signed. It was no longer possible for the Czechoslovak exiles to resort simply to a policy of *fait accompli* against the Hungarians.

On Czechoslovak prodding, Soviet Foreign Minister Molotov tried to include the transfer of Hungarians among the Allied armistice conditions with Hungary. The attempt was vetoed by the Western powers. Disappointed, Gottwald sent this message to London:

The Western powers have already rejected the notion of a transfer. During the debate over the armistice to be concluded with Hungary Balfour and Harriman objected to the inclusion of the question of transfer among the armistic conditions, in spite of Molotov's support. The Red Army may prove very helpful. But everything depends on the military developments. . . . There are more Hungarians in Slovakia now than before, because the Red Army had advanced from South to North, and the Hungarians had nowhere to flee. If we cannot send them elsewhere, we will place them in labor camps.[55]

The voice of the exiles, embittered by failures of their expulsion policies, became ever more aggressive against the Hungarians. The Slovak Communist Vladimir Clementis outdid Beneš in whipping up anti-Hungarian sentiments in his radio talks to the homeland: "The jackal of Budapest, following in the footsteps of the German tiger, is getting not just bones but large chunks of meat torn from the flesh of the subject nations."[56]

It is worth noting at this point that the text of all those notorious postwar Presidential decress of 1945 depriving the German and Hungarian minorities of their rights as citizens of Czechoslovakia were composed in the atmosphere of the summer optimism of 1944 in London and Moscow, at a time when it looked as if nothing could stop the solving of minority problems by military means.

It is worth mentioning too, that in the last months of the war disagreements arose between Beneš and the British Government over the entire problem of population transfer. Before leaving London, Beneš's last conversation with British Ambassador Nichols was not exactly friendly on this subject:

> We argued for a long time over the question of transfer. I was justified in expecting a clear and final formulation as to the borders and to the matter of transfer, so that we may issue our own laws. . . . Nichols demanded that we not issue such laws without prior consultations with the Allied Great Powers. When I explained to him what would happen at home if we were to refrain from issuing such laws (chaos, fighting, massacre of the Germans) he proposed that these laws be proclaimed as part of the government program, but before executing them, we must reach complete agreement with the Allies over method, scale of operations, etc., (since they too have a say in the matter, as they will be on the other side of Germany's border, and they will have to receive these Germans) and he stressed again that we may include our objectives as a maximum in our program. I rejected this solution and later, at the time our our saying good-byes, I brought up the matter once again with Eden and Churchill, but they have already been briefed by the Foreign Office in the matter and spoke in indefinite terms, without committing themselves, saying that we may deal with the matter only as a program,

and in no other way. . . . Before my departure I mentioned to
Nichols that I will discuss the matter in Moscow and may reach
an agreement directly with Moscow, and act accordingly.[57]

The first postwar Czechoslovak government assembled in Moscow in
March 1945 respected the British wish. The decrees on depriving the
minorities of their rights, signed by President Beneš already in London
in September 1944, were promulgated in Prague only on August 2, 1945,
following the joint decisions of the Great Powers on population transfers
at the Potsdam Conference. However, since the presidential decrees were
written in September 1944 (when hopes ran high that Germans and Hungarians could be treated the same way), the decrees affected the Hungarians as well, even though at Potsdam the Czecholovaks obtained no
Western approval to that effect. How this anti-Hungarian Czechoslovak
policy without approval of the Western Allies has bomeranged at the
peace conference, will be discussed in another chapter.

The anti-Hungarian intentions of the Czechoslovak exile government
were made public before Beneš's departure from London for Moscow.
In his radio address on February 16, 1945, Beneš for the first time publicly hinted that not only the German but the Hungarian minority as well
would be liquidated:

> All provinces inhabited by Germans or Hungarians will be from the
> beginning administered by government agencies until such time as
> the wartime and minority problems are solved. These agencies will
> be backed up, of course, by adequate military forces. Any kind of
> resistance will be ruthlessly smashed. This will be our guideline for
> the future . . . we are preparing the final solution of the question
> of our Germans and Hungarians since the new republic will be a
> Czechoslovak nation-state.[58]

After Beneš's arrival in Moscow, the Eastern and Western Czechoslovak
exiles deliberated from March 22 to March 29, 1945. Also a delegation of
the Slovak National Council from the home front joined them. They co-
ordinated their views and put together a National Front Government
which worked out a government program—or rather, approved one since

the program had already been put together by Klement Gottwald on the
basis of prior negotiations and agreements.

As a Communist Party chronicler, Václav Kopecký, put it: "Comrade
Gottwald asked if any of the parties present had worked out a proposal
for the government program, and it turned out that, except for our own
party, none had ready such a proposal. Then Comrade Gottwald announced that our party did draft such a program, and that he will introduce it
as a basis for negotiations. The proposal then became the program of the
National Front Government of the Czechs and Slovaks." [59]

Kopecký's account is not complete. A postwar collection of wartime
documents does speak of another proposal: ". . . the Social Democrats
from London brought along their statement of principles, approved at
their conference of February 18, 1945. This however, was not accepted
as a basis for negotiations." [60] The Social Democratic party was more
moderate than Beneš and his Communist allies regarding reprisals against
the minorities. This becomes obvious from the amendment they proposed
to the government's program:

> We demand that that portion of the German and Hungarian popu-
> lation which had been unfaithful to the Czechoslovak Republic,
> and which became a military prop of reaction and Nazism, should
> be expelled. The status of those Germans and Hungarian citizens,
> however, who had remained faithful to the Republic and its demo-
> cratic ideals, should be settled in the spirit of complete political,
> social, civil, and economic equality. [61]

The proposal of the Social Democrats conflicted with the principle
of a purely Czechoslovak nation-state. Essentially it presumed minority
rights, hence, it could not form the basis for discussions in the then prevailing chauvinist atmosphere. Furthermore, the leadership was already
in the hands of Klement Gottwald: "The fact that the deliberations began
on the basis of the proposal presented by the Communist Party has ex-
plicity proved that the Communist Party had become the leading political
force of the National Front." [62]

Beneš's dictatorial powers practically ceased with the formation of the
new government headed by Zděnek Fierlinger on the one hand, and with

the acceptance of the government program on the other. As one eyewitness in Moscow, the Slovak Communist Dr. Gustav Husák, recorded the scene: "He [Beneš] behaved as a constitutional president and took cognizance of the announcement with a cold expression. His dictatorial status in exile had come to an end. Anyhow, he had to leave quite a few of his illusions behind in London."[63]

One of the illusions Beneš had to part with was his concept of the Czechoslovak nation. He had always shied away from recognizing Slovak national sovereignty. He was an advocate not only of the continuity of the Czechoslovak state, but also of the continuity of the Czechoslovak nation. He did not recognize the existence of a separate Slovak nation. He considered the Slovak language merely as a variant, or a dialect of the Czech. Beneš held onto these views to the very end. In his own words, recorded by a Slovak Communist:

> I will never be persuaded to accept the existence of a Slovak nation. This is my scientific conviction, and I am not willing to depart from it. You as Communists may defend your own stand, I have no objections, but I will persist in believing and claiming that the Slovaks are Czechs, and that the Slovak language is but a dialect of the Czech in the same way as the Hanák language, or any other dialect.[64]

As an exile during the Second World War, Beneš had fought relentlessly not merely for the restoration of Czechoslovakia in its prewar size but also for making it into a purely Slav state of the Czechoslovaks by expelling the Germans and Hungarians. He returned home at the war's end by way of Moscow victoriously. But he had to give up territory, by ceding Subcarpathia to the Soviet Ukraine, and he had to face the fact that the Slovaks are not one nation with the Czechs but a separate nation. He still could hope, however, to be able with Soviet help to carry out the plans worked out in exile for the expulsion of the non-Slav national minorities. The government program promulgated in Košice on April 5, 1945, known as the Košice Program became the constitutional source of his Presidential decrees which deprived the German and Hungarian minorities of all their rights as citizens of the restored Czechoslovak state.

CHAPTER 3

RESISTANCE AT HOME AND THE MINORITIES

Not unlike among the exiles, among the Czechs and Slovak resistance movements at home, too, in 1943 the concept of a homogeneous Czecho-slovak nation-state began to gain acceptance. And beginning the summer of 1944, it is possible to discern within the country itself preparations for the postwar discrimination against the Hungarian minority, including plans for expulsion. In the course of these developments, the Communist switch to extreme measures against the Hungarians is of particular interest.

Until the summer of 1941, the war between Hitler and Stalin, the Slo-vak Communists were not enthusiastic at all about the restoration of a Czechoslovak state. In fact, they were spreading anti-Czech slogans and propagated the idea of a separate Soviet Slovakia.[1] Also, there was no mention in communist circles of an eventual postwar punishment of the Hungarian minority, let alone of the expulsion. At that time, Communist internationalism, class solidarity and tolerance towards the nationalities, was to a certain extent in harmony with the intial "democratic" phase of the Western exiles. This harmony, however, was not a matter of agree-ment between home front and exiles. Rather, it was the result of inter-national constellations which affected the same way both the exiles and the home fronts, at least as far as the question of minorities was con-cerned. In this period, before the summer of 1941, Beneš in exile occa-sionally promised more rights to the national minorities han they had enjoyed before Munich in 1938. And such promises actually matched the internationalist tone of underground Communist propaganda. For instance on July 15, 1940 *Hlas L'udu* wrote: "We protest most energeti-cally against the persecution of the Hungarian workers in our country, just as the Hungarian Communist Party objects to the persecution of the Slo-vaks in Horthy's Hungary."[2]

In the wake of Hitler's attack on the Soviet Union in the summer of 1941, the Slovak Communists promptly changed their attitude. They accepted the theory of Czechoslovakia's legal continuity and gradually they changed their views on the German and Hungarian minority questions as well. The changes corresponded to the direction nationality policy took among the exiles and also reflected the impact exile propaganda had on the home front, especially following the Allied recognition of the Czechoslovak Government-in-exile in London.

An important tactical goal of exile politics for gaining mass support at home was the formulation of common postwar national objectives, attractive to both Czechs and Slovaks, such as: recovery of Slovakia's lost territories from Hungary, elimination of German power in the Czech lands and, after 1943, the concept of a homogeneous Slav nation-state, which entailed the expulsion of the Hungarians as well. An ideological compromise on the Beneš interpretation of a centralist Czechoslovak concept was necessary in order to gain Slovak and Communist support in the common struggle. This need was clearly expressed in a letter written by the Communist V. Kopecký to J. Šverma in Moscow, on August 5, 1942: Military mobilization against the Germans will be more successful at home [in Slovakia] if carried out on a Slovak basis, rather than on a Czechoslovak basis. If done on a Slovak basis we may be able to include even the L'udák elements [followers of Hlinka and Tiso] in the united struggle against the Germans and the Hungarians. . . ."[3] This tactic proved fruitful in subsequent struggles, especially during the Slovak uprising in 1944.

From available domestic documents, it is not possible to reconstruct in all its details the evolution of the anti-Hungarian stance of the resistance movement nor its ideological or psychological motivations. A record of early manifestations of anti-Hungarian attitudes at home can be found mainly in the archives of the Czechoslovak government in London. The exiles have carefully appraised the desires, proposals, and reports received from the home front. There were often errors in their interpretations because the London exiles were obviously unable to evaluate the relative weight of resistance sources of information. Those who wrote the largest number of letters were deemed the strongest. The Communists, who remained relatively quiet, were underestimated. Half a dozen nationalist individuals reporting regularly were mistaken for a serious force, but

Communist revolutionary manifestations founded on internationalist class struggle were barely noticed. All letters received from home were systematically collected by Jaromír Smutný, Beneš's Presidential Cabinet Secretary.

Not until after the battle of Stalingrad did the correspondents from the home front begin to express views on the Hungarian question in the spirit of radical postwar retaliation. "Everyone is anti-German, and of course, anti-Hungarian as well,"[5] wrote one correspondent whom Smutný identifies only as "a participant of the Slovak resistance movement," though the letter came from Geneva. The anonymous letter's observations are debatable and the reference to "everyone" is certainly an exaggeration. Most likely, the letter came from intellectual circles, for at that time, the letter was dated March 9, 1943, anti-Hungarian sentiments had not yet reached the masses.

Another letter which makes reference to the Hungarians is dated Istanbul, June 23, 1943, and Smutný simply refers to the writer as "an informant." It says: "The inhabitants of the areas occupied by Hungary await impatiently the restitution of Czechoslovakia. This applies not merely to the Slovaks, but in part to persons of Hungarian nationality as well . . . ."[6] The reference to the Hungarians is hardly accurate. At that time Hungarians of "occupied" Southern Slovakia saw their salvation in the fall of the Horthy regime in Hungary, not in their return to Czechoslovakia. And if a few Hungarians did opt for Czechoslovakia, they certainly did not yearn for the nightmares that came with their return to Czechoslovakia.

The Communists correctly foresaw the eventual evolution toward the dictatorship of the proletariat. But, whatever their political coloration, nobody could foresee the anti-Hungarian terror following the victory over Fascism.

Until February 1945, the radical measures prepared against the Hungarian minority remained strictly confidential. The Hungarians at home were totally ill-informed about their future prospects. They knew nothing about the recognition of the legal continuity of Czechoslovakia by Allied diplomacy. They were convinced that a revolution would come in Hungary, and that this would solve their problems. A fundamental mistake on their part was the assumption that both Hungary and Slovakia, since both of them were Hitler's allies, would lose the war. They did not know that from 1942 on, Slovakia literally ceased to exist in Allied eyes. There was only a "Czechoslovakia," safely entrenched on the Allied side, thanks to Beneš's diplomacy.

Notions cherished by pro-Allied Hungarians that anti-Fascist resistance would earn dividends in the territorial conflict with Czechoslovakia, were to be proven illusory. By the spring of 1944, the Great Powers had already reached agreement on this matter. True, in May 1944, the Great Powers appealed to Hungary, Rumania, Bulgaria and Finland to withdraw from Hitler's war and to contribute to the common victory over Fascism. But, significantly, Fascist Slovakia was not mentioned, because it was considered non-existent and therefore not a member of the Hitler coalition.[7]

Slovak intellectuals at home in particular when talking to foreigners made no secret of their anti-Hungarian sentiments. In fact, by 1943, they openly expressed a desire for extreme reprisals against the Hungarians. Smutný quotes from the report on a visit to Bratislava by Colonel Edouard Chapuisat, representative of the International Red Cross, stressing the anti-Hungarian sentiments among Slovaks: "They hate the Germans and the Hungarians." Chapuisat did not elaborate on the causes of anti-Hungarian sentiments among the Slovaks. But there can be no doubt that the main reason for it was the loss of territory to Hungary in 1938. Though a Czech correspondent in Smutný's collection of letters also stressed different aspects of hostile Slovak sentiments at that time: "No one has forgotten yet how shamefully the Poles had behaved towards us during the days of deepest crisis. The people believe that the Hungarians had shown more moderation."[9]

Anti-Polish sentiments among Slovaks are also mentioned by the Slovak ambassador in Bucharest, J. Milec, a clandestine pro-Beneš diplomat who was informing the London government via Ankara on the mood at home. He wrote in a letter, in September 1943: "In Slovakia they do not like and do not trust the Poles, especially because of their friendly feelings towards the Hungarians." And he went on: "When the turn comes there will have to be a drastic purge not only in our own ranks. First of all, Slovakia will have to be ridden of the Hungarians. . . . People do not speak of the fate of the Slovaks in Hungary. Yet everybody expects that Slovakia will regain its southern boundaries of 1938, and that the Hungarian population of Slovakia will be resettled or exchanged for the Slovaks of Hungary."[10] A similarly biased report by a member of the former Czechoslovak Agrarian Party, V. Radákovič, is also noteworthy: "In Slovakia, they hate Hungary, they talk about how it might be possible to eradicate Hungarian influence completely in Central Europe, even at the price of deporting them to the Ural region. . . . As regards the minority issue, only the most radical solutions are discussed. The Germans will have to be expelled or possibly suffer an even worse fate. The Hungarians have to be expelled too, and exchanged for the Slovaks in Hungary and Austria."[11]

The political atmosphere at home was teeming with ideas how to liquidate the minority ethnic groups; and these ideas seemed to spread independently of any particular political ideology. But the basic objectives were always the same: acquisition of territories. Also, it should be noted that the population transfer idea as a means of territorial conquest was planted in so many Central European minds already by Hitler's and Stalin's practices following the Nazi-Soviet pact of 1939.

The idea of mass expulsions popped up in General Henrik Werth's head following Hungary's entry into the war against Soviet Russia. The pro-Nazi Chief of the Hungarian General Staff advised Regent Horthy in the summer of 1941 that "followng the restoration of Hungary's millennial frontiers," the Slavs, the Rumanians, and the Jews should be expelled for the sake of "definitive territorial security." The irrational proposal was rejected by Premier László Bárdossy, for the following reason: "The evacuation of such immense territories would result in an extraordinary decrease in national wealth. For most likely the expelled population would take its cattle and movable belongings along, as happened in such resettlement programs in the past elsewhere. The idea expressed in the memorandum of the Chief of the General Staff is so fantastic, that its practical application is inconceivable and, considering the strength of Magyardom, its realization would not at all be in the interest of the country."[12] It is worth noticing that, in 1941, the "Fascist" Bárdossy took it for granted that people forcibly transferred would be allowed to take their cattle and movable belongings. The postwar "democratic" concept of deportation with property confiscation was still unknown.

The Nazi-inspired idea of population transfer found early favorable reception in official circles of Tiso's Slovakia. As one chronicler noted:

"Thus in the fall of 1939, Hitler's resettlement policy of national minorities to make countries nationally pure aroused considerable hopes in Bratislava."[13] The leaders of the Slovak state at that time were quite confident that a German victory would lead to frontier rectifications with Hungary, to be followed by ethnic resettlements at the expense of the Hungarians.

The Nazi Germans were preparing similar plans for the removal of the Czechs from their Bohemian homeland. Bohuslav Ečer cites the following proposal made by Bohemia-Moravia's Nazi Reich "Protector," Baron Neurath: "The most radical and theoretically the most perfect solution would be the total resettlement of the Czech population, and the settling of Czech lands with Germans. . . . A total resettlement, however, is not necessary to achieve the desired end. Considering the racial mixing with the Germans over the past thousand years, Neurath believes it may be possible to leave a large part of the population on Czech territory . . . ."[14] Leaving the Czech population meant of course assimilation.

The Nazi Germans had secret plans on the liquidation of their friends and allies, the Slovaks too. According to a confidential report dated February 1943: "There is no need for a large scale resettlement [of the Slovaks]. On the contrary. [Such measure] may lead to resistance that would be difficult to repress. On the other hand, all conditions for assimilation are available to us."[15]

As can be seen, there was quite a variety of plans regarding population transfers circulating in Central Europe during the war. And the justification for all of them was "national interest." Such are the "just" causes of blind nationalism! For instance, if Henrik Werth's plan for expelling Hungary's "disloyal" nationalities would have been carried out, most likely historic Hungary's national minorities would have been accused of "collective betrayal," not unlike Czechoslovakia's national minorities had been by the Beneš plan. And, incidently, Werth's "national cause" would have been as "just" as was Beneš's—even the percentage of the "disloyal" populations in question were about the same.

Nobody could foresee clearly under what circumstances would the war end, where would the armies of the victors be at the time of Hitler's collapse. Nor could anyone foresee the mode of disintegration of the Hitlerian coalition. Not even the example of the Italian collapse in 1943 could provide safe answers to these speculative questions.

In 1943, prompted by the peace feelers put out by Miklós Kállay, Premier of Hungary, the Czechoslovak Government-in-exile in London became restless. They were worried lest the Hungarians somehow succeded in going over to the Allied side and thus creating an entirely new situation, endangering the existing agreements of wartime diplomacy. In September 1943, a message that Beneš had sent to certain non-Communist anti-Fascist Slovak resistance groups clearly reveals his worries regarding the Hungarian activities at that time: "The more automatic and natural the transition to the new power situation will be, the better for our country and for the solidity of our international position, especially with regard to the Hungarians."[16] Another Beneš letter, addressed to the Šrobár group, admonishes Beneš' former National Socialist Party followers of the precarious domestic situation:

> In any case, unity is needed, among you as well as among us [in exile].
> Our work can succeed only if we are united; then we need not fear
> that there will be chaos in Slovakia after the fall of the regime, a
> chaos which would be immediately exploited by the enemy, especi-
> ally the Hungarians. . . . In our opinion, not even for a moment
> should we allow the existence of an exclusively Slovak government,
> nor of something similar which might be regarded as the legal con-
> tinuity of independent Slovakia of today. The Hungarians and the
> Germans, and perhaps even some of the Allies, would immediately
> take advantage of such a situation, and would exploit it against us
> in the matter of boundaries and against our other aspirations.[17]

Not only the Czechoslovak government in London but others in Europe too, including the Hungarian government, assumed for a while that the war would end, not unlike in 1918, without the actual presence in Central Europe of the victorious armies of the Great Powers. However, after the Teheran conference in December 1943, the mood had changed. New perspectives opened up for the Czechoslovaks, both in exile and at home. In expectation of a total victory it also became possible to concretely contemplate the expulsion of the Hungarian minority. The issue was discussed simultaneously in exile and at home, through the effective unification of all resistance movements. Several resistance groups in Slovakia found links to one another, leading to cooperation and to the creation of a common revolutionary organ, the Slovak National Council (Slovenská národná rada) in December 1943. The minutes of the foundation were later named "Christmas agreement" because of its date, Christmas 1943. The Slovak National Council (SNC) originally consisted of eight members. At the time of the Slovak uprising, on September 1, 1944, two civilian and three military representatives (Golián, Ferjenčik, Marko Polak) were added, and thus the total membership was increased to thirteen.

The objectives of the SNC were worked out in line with the accurate assessment of the international military-political situation, and also in complete harmony with the policies of the exiles. This is particularly true of the issue of the national minorities. Point Four of the SNC program emphasizes complete agreement with the exiles: "The Slovak National Council shall act in harmony with the Czechoslovak government and with the entire resistance movement abroad; it recognizes and supports their work both on the diplomatic and military levels." Also, the program declares the desire of close cooperation exclusively with Slav states and Slav nations. Yet future developments are perhaps most clearly indicated by Point Six of Part Two, which guarantees freedom of religion, but does not even mention the national minorities.[19] No doubt, the success of Beneš's negotiations in Moscow at that time had an effect on this document, especially his declaration regarding the necessity of a homogeneous Slav nation-state. This opinion is corroborated by Jozef Jablonický: ". . . the final text of the Christmas agreement was determined by the Soviet-Czechoslovak treaty of friendship signed on December 12, 1943."[20]

Beneš himself voiced his opinion of the "Christmas agreement" on March 29, 1944: "He hailed the accord, and agreed with it in its general outline."[21] He deplored, however, the exclusion from the SNC of certain non-Communist groups (Kaviar, Muzeum, Flora).

It should be emphasized that in 1944 the united Slav stand against the Hungarian minority was limited to the highest levels of the Slovak National Council and to the intellectuals. The peasantry and the workers remained by and large indifferent to the anti-Hungarian propaganda. In fact, units of the Hungarian army were well received in the Slovak villages even after the defeat of the Slovak uprising in 1944, even though the occasion was not particularly conducive to fraternization.

In 1944, it seemed questionable in fact whether it would be possible to sway Slovak public opinion to accepting the idea of physical liquidation of the Hungarian ethnic community. Those who favored the expulsion, but doubted its successs, found encouragement in the smooth process of the deportation of Jews under the Tiso regime. Terrorized by an atmosphere of fear, the masses remained silent and indifferent at that time. It was possible to assume that at the end of the war, the anti-Hungarian propaganda would do what the anti-Semitic propoganda did during the Fascist period. These assumptions proved correct. After the war, public opinion responded with general passivity and cautious indifference to the persecution of Hungarians. Though the most likely reason could have been that there were but very few Slovaks who had nothing to hide in their political past. The majority had cause to remain silent, and those who might have wavered were brought in line by the force of nationalist propaganda.

No written proof exists (with the exception of two newspaper reports, which will be discussed in subsequent chapters) of anyone voicing after the war any kind of dissenting opinion against the expulsion policies of President Beneš and Prime Minister Gottwald, either on the grounds of a thousand years of Hungarian-Slovak coexistence or by virtue of humanitarian principles. Among the intellectuals, in particular, a stand against the Hungarians became a matter of national moral imperative. Workers and peasants did express disagreement individually according to eyewitness reports. But no other evidence of such "proletarian" dissent survived.

In July 1944, Beneš's political secretary P. Drtina, sent a message to the resistance groups at home in which he gave a foretaste of Beneš's tactics of accomplished facts: "It will be necessary for us to settle accounts with many Germans in the first days of liberation; to see to it that most guilty Nazis should flee our land out of fear, terrorized by the evolving revolution rising against them; and to beat to death most of those who would offer resistance."[22]

Even though Drtina advised this tactic explicitly only against the Germans, we must keep in mind that the advocacy of the German-Hungarian parallel had by then become a matter of routine. Moreover, if Drtina's advise was followed, it would be up to the crowd of lynchers to decide who was a Nazi and who was not, who was guilty and who was not, irrespective of nationality. There was a real danger that the method of punishing the Germans would be extended against the Hungarians as well, even though the exchange of populations was the only punishment Drtina had explicitly mentioned at that time with reference to the Hungarians.

The letters received in London at that time from the home front stress unanimity regarding the Hungarian question. And all the published letters demand deportation. One of them says: "Let the minorities be removed. We reject rapprochement with the Sudeten-Germans living in exile in England. There are no differences among them. They betrayed us. This applies also to the Hungarians."[23] Another letter by an unnamed member of a non-Communist resistance group reporting on the mood among students in Bratislava says: "They do not attempt to conceal their antagonsim towards the Hungarians, they grab every opportunity for anti-Hungarian demonstrations."[24] A report on the student groups by the clandestine information officer, Captain J. Krátky, is no more encouraging from a Hungarian point of view: "All these groups are united only in their anti-German and anti-Hungarian sentiments. They do not differentiate between Nazi and German, and as far as they are concerned, even a Hungarian Socialist is but a Hungarian."[25]

There was no direct contact between the home front in Slovakia and the exiles in Moscow until August 4, 1944, when a delegation consisting of Karol Šmidke and M. Ferjenčik was dispatched by the Slovak National Council to the Soviet capital. They returned a month later, on September 4. The dates are important, because the final solution regarding the Hungarian question—the principle of general deportation, that is—was brought home by Šmidke from Moscow, and was presented to the Slovak National Council on September 5. This was a turning point, proven by subsequent developments. Until September 4, 1944, the declarations of resistance organizations at home refer only to some kind of a population exchange, representing more or less democratic measures, whereas after September 5, 1944, the postwar ultra-nationalist slogans gained ground against the minorities, along with demands for property confiscation and denial of democratic rights.

The minutes of the 1944 negotiations at Moscow by Šmidke (officially published only in 1964) give a foretaste of the grim prospects. The text of the Moscow Accord between Šmidke and the leaders of the Czechoslovak

Communist party in exile did not augur well for the Hungarians of Slovakia:

> When the Red Army arrives on Slovak territory, in order to facilitate
> its advance, with its [Red Army] consent, there should be a general
> national uprising; the regime of traitors at Bratislava should be
> driven out; the powers of a provisional government should be ex-
> ercised by the Slovak National Council; with the help of the Red
> Army the Germans and the Hungarians should be driven out of
> Slovakia's occupied territories.[26]

It is not specified whether the Hungarians to be "driven out" from the
"occupied territories" are the Hungarian troops, or the civil administration
of the Horthy regime, or the Hungarian civilian population. There is reason to assume, however, that had the Moscow Accord meant only driving
out the Hungarian army units, the text would have specified that it meant
only that.

Be that as it may, the strategic precondition of this so-called "military
solution" of the Hungarian question was the assumption that the front
would advance in a north-to-south direction. Until August 1944 this
seemed not merely likely, but certain. Certainly the leaders of the Slovak
uprising based their plans on this assumption. However, by the end of
August the situation had changed. As a result of Rumania's switching
sides from the Axis to the Allies, a new front was opened against Hungary
in an east-to-west direction. This had severe consequences for both the
military and political prospects of the Slovak uprising: a large-scale Soviet
offensive moving from north-to-south became out of the question. This
was recognized by the military leaders of the uprising in the first days of
September. General Golián made a statement to that effect, recorded in
his recollections by A. Rašla: " . . . you had planned everything as if the
Slovak army could make [for the Soviet army] a rapid crossing of the
Carpathian mountains possible, and thus enable Slovakia's [Soviet] occupation as well as a rapid [Soviet] advance towards Vienna and Budapest."[27]

The military solution of the Hungarian question thus planned was also
mentioned in a memorandum sent to the Soviet government by General
Čatloš, Tiso's turncoat Minister of War: "The moment the Soviet forces

find a footing in the Krakow area, the time for a successful surprise attack against the Hungarians could come from Slovakia. . . together with possible further military operations against the Germans. The Slovak army would prepare and assist the rapid and unhampered advance of Soviet troops across Slovak territory, and would join in the attack against the Hungarians."[28]

In the summer of 1944, the reconquest of Southern Slovakia from the Hungarians was no longer a secret goal of the Slovak Fascist government but an open commitment of the anti-Fascist Slovak uprising. It was stated in the memorable proclamation of the Čapajev partison brigade: "The days of German and Hungarian rule are counted, the hour of liberty and settling of account has struck."[29]

The Hungarian resistance fighters who joined the Slovak uprising could hardly have felt encouraged by the nationalist spirit of the uprising. Nowhere in fact could Hungarians spot signs of encouragement that could have raised their spirit of anti-Fascist resistance. Everywhere the old Little Entente tactics of Hungary's hostile encirclement have threatened to block Hungarian efforts to forestall the approaching national catastrophe. National interests hostile to Hungary prevented above all the organization of an anti-Fascist Hungarian army under Soviet auspices, one of the last hopes of national resistance.

Despite expressed desire by thousands of captured Hungarian soldiers since 1943, no anti-Fascist army could be formed from Hungarian prisoners-of-war. Why not? Becuase such an army might have hurt the rival interests of Hungary's neighbors, it might have interferred with crucial decisions on conflicting claims to national territorial rights. The Hungarian Communist Zoltán Vas, a former exile in Moscow, was the only one ever to face this painful question honestly—twenty-five years later though—when he wrote:

> To organize a Hungarian army corps against Hitler and Horthy! This was, and remained, the objective of our prisoners of war movement. . . . It continued for more than a year. Yet the drive for setting up a Hungarian army corps ended in failure. Not because of lack of effort of the exiles in Moscow, or of the [prisoners of war] officers. The fact of the matter is that we never received from our Soviet comrades the permission to set up an army corps. Hence it was as if we

had been agitating in a vacuum. My conviction is that, had we received the permission, the corps could have been formed. Thus the Czechs, the Poles, the Rumanians were able to get ahead of us, while Horthy's Hungary stuck to the last as a satellite to Hitler's side.[30]

The "vacuum" Zoltán Vas spoke about was true not only of the struggle to form a Hungarian armed force abroad. The Hungarian resistance at home too was forced into a vacuum.

The Hungarian General Béla Miklós started seemingly fruitful negotiations with General Petrov, the commander of the Fourth Ukrainian Front, on the subject of an anti-Fascist Hungarian army. Whereupon, on November 1, 1944, and again on November 18, General Miklós sent a letter to Soviet Marshall Antonov, requesting authorization for the establishment of such an army. He received no reply. Then General Mechlis arrived from Moscow and informed General Miklós, to no small surprise of General Petrov, that according to Marshall Stalin's instructions no anti-Fascist Hungarian army should be set up.[31]

The fact of the Hungarian "vacuum" has been ignored by all historians, both in Hungary and abroad. Instead of explaining the dire reality of the Hungarian situation and the resulting mass psychology of the Hungarian people, we hear a hail of denunciations spread by the hostile nationalist propaganda of Hungary's neighbors. We hear of the Hungarian society's passivity, inaction, Fascism, cowardice, degeneration, obsequious submissiveness to the Germans, depravity, and so on. In actual fact, the feeling of "vacuum" determined the collective behavior of the Hungarian people toward the end of the war. It paralyzed the society at home, no less than it frustrated the efforts of the Hungarian exiles. But the historians are silent about it. And no one takes issue with such flimsy condemnations as those of Éva Teleki's, one of postwar Hungary's Communist historians who wrote: ". . .even the left was confused by the passivity of the masses. There is no excuse for this . . . ."[32] True, the historian should not look for excuses. But the historian should analyze and explain why the partisans in Slovakia and Serbia, or elsewhere fought bravely, whereas in Hungary—although the Hungarians are reputable fighters—the proletarian masses as well as the intellectuals remained paralyzed. Éva Teleki certainly did not explain the Hungarian "vacuun," the cause of the Hungarian paralysis.

Of course, it is depressing to read a report on the Hungarian situation sent to Nikita Khrushchev (then fighting in the Ukraine) by T. Strokač, a leader of the Ukrainian partisans: "According to partisan reports, the Hungarians are hostile to the partisans; they report our presence to the gendarmes or the military, and assist them in their attacks against us."[33] However, we should realize that we are dealing with a phenomenon which cannot be explained by the theory of "sinful passivity." For—and this is a fact—the class struggle, the coming social revolution, the defeat of the reactionary Horthy regime, everything that could have inspired the Hungarian masses had lost its meaning and importance to the Hungarian people. The Hungarians knew that Horthy's regime would not survive and Hungary would be defeated. However, in the "vacuum" of their desperate situation, through no fault of their own, the Hungarian people had no choice but meeting the inevitable with resignation.

Hungarian historians of the postwar Communist era, strangely enough, do not seem to understand the Hungarian situation. They do not look beyond the facts while condemning Hungarian "passivity." Communist Party historian Ignác Ölvedi notes that the propaganda of the resistance movement, whether that of the Communist Party or that of the Hungarian Front, was "unable to arouse the masses from their passivity."[34] Had Ölvedi noticed the wartime propaganda beamed to Hungary's neighbors and compared it to what was beamed to the Hungarian people, he could have easily understood the Hungarian "passivity." The fact of the matter is that the Hungarian people deemed not worth dying for another Trianon that humiliated and dismembered them.

Another Hungarian historian, Gyula Juhász, without really explaining it, actually sees the essence of the problem when he says: "From the beginning of the war, the national sentiment in Hungary could not become a moving force in the formation of an anti-Fascist independence movement as it did in other countries of Central Europe. The true face of German fascism . . . with all its horrors remained unknown to the country's population for a long time."[35] True enough. As a soldier in the Horthy army it was in September 1944 that I first heard of Hitlerite genocide; rumors reached us about the extermination camps around Katowcie. It is conceivable that, if better informed, the German orientation would have enjoyed less popular support than it did. However, the truth of the matter is that Hungarian national interests did not clash with Germany. They clashed with Czechoslovakia, Rumania and Yugoslavia!

To what extent national interests were the crucial factor in the final stage of the Second World War was duly noted by the Slovak historian Motoška. He even attempted, better than the Hungarian historians, to analyze the complex situation of the Hungarian masses:

> When the Arrow-Cross rule of terror was nearing its end, resistance among the ranks of Hungarian soldiers increased. But there were no forces at work which could have given the Hungarians new direction out of their state of passive resistance.[36]

Current Hungarian official historical writing indiscriminately compares resistance movements of different nations without explaining the causes that accounted for their differences. Shameful as it is, we have to turn to Motoška, the Slovak historian in order to understand the different context of the Hungarian and Slovak resistance movements:

> Unlike in Hungary, the Slovak resistance movement was united. It was the national movement of all classes and groups. . . . Even the leftists worked in a nationalist spirit. Hence the conflict between the views of Slovak and Hungarian Communists regarding the solution of the question of national minorities after the war. . . . The Hungarian Communists counted on proletarian solidarity with the Slovak Communists. No wonder that, after the war, the Hungarian Communists had a hard time to resign themselves to the events [in Slovakia] of the years 1945-48. . . .[37]

One wonders only: How could any Hungarian at any time, and during the period of 1945-1948 in particular, look for any signs of "proletarian solidarity" on the Slovak side? Persecution hit the Hungarian working class indiscriminately, and the poor peasant often more severely than the well-to-do.

Motoška recognizes the same phenomenon in Slovakia's Hungarian regions that the Strokač-report of the Ukrainian partisans did in Hungary proper—namely that the Hungarian people, including the working class, were not aware of them being "liberated;" moreover, that they were hostile towards the Soviet "liberators." But Motoška, disingeneously, does not admit that the "hostile" Hungarian attitude in liberated Slovakia reflected the anti-Hungarian attitude of the Slovaks. He disparages the Hungarian masses for their "essentially passive resistance" in the face of "the arrival of the liberation army."[38] Thus, not unlike the postwar Hungarian historians, Motoška too sees only the facts, but fails to explain them. He fails to face the question: Why should Slovakia's "liberated" Hungarians have felt enthusiasm when the anti-Hungarian leaflets berated them and condemned them to loss of freedom?

The anti-Hungarian objective of the Slovak uprising of 1944 was eagerly promoted by actions of the Czechoslovak government-in-exile. On August 29, 1944, consistent with Beneš's anti-German *and* anti-Hungarian ideology, the London government had sent a message to Slovakia via Army Commander-in-Chief Ingr: "We find it self-evident that you should declare yourself part of the Czechoslovak army at the moment of launching the struggle against the Germans and Hungarians." Another message from London to General Golián of the partisan army emphasized the ideology of Czechoslovak unity: "Declare yourselves part of the Czechoslovak army."[39] And without waiting for a reply, the London government actually announced that the military units fighting in Slovakia are units of the Czechoslovak army.[40]

At the end of August, Beneš did not know yet that after Rumania's surrender to the Soviets, the main thrust of the wrar in the Danube region had shifted to the south-east, and that the general Soviet offensive across the Carpathians from the north would not be mounted against Hungary. Unaware of the change, the London government sent new instructions to General Viest in Slovakia on September 8: "In case of the collapse or surrender of Hungary the annexed Slovak territories [annexed by Hungary in 1938] must be reoccupied!"[41] In those days, the London exiles still counted on a quick success of the Slovak uprising with the support of a Soviet offensive in a north-to-south direction toward the Hungarian mid-Danube region.

General Pika's instructions dispatched from Moscow on September 18 attest to a more realistic assessment of the situation: "We [fighters of the Slovak uprising] must not launch an offensive against Hungary until the arrival of the Red Army and of the Czechoslovak units [fighting together

with the Red Army]!"[42] The limited extent of the uprising, and the inaction of the so-called Malar-division in Eastern Slovakia, as well as the un-
reliability of the Slovak garrisons at Trnava and Nitra in the West, made in
fact the launching of an offensive not possible at all without Soviet support.

The Banská Bistrica headquarters of the Slovak uprising issued its first
measure against the Hungarians on September 6. This directive 6/1944 of
the Slovak National Council eliminated Hungarian secondary education,
leaving the Hungarian minority only with elementary schools. It also abol-
ished any Hungarian school set up after Munich in 1938. Actually, the
directive had no practical implications at that time because the Slovak uprising never extended to Slovakia's Hungarian-inhabited regions. Yet, this
first measure started the large scale civil rights and cultural suppression of
the Hungarian minority, although it has often been called a "democratic"
gesture (perhaps by way of comparison with later developments).

Anyway, the real turning point in dealing with the Hungarian question
in liberated Slovakia should be dated from the September 5, 1944, session
of the Slovak National Council which adopted the Šmidke-Ferjenčik
report on their Moscow mission. From that moment on the radical policy
of anti-Hungarian discrimination took effect, as determined by the leaders
in exile both in London and Moscow.

After September 5, the gist of the policy against the non-Slav nationalities was deportation coupled with property confiscation. If any democratic illusions survived, they were dispelled by the proclamation published in mid-September, designed to persuade Slovak public opinion
that anti-Fascism and national revolution meant deportation of the Hungarians. The new concept of the Slav nation-state eliminated the Hungarian minority from the legally recognized ranks of the country's inhabitants. The tone of the September appeal already anticipated the 1945
Košice program of total discrimination: "The National Committee, in a
most ruthless manner, will confiscate the property of the traitors, Germans and Hungarians, the wealth of those who committed crimes against
the nation."[43] As interpreted in practice, the entire Hungarian ethnic
group was collectively declared guilty and condemned to loss of civil
rights and property confiscation. The principle was the same as that of
the later Presidential decree 108/1945, which served as the basic law for
carrying out the Košice program of total discrimination against the national minorities of liberated Czechoslovakia.

The naive and uninformed, who believed in Soviet liberation as a social revolution, thought that the class of exploiters alone had been affected by the September proclamation. They should have been enlightened by the text of the proclamation itself which precluded all possible misunderstandings: "All the property of the Germans, Hungarians and traitors, acquired at our expense will be confiscated, and will be provisionally transferred to the care of the National Committees."[44] There could be no doubt. "All the property" included the property of the Hungarian working class as well.

Historians later argued that the principle of discrimination was yet unknown in 1944, and that the leaders of the Slovak uprising were led by "democratic" sentiments toward the Hungarian minority. The "uprising measures" were described as having been "internationalist." Some authors found concrete evidence in support of this interpretation. For instance, J. Purgat quotes the report of information officer Špáta regarding a statement by Laco Novomeský, a prominent Slovak Communist writer: "Our view is that we cannot adopt a uniformly negative attitude towards every German and every Hungarian. Many Hungarians have remained more faithful to the Republic than any number of Slovaks or Czechs. . . . They must not be abandoned and betrayed in the struggle."[45] Historian Purgat believes that with this quote he has furnished solid evidence in support of the "democratic" measures taken toward the Hungarians during the Slovak uprising. However, he ignored the next sentence of information officers Špáta's report: "Of course I don't know how he [Novomeský] might fare with such noble humanistic sentiments in present-day Slovakia."[46]

The measures taken against the Hungarian minority were clearly rooted in the new Slav ideology of Czechoslovak nationalism. Yet a view, still popular among Slovaks, maintains that discrimination against the Hungarians was caused by the Hungarain political climate of 1944: "The road which might have led to mutual understanding was barred by the wavering Hungarian attempt to surrender, and especially by the dreadful Arrow-Cross terror in Hungary which also engulfed Slovakia's territories under Hungarian occupation."[47]

By the fall of 1944, the Slovak revolution had been openly transformed from a class struggle into a nationalist war against the Hungarians. A Slovak capitalist was an ally of the revolution, provided he was not a *known* collaborator (which was hard to know under the circumstances). But a Hungarian proletarian, unless he could *prove* (which was not easy under the circumstances) that he had been an active fighter against Fascism, was regarded as an enemy. On September 22, 1944, the Slovak *Pravda* wrote: "The landed estates of the Hungarians and Germans have to be confiscated right away and without compensation." The land reform in fact became a radical tool of nationalist discrimination against the Hungarians. It preserved the large estates of Slovak landlords, but excluded the landless Hungarian peasants from the benefits of land distribution. In the course of socialization of industry, too, the ethnic bias of nationalism prevailed. Characteristically, the Slovak *Pravda* consistently attacked only the factories of Germans and Hungarians as targets of struggle against "big business."[48]

Theories of Slovak historians claiming that the discriminatory policies against the Hungarian minority were spontaneous outbreaks of some kind of popular rage against Horthy's failure to leave the war, or against the subsequent Hungarian Arrow Cross terror, are altogether contrary to the facts. A new, purely Slav concept of Czechoslovak nation-state was declared at the time of the Slovak uprising, in accordance with the nationalist directives received from the exiles. The groundwork for the later "constitutional" discrimination against the nationalities was already laid at that time in exile, even though it was published at home only in 1945. Historian Marta Vartíková is correct in pointing out: "The decree [of 1945] concerning the confiscation of the enemy properties of Germans and Hungarians was worked out at the time of the uprising by the Slovak National Council [in 1944]."[49]

To discover some sort of "internationalist" spirit in the Slovak uprising just because several hundred Hungarians had fought in it would amount to a distortion of history. (More recent literature, as seen from Vartíková's work no longer makes such "internationalist" claims.) Certainly, the Hungarians, joining the Slovak uprising in a struggle against Nazism and the Germans did not know that they were fighting for their own and their fellow Hungarians' deportation from Slovakia and confiscation of all Hungarian property. Nobody told them right away that the objective of the Slovak uprising was to establish a purely Slovak nation-state.

In retrospect, however, it should be clear that the main motivation behind the Slovak uprising was the expectation to create favorable conditions for the liquidation of the Hungarian minority living within Slovakia's pre-Munich frontiers. Otherwise, from the Slovak point of view, the uprising itself made little sence. After all, the Allied had already pledged the restoration of Czechoslovaki's prewar frontiers. Moreover, militarily, as we now know, the uprising was not even brought into line with the Soviet strategic plans of that time.[50]

The composition of the Slovak National Council was limited to two parties, the Communist and the Democrat, while General Golián was a so-called Independent. The power of the Democrats, however, was secondary, as evaluated by the Communist Šverma in a letter sent to Moscow in October 1944: "The Democrats (Šrobár, Ursíny, Zaťko) do not yet have a party. They have some kind of central committee, and they publish the *Čas*. But they do not have positions within the bureaucratic structure and they hold the union of farmers in their hands through Ursíny. Today they are united with us, though they back down and are afraid of us."[51]

Incidentally, the Democrats at that time (but not later) were somewhat uncertain regarding the anti-Hungarian objectives of the national revolution. Will any Hungarians remain at all within the restored Czechoslovak Republic and, if so, what will happen to them? The program of the Democratic Party addressed itself to that question at the beginning of October: "The national minorities, in case they cannot be transferred from the Republic within the framework of a large-scale exchange of populations program, will receive whatever rights the new international order guarantees them, and corresponding to the rights guaranteed to the Slovaks in the motherland of the minorities."[52]

Such "democratic" considerations were actually out of date already at that time. The information the Communist Šverma brought from Moscow rendered any democratic plans regarding the minorities illusory. Nevertheless, postwar historians have been fond of citing the Democratic Party program as a proof the "internationalist and democratic" spirit of that time. The October program of the Democratic Party, in fact, had but marginal significance. Its authors might have believed that some kind of international agreement would guarantee the rights of the national minorities after the war. But since September 5, the realities of power

were represented by the instructions handed down by the Czech Communist Gottwald and forwarded from Moscow by Šverma: "As regards the
question of the Germans *and* [italics added] the Hungarians within the
new Republic: Radical measures will be taken to reduce the German population of the Republic. I declare that we will raise no obstacles of any
kind to a radical solution of *all* [italics added] these questions."[53]

At the same time, the Slovak National Council also received identical
information regarding minority matters from the Czechoslovak government in London which said: "Among others, a decree is under discussion
now by which the Germans *and* [italics added] the Hungarians will be
shorn of their citizenship, with the exception of those who fought for the
Republic."[54] This information received on September 24 from the London government came as no surprise. Several resolutely anti-Hungarian
measures had been already in the making against the Hungarian minority
(though premature at that time for lack of power to carry them out)
in the directive pertaining to the so-called "democratic transformation
of society." According to a directive dated September 17, 1944, the national committees were to be organized in the spirit of anti-Hungarian
discrimination by excluding the Hungarians unequivocally from all civil
rights. Paragraph Six of the directive issued by the interim representative
in charge of internal affairs declared: "The local national committees
may not include German or Hungarian members." In other words, the
Hungarian minority was ordered to be excluded from self-government
and from the exercise of basic civil rights in general. Legally speaking,
the Hungarians should have been first deprived of the Czechoslovak
citizenship. The Presidential decree 108/1945 caught up with that omission.

By the middle of October the tone of public utterances became even
sharper. In particular, class solidarity preached by the Communists vanished altogether. At a gathering of farmers, the Communist Marek Čulen,
speaking of the coming "national and democratic revolution," advocated
the confiscation of the land of the Hungarian peasants, outlining thus
the new form of socialist ideology of extreme nationalist content: "We
must seize without delay all the lands owned by Germans and Hungarians,
or by their treacherous helpers, and distribute them without compensation
among the Slovak farmers."[56] Thus began the war against the Hungarian
proletariat. Resistance at home aligned itself with exile policies.

The new tone encountered no obstacles. All that was needed was to apply the anti-Semitic slogans of the Tiso era to the Hungarians. The worn-out denunciation of "Jewish capital" turned into a denunciation of "German and Hungarian capital." This curious new spirit of "class struggle" captivated the congress of the labor union committees at Podbrezová: "We do not raise the issue of property rights, but we do insist that it is necessary to nationalize the wealth of German and Hungarian capitalists, and everything which is in the hands of our enemies at home or abroad."[57] Class in Marxist sense ceased to exist. Capital meant German and Hungarian capital. The international revolution was taken over by the Slav proletariat, solely entitled to receive the rewards of the revolution.

By the middle of October, militarily the uprising was in deep trouble. Nevertheless, on October 17, Jozef Lettrich, Chairman of the Democratic Party, still struck on optimistic note. In a debate at a meeting of interim representatives, he spoke of the impending annexation of Slovakia's lost territories: "We must carefully prepare the occupation of this area. Many serious issues will arise then. We must be ready for action any day now."[58]

Actually, this might have sounded realistic just a couple of days earlier. For, as the Hungarian Communist A. I. Puskás pointed out: "Horthy knew full well that all he had to do was issue the order for the execution of the conditions of the armistice and the Soviet troops would reach Budapest within a few hours."[59] The Nazi Germans, too, seemed to share that view. Former German ambassador to Hungary Veesenmayer spoke to that effect at the trial of the Hungarian Fascist Andor Jaross: "Had the Hungarian army surrendered on October 15 [the day of Horthy's miscarried attempt to leave the war], the Germans would have been forced to withdraw their forces from the Danube basis."[60] And, indeed, according to the terms of the Soviet-Hungarian armistice signed in Moscow on October 11, 1944, the Hungarian troops and the Hungarian administration were to be drawn within ten days to the Trianon boundaries, which would have meant recovery by the Slovaks of the lost territories, as Lettrich hoped that it may soon happen.

The Hungarian army's failure to obey Horthy's order and surrender became later a factor in condemning collectively Slovakia's Hungarian minority. Ferenc Szálasi's Arrow Cross regime became full proof of the "Fascist nation" charge against the Hungarians. In this connection, a report of the Czechoslovak government in London dated November 16, 1944, is of particular interest:

> In the second week of October we still hoped to establish a link between our soldiers and the Soviet forces in the Southeast where the army of Malinowski crossed the Transylvanian Alps and created a serious military and political crisis in Hungary by crossing the Tisza River as well. It was generally assumed everywhere among the Allies that the Hungarian army would collapse, and make it impossible for the Germans to carry on a sustained defense. However, contrary to all expectations, by their rapid intervention, the German units and the Gestapo succeeded in preventing Hungary from stepping out of the war. It is interesting, and instructive for the future, that even after such an upheaval the Hungarian army did not lose any of its combativeness and its inclination to continue the war, and kept on fighting alongside the Germans under hopeless conditions. . . . Therefore, after a brief spell of optimism, nurtured by the possibility of the eventual collapse of Hungary, a grave and far reaching crisis occurred in Slovakia, leading to the collapse of [Slovak] military resistance.[61]

The Czechoslovak view was wrong only in believing that the Hungarian army held out alongside the Hiterlite coalition solely because the Gestapo and the German units prevented the switch to an anti-Fascist stand. The fact of the matter is that the Hungarian Army had no inclination to switch sides. This was also the mood of overwhelming majority of the officer corps.[62] And I have already clarified the reasons for this deplorable attitude in my discussion of the Hungarian "vacuum."

However, had the leaders of the Slovak uprising in Banská Bystrica, in September and October 1944, sought the helping hand of the Hungarian working class instead of proclaiming the policy of discrimination against the Hungarian minority, the Slovak uprising itself might have fared differently. A new friendly tone might have perhaps affected even developments in Hungary. All this of course is only guesswork—idle speculation. Only two things are certain: Local fraternization with Hungarians fighting in the Slovak uprising had no positive impact whatsoever on Slovak-Hungarian relations. Alleged participation of Hungarian units in suppressing the uprising, on the other hand, had an exaggerated negative effect.

The role of the Hungarian units in the defeat of the Slovak uprising is not clear. Yet, in the hysteria of anti-Hungarian reprisals exaggerated charges have recklessly been levelled: "It is not possible to erase this Hungarian crime from history. Hungary contributed to the subjugation of our liberated lands, not to mention those Hungarian divisions which combed the partisan-controlled areas with the help of SS troops."[63] The term "combing," incidentally, had several meanings in those times. It might have meant checking identifications—but also mass murders.

Later historical literature knows of no atrocities committed by Hungarian units against the civilian population. Moreover, it is common knowledge that Hungarian troops took no part in the military operations: "Hungarian units did not participate in the attack. . . . It was only at a later phase of the uprising that Hungarian units entered Slovak territory, and performed guard duties. . . ."[64]

Following the German defeat of the Slovak uprising, more than ever the recapture of Southern Slovakia has fired Slovak hostility against the Hungarians. The repossession of the "lost territories" became the battle cry! German diplomacy took due notice of the Slovak mood: "Broad masses of the Slovak population expect that in the context of a new political and international order the Vienna Award of November 2, 1938, according to which the southern areas of Slovakia had been attached to Hungary, will be rectified. Faith in the revision of the boundaries had found deep root in the Slovak nation. This was taken advantage of by the enemy propaganda claiming that the new Czechoslovakia will reestablish the borderline prior to the Vienna Award of 1938 and bring about an aggrandizement of Slovakia."[65]

In sharp contrast to Slovak hopes, Hungary, collapsing into a "vacuum," faced the grim fact that any sacrifice would be rewarded by a bitter retreat to the Trianon boundaries. Already in the summer of 1944, the Hungarian government was well aware of this, but no one dared to say it publicly. The chief of the General Staff reported the "Anglo-Saxon position" according to which "Hungary will return to its Trianon boundaries."[65] And at a cabinet meeting, Minister of the Interior Miklós Bonczos, while pondering the chances of withdrawing from the war, was musing about "merits" and "interests" in international politics. The Allies, he said, "considered only their own interests."[66] Others knew this truth well before the Hungarian minister discovered it. The greatest expert of all time in that respect, Edvard Beneš, recorded in his First-World War memoirs: "One must always adjust one's tactics to the interests of the victorious Great Powers, and make use of their interests for one's own goals."[67]

For reasons already mentioned, at the time of the Slovak national uprising, Hungarian resistance activity was but sparse. Stemming from the mood of national "vacuum," Hungarian passivity prevailed everywhere, even in the immediate vicinity of the Slovak uprising. Both the Hungarian civilian population and the army remained passive.

Instead of searching the true causes, some Slovak historians devised contrived theories to explain Hungary's apathy: "An important role was played by a feeling of aristocratic pride and of dumb anti-Communism," suggested one of them.[68] This hardly could explain the passivity of workers and peasants. After all, the Hungarian working class did have revolutionary traditions. They certainly did not suffer from aristocratic pride.

In addition to the Hungarian feelings of a "vacuum," among the causes of passivity were also the news from the liberated territories of Czechoslovakia.

After the liberation of Eastern Slovakia in late 1944, discrimination against the Hungarian population got immediately under way. Hungarians were summarily barred from the exercise of civil rights. When elections for the national committees took place in the liberated areas of Eastern Slovakia at the end of 1944, the "Germans, Hungarians, and the traitors" were deprived of the right to vote.[69] It cannot be doubted that the exculsion of the Hungarians from political rights happened at the instigation of higher authorities rather than on the initiative of the local population.

By November 1944, the resistance leaders of the home front and the exiles were in full agreement on the expulsion of the Hungarian minority. A delegation of the Slovak National Council arrived in London in November 1944 to confirm the agreement reached between the London exiles and Moscow, on the transfer of the Hungarian population.[70]

What some historians refer to as "democratic" initiatives in the matter of the Hungarian minority simply did not exist. Ever since the September directives which ordered the Hungarian secondary schools to be closed the course of actions was anti-democratic, though not yet to the same degree as the moral nihilism of 1945 and of subsequent years. But there is no trace of a "humanistic stand," or of an "internationalist class solidarity." There is no democracy, only in some pages of the Slovak memoir literature. The goal of the Slovak political leadership with regard to the Hungarian minority was simply ethnic elimination, the strategy of liquidation.

After the war the leading politicians cleverly claimed: "It was the wish of the people, expressed in the Slovak uprising, that the Hungarian minority should be liquidated." According to Dr. Lettrich, Chairman of the Democratic Party: "At the time of the uprising the Slovak masses expressed their wish that they want the new Czechoslovakia to become not a multinational state but the national state of Czechs and Slovaks alone, with no minority rights for other nationalities. We based our program on the principles of resettlement, expulsion, and re-Slovakization as the new form of solving the problem of Hungarians in Slovakia. Hence the uprising has the character of a national revolution for which there is no precedent in our history."[71] Viliam Široký, speaking on behalf of the Communist Party, concurred: "It follows from the sad experiences we have had with the Germans and the Hungarians that, since they had betrayed the Republic at the moment of gravest crisis, our people demanded already in their struggle for liberation that the Germans and Hungarians be expelled from the Republic, in order to make the Czechoslovak Republic into a strong Slavic state."[72]

Thus was the myth of the will of the people born in support of the policy of the Hungarians' expulsion—a policy actually imposed from above. The following chapters will deal with the efforts to carry out this policy, which did not lack nationalist support—but hit on some international stumbling blocks.

CHAPTER 4

1945: THE YEAR OF PEACE

As the first hostile blows hit the Hungarian minority in the early days of liberation in 1945, the nationalist excesses, not uncommon in the Danube region, have been thought to be passing acts, intended to intimidate the Hungarians—or manifestations of pent-up revolutionary passions, heightened by the presence of the Red Army as liberator. Little or nothing had then been known of the carefully prepared Czechoslovak policy behind most of these seemingly chaotic events, considered to be as nothing unusual under postwar conditions.

The Czechoslovak policy of liquidation conceived in exile against the Hungarian minority was unknown to the Hungarians. It remained hidden in fact from the Slovak public opinion at large as well. Thus, for a while, the Hungarian minority observed the unpleasant events with relative calm, awaiting the prewar rule of law to return. Not until the proclamation of the Košice government program in April 1945 did both Slovaks and Hungarians fully realize that a historical initiative was unfolding which would radically alter their mutual relations. In retrospect, the opening of this new era in Hungarian-Slovak relations was fittingly described by the Slovak Marxist theoretician Ladislav Szántó: "I knew already than that we will not be able to avoid the nationalist wave. The new world will not be born the way it is written in the textbooks but, rather from the heap of physical and spiritual ruin left behind by Fascism and the war."[1]

Given the emotional antecendents since Munich in 1938, it was not difficult for the new authorities that emerged after liberation in 1945 to channel Slovak nationalist passions in an anti-Hungarian direction. In the first days of liberation, sundry revolutionary demands began to appear, all directed mainly against the Hungarians. The Germans of Slovakia (always much smaller in number than the Hungarian minority) were much less a target, since with few exceptions, they had fled west with the retreating Nazi armies.

A "socialist" demand that emerged fairly early was an utterly un-Marxist proposition that the needs of the Slovak working class should be satisfied from properties of the Hungarian bourgeoisie—and at the expense of the Hungarian working class. Another noteworthy phenomenon was the meaning of the popular term "traitor." It has been understood to mean only minorities. Attacks against Slovaks or other Slavs were carefully avoided. Thus in January 1945, in liberated eastern Slovakia, at a rally at Humenné, the Slav population unanimously accepted a decision which declared "the immediate confiscation of the lands of the Gemans, Hungarians, and traitors, and the distribution of these lands to the poor farmers."[2] Although tied to the word "and," the term "traitor" was meant to be applied to minorities only, as made clear in a similar proclamation issued at a meeting in the Eastern Slovakian town of Prešov: "Let the property of the traitor Hungarian and German owners be confiscated."[3] Such demands anticipated the official policy which later explicitly declared the Hungarians alone as traitors and enemies of the Slovak people.

During these early days of liberation, the Slovak National Council had been heard from also. On February 4, 1945, the Council issued a so-called "Manifestum." Its tone was mixed. It started with some democratic promises and ended with totalitarian threats. It read in part: "The situation of the Hungarian citizens of this land depends on how they themselves will define their relationship to the Slovak nation, to the new Czechoslovak Republic, to the democratic and Slav orientation . . . ." This could have been interpreted as a promise of fair play. But then the "Manifestum" concluded with the threatening words: "From our economic life, we will eradicate the influence of Germans and Hungarians, of Slovak traitors who aided them, and of all anti-Slovak elements."[4]

The explanation for the mixed phrasing of the "Manifestum" might have been that, in February 1945, prior to the publication of the Košice program in April, there were quite a few doubts manifest regarding the success of an all-out radical solution of the Hungarian problem. For that matter, not even the Košice program mentioned the minorities' expulsion among the objectives of the Government. This might have been a tactical move, in order not to create panic. Anyway, as it turned out the loss of citizenship of the minorities, proclaimed in the Košice program, was a preliminary stage only in the policy of total liquidation of the minorities.

This preliminary stage of policy regarding the Hungarians is well reflected in the instructions sent by the Slovak National Council to the people of Lovinobaňa on February 5, 1945. It is almost tolerant in tone, proposing collaboration in administrative matters with "democratic" Hungarians: "Let the National Council work together with the democratically inclined Hungarians, in areas inhabited predominantly by Hungarians."[5]

The practice in Hungarian populated regions of Slovakia to attach to local Slovak committees Hungarians of so-called "democratic persuasion" as "advisors" continued throughout the postwar years, even at the time of the worst persecutions. This pattern was not practised at all in the case of the Germans in the Czech lands. However, resorting to Hungarian advisors had its drawbacks too. Hungarians who accepted such appointments, found themselves as collaborators with the enemies of the Hungarians in carrying out instructions against their fellow Hungarians—compiling, for instance, lists of Hungarian persons to be deported or expelled. No wonder, these Hungarians of "democratic persuasion" aiding the enemies of the Hungarians were less than popular among Hungarians. In fact, the practice elicited only despair and resentment among the entire society of the Hungarian minority.

It should be recalled that the transfer policy against the Hungarians reached an impasse during the war because of a lack of unanimous approval by the Great Powers. The Hungarian population did not flee either, as expected by those who hatched plans for the liquidation of minorities by a military *fait accompli.* The expected direction of fronts had changed in the closing stages of the war, and the Hungarians of Slovakia, mostly peasants, stayed anyway, never thinking of leaving the land where they lived since time immemorial. Thus, in the first months of 1945, those Slovaks who hoped for either of the two "solutions"—flight or forcible transfer —it looked as if they had to count with the continued existence of a Hungarian minority in Slovakia. Even in retrospect, the situation as it evolved, makes the Slovak historian Samuel Cambel most unhappy. He deplores both that the Hungarians did not flee and that the Western powers did not endorse the expulsion of the Hungarians. In his book on postwar "land reform," which is often a euphemism for land confiscation in Slovakia's Hungarian inhabited regions, Cambel explains: "The complexities which hampered land reform were connected mainly with the direction of the fronts; but the veto of the Western powers, at the time of the armistice with Hungary, regarding the deportation of the Hungarian minority from Czechoslovakia also played a part."[6]

Doubts among Slovaks at home concerning the success of the transfer policy did not bother the leaders in exile. Both in the West and in the East, they still believed that it would be possible to extend the transfer policy to the Hungarian minority by means of international agreements. The postwar Czechoslovak government program written in London and Moscow, was visibly inspired by such conviction.

The Hungarians of South Slovakia themselves at that time were waving between optimism and ill forebodings. They expected a democratic social revolution to follow the Horthy and Nazi era. The initially mostly halfhearted executed anti-minority measures encouraged Hungarian hopes that the chauvinistic excesses were simply a matter of a temporary flareup of intolerance. Hungarian optimism, however, received a cold shower when directive 4/1945 of the Slovak National Council in late February confiscated holdings in excess of 50 hectares of land of both Germans and Hungarians. Slovak "traitors" too were affected by the directive, but the number of Slovak landowners declared "traitors" was negligible.

The new Czechoslovak government formed at Košice in April hailed the local seizures of landholdings of "the enemy and of the traitors" for the benefit of the "poor Slovak peasants," and extended it to the entire territory of the state.[7] The postwar revolution thus turned its full force against the Hungarian peasant. Even the poor peasant was considered an enemy, if he was Hungarian. Almost all land in fact owned by Hungarians became subject to confiscation. The Presidential decree 12/1945 dated June 21, 1945 exempted from confiscation only the agricultural property of those persons of Hungarian nationality "who took an active part in the struggle for the defense of the Czechoslovak Republic."[8] Theoretically, this meant that perhaps 0.1 percent of the Hungarian-owned land would be exempt. In practice, however, no Hungarian land was safe against confiscation.

Another insiduous early onslaught against the Hungarian population was the decision of the Slovak National Council, issued on February 13, 1945, ordering all former civil servants to submit applications for reemployment.[9] The directive mentioned no nationality. Nevertheless, it resulted in the elimination of all government employees, including state-employed teachers of Hungarian nationality. Namely, in April the Slovak National Council ordered the firing of all Hungarian employees,[10] and the order having been completely carried out by May.[11]

Meanwhile, the liberated Slovak press was giving full support to the anti-Hungarian measures. A typical example was this harangue published by the Slovak Communist Party, entitled *"Ohlas"*:

> The Communist Party of Slovakia expects that the southern border regions of Slovakia which, in the past, were Hungarianized by force, will again be systematically Slovakized. The rich productive areas of Southern Slovakia whence the Hungarian feudal lords forced the Slovak farmers into the mountains, should be returned to the Slovak people. We expect that administrative commissars will be appointed to the towns and cities with a Hungarian majority.

To add insult to injury the Communist *"Ohlas"* declaration also expected the Commissars to be aided by "the democratic and actively anti-Fascist elements among the local Hungarian citizens" in advisory capacity.[12]

The historical argument of *"Ohlas"* that the southern borderlands of Slovakia were forcefully Hungarianized has no foundation whatsoever in fact. Nineteenth century Hungarianization (also known in English as "Magyarization") affected only the urban areas, while, if anything, in most cases Slovakization had taken place in the rural areas. This is a fact confirmed even by Czechoslovak scholarly sources: it is certain that

> during the 150 years preceding 1921, the Slovak-Hungarian language frontier changed rather in favor of the Slovaks, despite all the political pressures [of Magyarization]. Of the 319 communes in the language frontier areas, 73 changed their nationality; of these 49 changed in favor of the Slovaks.[13]

The government program proclaimed in liberated Košice on April 5, 1945, the so-called "Košice program" sanctioned the nationalist revolution in progress. For all practical purposes, the Košice program declared the entire Hungarian minority guilty of treason. The composition of the new government, formed at the same time, corresponded to the results of the negotiations in Moscow. It was appointed in Košice, on April 4,

1945 by a Presidential decree, "as the Government of the National Front of the Czechs and Slovaks." The cryptocommunist Czech Social Democrat Zděnek Fierlinger became Premier of the new government.

Chapter Eight of the Košice program dealing with the national minorities, deprived the Germans and Hungarians of their citizenzhip. The "exemption" promised to "anti-Fascists" was an illusory mitigation of the government program not unlike a similar clause of the earlier land confiscation measures. The pertinent passage of the Košice government program reads as follows:

> The terrible experiences of the Czechs and the Slovaks with the German and Hungarian minorities, the overwhelming majority of whom became the tools of invaders from the outside aiming to destroy the Republic. . . compel the new Czechoslovakia to intervene profoundly and for good. . . . The citizens of the Czechoslovak Republic of German and Hungarian nationalities who had Czechoslovak citizenship before the Munich decision of 1938, and who are anti-Fascists, will have their Czechoslovak citizenship confirmed and their return home shall be facilitated; the same applies to those who carried out an active struggle already in the period before Munich against Henlein or the Hungarian irredentist parties, for the defense of Czechoslovakia, and who, after Munich and March 15 suffered persecution at the hands of the German and Hungarian authorities because of their fidelity to the Czechoslovak Republic, to those who were imprisoned or sent to concentration camps, or were forced to flee abroad from German and Hungarian terror, and actively participated there in the anti-Fascist struggle for Czechoslovakia. The Czechoslovak citizenship of the remaining Czechoslovak citizens of German or Hungarian nationality will be invalidated. These citizens have the option to request Czechoslovak citizenship, and the agencies of the republic reserve the right to adjudicate each and every request on an individual basis.[14]

The mercy accorded to perhaps three percent of the minority population does not mitigate the mercilessness meted out to the remaining 97 percent. The government program also ordered complete purification of the administration from non-Slavic elements: "In those counties where

the population is unreliable and not of Slavic nationality, the adminis-
trators shall be appointed from the outside." [15]

The classification of people according to "Slav" and "non-Slav," reminiscent of the Nazi differentiation between "Aryan" and "non-Aryan," thus
became a permanent feature of government policy in Czechoslovakia,
without arousing the slightest concern or reflection abroad on the question: What had the Second World War actually been fought for? The
government program also explicitly declared the confiscation of the Hungarian landholdings, [16] and ordered the closing of German schools. [17] Most
of the Hungarian schools were closed already anyway.

The Košice government program was not published in Hungarian. But
rumors of its contents spread rapidly among the Hungarian population.
Those who heard the rumors refused to believe them. This amused the
Slovak historian J. Purgat who noted mockingly: "How great was their
surprise when it was no longer a matter of rumors, but even the government program proclaimed that only a Slovak person may receive land,
that there will be only Slovak schools, etc.!" [18]

Thus did liberation turn into tragedy for the Hungarian minority of
Czechoslovakia. Those who had expected from the defeat of fascism a
return to democracy were understandably astounded.

The unexpected was most unexpected for the Leftist Hungarians. It
is worth quoting briefly from the confessions of Rezső Szalatnai, a prominent progressive Hungarian writer. Rumors about the anti-Hungarian
measures in the liberated parts of Slovakia reached him before he himself
was liberated:

> We sit here in the shelter, a few feet underground . . . . My [Slovak]
> neighbor smilies, he knows a lot, he is not worried, he is sure of his
> thing. . . . But you will be in trouble, he keeps telling us. He has
> good information. The future, he says, belongs to our race, those
> who are not part of us will be deported. The Hungarian question is
> a matter of railway wagons. We look at him in astonishment: is he
> stupid or is he trying to create panic. The matter is settled, he
> whispers, courageous behavior counts for nothing. I am very sorry
> for you, we all know how bravely you behaved. But the matter is
> settled. . . . " [19] [The frightening rumors are spreading fast:] "B.

is coming, like every evening, and I let him know what I heard in the shelter. He says not a word, only drops his eyes. It turns out that in the morning he had met our mutual [Slovak] friend, a poet, who told him exactly the same thing.[20]

Despite the fast spreading rumors about the Košice program later that year, the Hungarian population did not fully believe in the impending danger. The ruthless tone attacking the Hungarians, the demand for their expulsion was everywhere, on the radio, in the press, on the posters. Yet the execution of these threats was still not believed to be possible. Rumors had spread that the Great Powers did not agree with the anti-Hungarian measures. Help was expected from the newly installed provisional revolutionary government across the border in Hungary.

The war was still on. Early in May, general mobilization was ordered in Czechoslovakia which did not apply to the Hungarians. Naively, the peasant population took this as an indication that the new Czechoslovakia did not want soldiers of Hungarian nationality, because the Hungarians will belong to Hungary.

The war was still on when the reorganization of the administration began along the lines of the Košice program. The Slovaks set up their National Committees everywhere where the Slav population was at least one-third of the total. In the Hungarian communes of southern Slovakia, so-called commissars or national representatives, and committees of administration were substituted for the National Committees. On April 7 the Central Slovak National Council issued a directive which excluded the non-Slavs from the exercise of democratic rights in the new administration: "Only a Czechoslovak citizen who belongs to some Slav nation" was declared eligible for membership in the National Committees.[21] The same directive regulated the appointment of commissars in the communes inhabited by Hungarians.[22] Unlike some earlier measures, this directive no longer made mention of including in an "advisory capacity" Hungarian anti-Fascists in the new administration.

May 1945 was no longer the time of confused ambiguities. The execution of the Czechoslovak nationalist program became crystal clear. On May 9, 1945, President Beneš made his memorable declaration: "The overwhelming majority of the Germans and Hungarians will have to leave our land. This is our final decision. . . . Our people can no longer live in the same country with Germans and Hungarians."[23] Soon thereafter, head of the Czech Communist Party, Klement Gottwald declared in a broadcast: "The Germans and the Hungarians, who had sinned so gravely against our nations and our republic, will be deprived of their citizenship and will be severely punished. Let the National Committees set on the tasks immediately."[24]

Then the Presidential decrees, so called because President Beneš issued them, started coming to implement the government program of Košice. The first such Presidential decree in May excluded the non-Slav population from the economic life.[25] Class considerations played no part. Not unlike the large enterprises, the small industrialists and small merchants as well as landholders of any kind, came under Slav control by virtue of a system called "national caretakers." The same Presidential decree declared the Germans and Hungarians politically unreliable. It defined the persons who were to be considered German or Hungarian as follows: "Those persons who have declared themselves Germans or Hungarians in any census since 1929, or have become members of a national group, organization, or party which consisted of Germans or Hungarians."[26] The decree exempted from discrimination only those who were able to prove that they had remained "faithful to the Czechoslovak Republic" or had become "victims of political or racial persecution."

It should be pointed out that in many instances, persons to fill the posts of "national caretakers" in Hungarian inhabited areas corrupted the entire system. Caretakers collaborated with the Hungarian entrepreneur; they became part of the enterprise by mutual understanding; often they were members of the family who made use of their political contacts in the interest of the joint enterprise. Thus, fortunately, this particular system caused no substantial harm to Hungarian minority society.

The story was different regarding the Presidential decree regulating so-called "internal resettlement." This decree issued in July 1945, was meant to place all land into Slav hands: "We mean by internal resettlement the totality of those regulations which will make it possible, by means of special prescriptions, to return all land in Czechoslovakia into the hands of the original Slav element."[27] (It should be noted that the reference to "original" Slav ownership was not a fact but a figment of nationalist imagination.) A Settlement Bureau with offices in Prague and Bratislava was to be set up. The head of the Bureau in Prague, with the rank of a Counselor in the central government was to be appointed by the President of the Republic on the recommendation of the Cabinet.

Most of the sufferings of the Hungarian minority from July 1945 on were closely tied to this Bureau in Prague and in its branch office in Bratislava. The Bureau ruthlessly exploited its authority; it was clearly the initiator of certain barbaric actions such as the winter deportations of 1946-1947.

In May 1945, when the mass firing of Hungarian civil servants took place pursuant to directive 44/1945 of the Slovak National Council, the overwhelming majority of the fired Hungarians remained without earnings overnight. Yet they did not dispair. They had faith in the coming peace treaty. The situation, however, changed by the fall. In September, all Hungarian schools remained closed and the mass expulsion of Hungarian teachers to Hungary began. Those who escaped expulsion found work mostly in construction. Concurrently with this fatal blow against Hungarian cultural life, all retirement payments to Hungarians were halted. The purge was not limited to government employees. Directive 69/1945 of the Slovak National Council ordered all "unreliable" Hungarians to be fired from private employment as well.[28]

A person of Hungarian nationality could be considered "reliable" if he was issued a so-called National Reliability Certificate. No particular legal procedure regulated the issuance of these certificates; it was simply a revolutionary practice. The certificates were issued at the discretion of the local Slovak National Committees. The custom was to grant certificates for three months at a time.[29] It is estimated that about three percent of the Hungarians succeeded in getting such certificates. In the summer of 1946, when the so-called "re-Slovakization" process was under way, a condition for issuing reliability certificates was the acceptance of "exchange" under the provisions of the Czechoslovak-Hungarian agreement on population exchange. In other words, a Hungarian who declared himself willing to leave the country was rewarded with a certificate of reliability, a rather cynical procedure.

By the summer of 1945, the Hungarian population recognized the seriousness of the situation. Many of the Hungarian anti-Fascist intellectuals became sharply critical of the anti-Hungarian measures. Some of them took the advice to leave for Hungary. But many left-wing intellectuals were deported against their will.[30] Had they remained, the cultural destruction of the Hungarian minority might not have been as extensive as it actually had become. The reason why so many anti-Fascist Hungarians had left was readily admitted by the Slovaks themselves; in the words of J. Purgat: "They became convinced that it was not only a matter of punishing the guilty, but the Hungarians in general."[31]

In its misery, the Hungarian minority expected anti-Fascist help from the postwar democratic government of Hungary. Verbal help did come from both the government and the press. However, the only means of international help Hungary could muster in this matter was through the Allied Control Commission in Budapest. Between April 1945 and July 1946, the Hungarian government sent 184 notes to Marshal Voroshilov, President of the Allied Control Commission in Budapest, protesting discriminations contrary to Czechoslovakia's international obligations against the Hungarian minority.[32] The Hungarian government protests had no effect whatsoever. On the other hand, the Hungarian press campaign had some impact. The reports on the persecutions may have occasionally resorted to exaggerations. But what mattered most was they that succeeded in arousing world public opinion to the plight of the Hungarian minority in Czechoslovakia.

Particularly insidious was the Czechoslovak policy against the Hungarian schools. The schools were not closed by any particular law. In 1945, the whole system of Hungarian minority education simply ceased to exist because of the dismissal and expulsion of the teachers.

The dismal stroy goes back to the time of the Slovak uprising. On September 6, 1944, the Slovak National Council ordered all Hungarian schools closed which were not in operation prior to October 6, 1938.[33] Then a memorandum sent by the London Czechoslovak government to the allied Great Powers on November 23, 1944 stated that no Hungarian public schools would be tolerated in liberated Czechoslovakia. Despite this threat, instruction in Hungarian schools continued in liberated Slovakia till the end of the war.

The Košice government program in April 1945, declared the closing of German schools only. In May, however, with the mass firing of Hungarian teachers without any legal grounds, the Hungarian school system automatically collapsed. What did kill the Hungarian schools was in fact the vituperous anti-Hungarian propaganda. Reportedly, the government representative in charge of education in Slovakia, Ladislav Novomeský did make attempts to ensure continuing instruction of Hungarian children in their mother tongue, but his proposals were turned down.[34]

The end result of Czechoslovak policy against Hungarian education was that from 1945 to 1949, Hungarian children were excluded from public schooling for four years. And even in 1950, when Hungarian schools reopened, half of the school-age Hungarian children did not attend Hungarian schools.[35]

After liberation, the most disillusioned members of the Hungarian minority in Czechoslovakia were the Hungarian anti-Fascists. Ferenc Molnár, a functionary of the Hungarian Communist Party at Nagyabony, returning from a district conference of the Slovak Communist Party in Bratislava, declared: "The conference smacked of Fascism."[36]

When the Hungarian anti-Fascists became aware of the situation, whether Communists or not, they had three choices: (1) Move to Hungary, (2) To retreat into passivity, (3) To change their nationality from Hungarian to Slovak. The government encouraged the change of nationality on a large scale by launching a so-called "re-Slovakization" campaign. The pretext of this campaign was that many Hungarians were of Slav ancestry. Actually, it was a part of the strategy to "solve" the Hungarian problem. Through "re-Slovakization" the number of Hungarians was to be reduced by 200,000. Another 200,000 would be "exchanged" for Slovaks from Hungary, still another 200,000 would be transferred to Hungary by the peace treaty—and the Hungarian question would be solved.

How did "re-Slovakization" work? In November 1949, I asked István Major, a longtime Hungarian member of the Communist Party in Czechoslovakia, whether he was allowed to vote in the first prewar elections. He answered: "Yes, but first I had to declare in writing that I am a Slovak."

Slovak Communists in general believe that there was nothing wrong with depriving the Hungarians of their rights. They thought, rather, that there was something wrong with their Hungarian comrades: "The Hungarian comrades did not show sufficient alertness and consistency in the observance of the party line, when it came to nationalities policy."[37] First Secretary K. Bacílek condemned the attitude of the Hungarian Communists, branding it as divisive:

> Many Hungarian comrades, unfortunatley old Communists among them, including some who had spent years in concentration camps, cannot understand the meaning of our nationalities policy, now that the nationalities question has to be subordinated to the general requirements of progress. They often take a stand as alleged defenders of the policies of Stalin, and demand minority rights, schools, and a press on behalf of the Hungarians. These comrades have gone so far of late that their activity resembles divisive activity . . . . They even organize mass meetings with the participation of five or six thousand people, where they speak Hungarian, and demand the publication of anti-Fascist Hungarian newspaper.[38]

By the end of 1945, the year of liberation by the Red Army, Slovak-Hungarian relations within the Communist Party of Czechoslovakia deteriorated to a point that the Slovak party chairman, Viliam Široký declared: "It is no longer possible to collaborate with Hungarian comrades." And he added: "After all, if we solve the Hungarian question . . . it becomes natural to ask our Hungarian comrades to leave voluntarily for Hungary."[39]

Communist internationalism was dead as far as Slovak-Hungarian relations were concerned. Lest the Hungarians get ideas to the contrary, the slogan "Proletarians of the world, unite!" disappeared already in May from the masthead of the Bratislava *Pravda*. In the once Hungarian town of Rimaszombat (Rimavská Sobota) delegates of the Communist Party from six counties accepted a resolution on June 3, 1948, condemning the Hungarian minority and demanding complete de-Hungarianization:

> We demand the immediate solution of the Hungarian question. The Hungarians failed the historical test because all of them, with few exceptions, accepted the policies of the feudal lords. We demand that the resettlement of Slovak farmers from the poor and mountainous regions begin right away to the lands in the South of the Hungarian landlords, settlers, and Fascists, who have no business here in Slovakia! . . . We want a Slovakia without Hungarians![40]

A Slovakia without Hungarians meant deportation, the use of force against Hungarian workers, peasants, artisans who constituted 90 percent of Hungarian minority society.

No wonder the Hungarians showed no enthusiasm toward the "national and democratic revolution" in liberated Czechoslovakia. Writing in a "liberalized" mood in 1965, even the Slovak historian Samuel Cambel appreciated the reasons: "The [Slovak] settlers acquired their cattle and their equipment from the poor Hungarian peasants by means of confiscation. . . . It is understandable that in the areas of colonization the [Hungarian] inhabitants greeted the [Slovak] newcomers with hostility."[41] A few years later, the same historian became less understanding. Writing in 1972, he scolded the Hungarian peasants for their hostility: "[They] did not greet the liberation and the restoration of Czechoslovak independence. . . it is a historical fact that in they years 1945 and 1946 the Hungarian population behaved antagonistically towards the Republic, sabotaged the program of the government, and terrorized the [Slovak] settlers. . . ."[42] Confronted with open distrust of the Hungarian population—Cambel's colleague Jozef Jablonický, wrote indignantly—the government representative in charge of domestic affairs ordered to "intervene most harshly against all those persons who bear an irredentist or chauvinist attitude in Slovakia."[43]

The decisions of the Potsdam Conference of the Big Three, published on August 2, 1945, caused disappointment to the Czechoslovak nationalists bent on expelling both the Germans and the Hungarians in order to make Czechoslovakia into a purely Slav state. Potsdam approved the transfer of the Germans from the Czech lands, but not the transfer of the Hungarians from Slovakia. Yet, despite disappointment, Potsdam did not slacken the Czechoslovak effort to get rid of the Hungarian minority. In fact, Potsdam was not altogether a defeat for the Czechoslovak policy to expell the Hungarians.

On of the Potsdam decisions was the transfer of Hungary's German population to Germany. This decision, in a roundabout way, was to promote Czechoslovak policy since the Germans expelled from Hungary were to make room for the Hungarians marked for expulsion from Slovakia. This strategy (whose author behind the scenes was most likely President Beneš himself in collusion with the Soviet Union) became clear for everybody only during the Paris Peace Conference in 1946 when both Czechoslovakia and the Soviet Union were trying hard to win endorsement for the transfer of 200,000 Hungarians from Czechoslovakia to Hungary. According to Czechoslovak strategy, the "transfer" would have been the final stage of liquidating the Hungarian minority, following "re-Slovakization," and the population "exchange" agreement with Hungary which was expected to be concluded before the Peace Conference.[44]

Although Potsdam failed to approve the transfer of the Hungarians, the campaign for the expulsion of the Hungarian minority from Czechoslovakia continued unabated after Potsdam. Concurrently with the publication of the Potsdam decisions, Presidential decree 33/1945 was issued on August 2, 1945 depriving the Germans and Hungarians of their citizenship. On August 7, 1945, the Bratislava *Pravda* published a front page banner in large type: "The Germans and Hungarians have been deprived of Czechoslovak citizenship." The subtitle offered the promise: "Those who fought against Fascism will remain Czechoslovak citizens." The news story itself stressed that in Slovakia the Slovak National Council would decide on the return of citizenship.

The details of the *Pravda* report mostly rehashed the Košice government program, but in a new context which is worth quoting as an illustration of the Czechoslovak perception of the situation after Potsdam:

> The program of the National Front of the Czechs and the Slovaks declares, among other things, that for the sake of purification of the Czechoslovak Republic from the unfriendly German and Hungarian minorities, the Germans and the Hungarians have to be deprived of Czechoslovak citizenship, with the exception of the explicitly anti-Fascists. It was also mentioned in the government program that the other Germans and Hungarians will have the possibility to apply for the restoration of their citizenship. These applications will be adjudicated on an individual basis. . . . The presidential decree 33/1945 of August 2, 1945 signed by the President has now converted these principles into law. It is necessary to underscore that this decree appeard simultaneously with the conclusion of the Potsdam conference. In its decision the Potsdam conference accepted in principle the stand taken by the Czechoslovak government from the beginning.

The *Pravda* story was deliberately slanted because the Potsdam conference did not approve the Czechoslovak request to expel the Hungarians along with the Germans. Nevertheless, the Czechoslovak government, assuming an ultimately "favorable solution," applied to the Hungarians all laws regarding general deprivation of minority rights and confiscation of minority property. And this led to a total discrimination for years to come.

Historically, more interesting than the headline story of the Bratislava *Pravda* for August 7, 1945, was the report in the same issue on a statement made by Minister of Interior Václav Nosek. It supplied some missing information from official sources on what went on at Potsdam:

> On Friday, Minister of Interor comrade Nosek informed the representatives of the press about the diplomatic note which the Czechoslovak government sent to the three Great Powers at Potsdam, requesting approval in principle of the expulsion of the Germans and Hungarians from Czechoslovakia. The Potsdam conference accepted this measure in principle. Now the President of the Republic issued a decree regarding the citizenship of persons of German and Hungarian nationality, according to which these persons lose their citizenship. This measure is justified by the cruelty of our experiences in the past and in the present. Those who were responsible for the disintegration of the Republic may not remain without our borders. The realization of this government program is guaranteed by the decree presently signed. The Minister of the Interior has already worked out the plan for the expulsion of the Germans and Hungarians in complete accord with the Potsdam decision. According to the Prague correspondent of *Čas,* the expulsion of the Hungarians will take place mostly in the form of an exchange of populations.

The Czechoslovak strategy, as it soon became clear, was to force the democratically-elected Hungarian coalition government to accept an "exchange" of populations agreement, and then to achieve the expulsion of the so-called "remaining 200,000 Hungarians" at the Peace Conference. (The actual number of the "remaining" Hungarians should have been by any fair count closer to half a million.)

The Potsdam decision that the Germans should be resettled from Hungary came as a surprise to the Hungarian Government. Hungary did not ask for it, nor were other defeated satellite states—Italy, Rumania, Finland, or Bulgaria—obliged to carry out similar measures. It did not take long for the Hungarians to recognize that the intention behind the Potsdam decision to remove the Germans from Hungary was to make room for the Hungarians of Czechoslovakia.

Contemporary Communist Hungarian historiography too recognizes that the resettlement of the Germans served no Hungarian interests. According to Ágnes Ságvári, the Potsdam decision had "harmful consequences for the Hungarians." She also reminds us that the Hungarian Social Democratic Party objected to it because organized labor in Hungary included many Germans. Furthermore, the resettlement would hurt disproportionately the poor peasants who had been misled by Fascist demagoguery. At the same time, the right wing of the Hungarian coalition government argued against the transfer, mainly because expulsion of Germans from Hungary, when Hungarians were threatened with expulsion from Czechoslovakia, was simply regarded as irresponsible from the point of view of national interests. Nevertheless, the weight of the Communist-dominated "Bloc of the Left" prevailed over the majority opinion in the Cabinet. The Hungarian Government grudgingly obeyed the Potsdam decision of the Great Powers on the resettlement of the Germans.[45] Not all of Hungary's German population, though, had been transferred—as Czechoslovakia would have wished, "to make room" for the Hungarians from Czechoslovakia. Yet, contrary to the national wish and interest, Hungary joined the postwar totalitarian movement of population transfers, compromising thus some of the new regime's truly democratic and socialist achievements.

The Hungarian Communists, presumably in collusion with their Czechoslovak and Soviet comrades, tried to turn the transfer of Germans from Hungary into an ideological issue. They pretended to take a "progressive anti-Fascist" stand in support of the Potsdam decisions. In reality, they obediently supported the Soviet policy which, in turn, gave full support to postwar Czechoslovakia's Slav nationalist objectives, including the expulsion of the Hungarians from Slovakia.

In the context of East-West diplomacy, the Potsdam decision to transfer the Germans from Hungary was, to all evidences, a compromise. The

Western Powers vetoed the transfer of the Hungarians from Czechoslovakia, whereupon—presumably as a compromise, and in support of the Czecho-slovak strategy at the forthcoming peace conference—the Soviet Union proposed the transfer of the Germans from Hungary.

Details of the actual proceedings leading to the compromise at Potsdam on Czechoslovakia's demand to expell the Hungarians are still unknown. The published documents on the Potsdam conference do not cover this aspect of the Hungarian-Czechoslovak conflict. Yet, from Czechoslovak sources we do know that the question had been discussed at Potsdam at Czechoslovakia's request and that the Government of Czechoslovakia actually submitted a request for the transfer of the Hungarians to the conference of the Great Powers.[46]

For a while after Potsdam, a certain confusion got hold of the Czecho-slovak government regarding the transfer of Hungarians. I. Pietor, Min-ister of Domestic Commerce, expressed in a Cabinet meeting his doubts about the realism of such a measure. His doubts were shared by Foreign Minister Ján Masaryk and his Communist Undersecretary Vladimir Cle-mentis. As reported, their reasoning was as follows:

> Czechoslovakia had attempted to win over the Potsdam conference in the matter of the Hungarians, but the United States promptly rejected the [Czechoslovak] point of view, whereas Great Britain remained silent. The Soviet Union was now establishing diplomatic relations with the Hungarian Government, thus it seems probably that it will be able to modify the situation in favor of the Czecho-slovak view. Vl. Clementis informed the [cabinet] meeting that he had sent a proposal to Marshal Voroshilov, Chairman of the Control Commission at Budapest, that he would like to discuss with him the matter of the exchange of population and resettlement, and might even negotiate with the Hungarian Government, but so far has received no answer. According to confidential information, the Hungarian Government is willing to consider only an exchange of population. Nevertheless, the majority of the cabinet held that the projected law [on the confiscation of Hungarian property] be dis-cussed in its original form. Clementis proposed that the decree be issued, but that those Hungarians who emigrate voluntarily or who

will be exchanged should be promised restitution of part of their property.

The Cabinet accepted the Clementis proposal and, along with the confiscation decree, issued instructions suspending further confiscations of Hungarian property in order to facilitate negotiations with Hungary and, also, in order to "interest the Hungarian population in the reconstruction of Czechoslovakia."[47]

In the fall of 1945, Czechoslovakia's chances for negotiations with Hungary's democratically-elected government were problematical. The Potsdam decision regarding the Germans of Hungary could only benefit Czechoslovakia. This must have been clear to the new Hungarian Government if it examined the question, as it no doubt did, from the point of view of Slovakia's Hungarian minority under the threat of expulsion. The democratically-elected Hungarian government, in a stronger position to defend Hungarian interests than the provisional one, showed no inclination for negotiations which would benefit only Czechoslovakia.

In face of Hungarian tactical resistance, the Czechoslovak press demanded negotiations without delay. However, there were skeptical voices too:

> The Berlin decision gave Hungary the opportunity to rid itself entirely of the German minority. It is difficult to predict today whether or not they will take advantage of this opportunity, and to what extent. According to law, they would have to deport some 430,000 Germans to the West. The first attempts, however, remained unsuccessful. Of 12,000 deported persons, 4,000 are presumed to have turned back even before they reached the border. It seems the measure will be sabotaged. . . . The Hungarians shilly-shally because they are afraid that by expelling the Germans they are creating room for the Hungarians from Slovakia and Yugoslavia. They want to leave the Hungarian minority with us at any price.[48]

The Hungarians avoided the Potsdam trap by procrastination and by open opposition. They were helped, too, by the growing European disgust with the mass transfers of populations. Also the secrecy surrounding the Potsdam decision regarding the Germans of Hungary was thought to be distasteful. Anyway, the Hungarians did not cherish the idea of "exchanging 650,000 Hungarians from Czechoslovakia for 100,000 Slovaks from Hungary." (The figures are based on the last prewar census of the two countries.)[49]

By the time of Potsdam in the summer of 1945, the Slovaks had evicted all the Hungarians who settled in Southern Slovakia after November 2, 1938, the date of the Vienna Award. Every one of them (31,780 according to Czechoslovak sources[50]) had been transferred across the border to Hungary with whatever they could on a short notice carry with them. Their deportations carried out by the Czechoslovak Settlement Bureau, was completed by July 1, 1945.

The Presidential decree of August 2, 1945, depriving almost all Hungarians of their citizenship rights was designed to continue the process of expulsion. It is estimated that the decree terminated the citizenship of about 97 percent of Slovakia's Hungarian population. Also, it ushered in a whole series of anti-Hungarian measures, such as the cessation of retirement payments, the prohibition of any kind of welfare services to them, including public health care, etc. The evil spirit of the dreaded "Decree 33" poisoned the life of the Hungarian minority for over three years to come.[51] (The decree was revoked in October 1948, following the Communist take-over in February.)

In order to be exempt from the discriminatory measures, Hungarians had to prove "anti-Fascist" activities. Slovaks, of course, needed no proof of anti-Fascism in order to enjoy full citizenship rights. The Hungarian population at large did not even petition for exemption, viewing such procedures as useless. Most of those who did, in particular dismissed civil servants, were turned down anyway. They received a resolution signed by local heads of the Slovak National Council that read: "I feel no justification for considering you exempt from the provisions of the 3rd paragraph of the regulation 99/1945 issued by the Council. I hereby so inform you."[52]

Yet, after Potsdam, one last hope sustained the Hungarians, and everyone clung to it: The peace conference! Meanwhile, they were naive enough not to notice the new menaces closing in on them.

The determined Czechoslovak policy to eradicate the Hungarian minority continued with the Presidential decree 108/1945, issued on October

25, 1945, regarding the confiscation of German and Hungarian property. The decree legalized the confiscation of "all movable and immovable property" belonging to Hungarians unless they were exempted by virtue of the hypocritical anti-Fascist clause.[53] Considering that 67 percent of the Hungarians were living from agriculture, 14.5 percent from industry and mining, the projected measures would have confiscated primarily the belongings of the workers and peasants.

Talks began, in the meantime, with Hungary on population "exchange," and an order of the Minister of the Interior, dated February 14, 1946, instructed the Slovak authorities that "in case of Hungarian persons it will be necessary to wait for further instructions." However, the order did not suspend confiscation of property. Whenever a Hungarian was declared a war criminal it was possible to confiscate the goods of Hungarians administratively, without judicial procedures. And the number of Hungarian "war criminals" was growing unchecked to about a hundred thousand! Not until after the signing of the population exchange agreement on March 31, 1946, did the Minister of the Interior issue an order which stopped the practice of indiscriminately declaring Hungarians administratively "war criminals."

While negotiations were going on between the governments of the two countries, a lively war of words was taking place between the Czechoslovak and the Hungarian press. Grievances were aired on both sides, invectives exchanged, mutually declaring each other's charges as exaggerated or unfounded. A particular favorite theme of reciprocal accusation was the questioning of each other's democracy. The Hungarians kept attacking the Czechoslovak policy persecuting the Hungarian minority as anti-democratic while the Czechoslovaks kept repeating that accepting the principle of population transfer alone could prove the Hungarians' devotion to peace and democracy.

In Czechoslovakia, the slogan branding the Hungarians a "Fascist nation" continued to be broadcast relentlessly by all means of public communication. Members of the highest state authority referred to the Hungarians as "Fascists." Said Karol Šmidke, Chairman of the Board of Delegates in charge of administration in Slovakia: "It would be in the interest of further coexistence between the peoples of Central Europe if the question of minorities would be solved by deportation of the Fascisized German and Hungarian population."[54] At the same time, the Czechoslovak state authorities continued their lenient attitude towards the Fascist Slovak past. Only a few Slovaks were held responsible for establishing and supporting the Fascist Slovak state during the war. To this very day, distinction is made between Hungarian "popular Fascism" and Slovak "political Fascism." The Slovak Fascists supposedly were merely a political sect, "a narrow stratum of Ľudák collaborators."[55] The Slovak Fascists are never identified with the Slovak people.

In the fall of 1945, the Slovak press was greatly dissatisfied with the insufficiency of anti-Hungarian measures. It advocated measures similar to those applied in Bohemia against the Germans.[56] Perhaps the best description of the Slovak aspirations was the speech on November 7 by Karol Šmidke:

> Historical facts prove that it was precisely the Hungarian minority which appreciated least the democratic rights and opportunities in Czechoslovakia and, in the difficult days of 1938, it became a fifth column on behalf of Hungarian imperialism, the purpose of which was the disintegration of the Czechoslovak Republic and the subjection of the Slovak people. Historical facts also prove that during the six-year occupation of our southern territories the Hungarians had ruthlessly and crudely deprived this area of its Slovak character, chasing the Slovaks aways from the towns and villages. And, it should be added, that it was not merely the Hungarian intruders who behaved thus, but the overwhelming majority of the local Hungarians as well; they became a reliable support for any [Hungarian] regime, including the Fascist Arrow-Cross rule; they were willing tools of the policy of denationalization directed against the Slovaks. If we now insist that Slovakia be freed of this irredentist [Hungarian] minority, which had always been a tool of the conspiracies directed against the Slovak people and the Czechoslovak Republic, we are not only following the interests of the sovereign rights of our state and of our nation, but also the interests of peace and consolidation in Central Europe. Thus I propose the truly democratic solution, that the Hungarian minority of Slovakia be exchanged for the several hundred thousand Slovaks in Hungary who want to return to their own home. If the Hungarian side slyly and stubbornly

rejects this worthy solution, which is in accordance with the principle of national self-determination, then the accusation of being
anti-democratic cannot be levelled at us. Undaunted, we insist on
this demand of ours because it is of prime importance to us. We also
believe that after its realization no obstacle will remain to friendly
and goodneighborly relations between Hungary and Czechoslovakia.[57]

I am quoting Šmidke's speech at length not only because of its relevance at the time he delivered it, but also because its concepts continue
to dominate Slovak historiography on the subject.

Among many other distortions, Šmidke pretended as if all Slovaks had
been chased away from "Hungarian occupied" South Slovakia. The fact
is that no more than 5,000 were expelled while some 300,000 stayed. If
Šmidke would consider as "expelled" those who left on their own as
recent settlers, even so, the figure would not be higher than several tens
of thousands. And Šmidke's statement that the overwhelming majority
of the Hungarian population supported the Fascist Arrow-Cross rule is
pure fabrication.

Toward the end of the year 1945, the Czechoslovak nationalist land
reform ran into difficulties. Because of the halt in the expulsion of the
Hungarians, ordered during the Czechoslovak-Hungarian population exchange negotiations, the land issue became a major concern of the central
Government in Prague. J. Ďuriš, Minister of Agriculture, expressed the
Government's worries over expecting too much from seizure of the minorities' land in general:

Even if it were possible to expell every German and Hungarian from
the Republic, there wouldn't be enough land to ensure the adequate
economic and cultural development of our farmers. In Slovakia,
after the total deportation of Germans and Hungarians, only 6
hectares of land would be available for each agricultural unit, whereas in the Czech lands even less, 5 hectares in Bohemia, 4 in Moravia.
Up to now, we have confiscated 150,000 hectares of land in Slovakia, and relocated 4,000 persons. There are difficulties with the
resettlement of the Hungarians. If it were possible to speed up the
confiscation of the estates of reactionary Hungarian landlords, in

accordance with the provisions of regulations issued by the [Slovak National] Council, we would not have to wait for an exchange of populations and for deportations. . . . The Fascist Hungarians should have been expelled long ago from their estates and transported to labor camps, or allocated as farm laborers.[58]

Ďuriš seemed to have been ignorant of the fact that the number of so-called Hungarian landlords in South Slovakia was relatively negligible. Ninety-nine percent of the Hungarian farmers were kulaks or poor peasants. The Czechoslovak land reform of 1945 was consistently nationalist favoring the Slavs. Large landowners of Slav nationality, as long as they had not compromised themselves publicly by collaboration with the Nazis, were exempted from land reform, whereas the estates of the non-Slavs were taken away regardless of class or past behavior.

Fortunately, at that time, the Communist Party had not been united in the demand for a radical and general land reform. In Slovakia, an additional obstacle to a sweeping land reform was the opposition of the Democratic Party, which was the more effective since a member of the Party, Dr. M. Kvetko, was the Minister of Agriculture. A situation, rare at that time, favoring the Hungarians was the result. The first round of land reform in 1945 protected many Slovak estates in mixed or purely Hungarian inhabited areas, thus making these regions safe against Slovak colonization by the familiar means of land distribution rigged by nationalist preferences. After the Communist takeover in 1948, when the second round of land reform came, the Slovak estates too were subject to division. But by then the Hungarians were entitled to receive land.

The first round of Hungarian-Czechoslovak negotiations on population exchange ended in a deadlock. The Prague meeting on December 3-6, 1945, was adjourned with no results. The Hungarian public opinion greeted the failure of negotiations with relief, hopeful that the peace conference may settle the conflict between the two countries in the spirit of fairness. The relief did not last long. Under pressure from the Allied Control Commission in Hungary, after eight weeks of recess, the Hungarian-Czechoslovak negotiations were resumed.

In the meantime, the discrimination against the Hungarians in Slovakia (still thought to be by many Hungarians only temporarily) was developing into a system. It became an established policy producing unending series of social and cultural blows against the Hungarian minority. But its theory and its practice resembled Nazism. Actually the two fundamental principles of the constitutional law of 1942 under Fascist Slovakia against the Jews were no different from those of the Presidential decrees of 1945 against the Hungarians—loss of citizenship and confiscation of property. Czechoslovak policy against the Hungarian minority from 1945 to 1948 became a political system which, not unlike Nazism, repressed all humanism and internationalism in the name of the purported interests of the Nation and of the State.

There were a few people in the highest government circles who saw the nationalist shortsightedness of this policy. Such was the case of Jan Masaryk. He anticipated difficulties in expelling the Hungarians even before his return from exile: "It was clear from the beginning that the problem of the Hungarian ethnic group of Slovakia, although an insignificant matter in comparison with the resettlement of the Germans would mean a much more serious problem on international and diplomatic levels."[59] Jan Masaryk, unlike President Beneš and the majority of those in leadership, was no prisoner of anti-Hungarian hatred. Yet dissent or even counsel of moderation had no chance to assert itself in an atmosphere of massive emotional nationalism. Thus it was easy all along to preserve the semblance of unanimity in support of Czechoslovak policy against the Hungarian minority.

From the moment of liberation, the Czechoslovak Government was determined to follow the same policy against the Hungarians as it did against the Germans. Yet, from the moment of liberation, it was obvious that popular sentiment was different in Slovakia from that in the Czech lands. Anti-German sentiments broke loose in Bohemia, whereas a certain calmness reigned for awhile in Slovakia. There were no lynchings of Hungarians. It took the harsh measures decreed from above to arouse mass nationalist hatred. In this respect, the situation in Slovakia was different too from other Danubian countries with Hungarian minority populations. In Rumania, in the fever of reprisals, the members of the Maniu guard carried out a whole series of bloodbaths against Hungarian communities. In Yugoslavia, it was with the murder of more than a thousand Hungarian peasants that the Yugoslavs evened the score for the mass murders perpetrated by the Hungarians at Ujvidék (Novi Sad) and Zablya during the war.[60]

The hate campaign unleashed against the Hungarians in Czechoslovakia in 1945 has been stepped up, rather than allowed to subside, as the years went by. The literature of discrimination against the Hungarians has grown to enormous proportions. It would fill volumes to collect the laws, regulations, decrees, instructions, and guiding principles issued against the Hungarian minority. The Central Settlement Bureau at Prague has published a 700-page book merely to explain the measures dealing with property confiscation.[61]

Slovak historiography continues to indulge in anti-Hungarian interpretations. There is a noticeable effort to keep the anti-Hungarian edge of Slovak nationalism alive. Writing of the postwar years, V. Jarošová and O. Jaroš approvingly remarked in a study published in 1965: "Anti-Hungarian nationalism marked something special during those years—a significant portion of the Slovak nation, including the working class, fell under its spell."[62] The authors failed to mention that it was the result of planned mass manipulation.

Only after the Communist takeover in 1948 has postwar nationalism come under criticism for a while as a "bourgeois" aberration. However, anti-Hungarian Slovak nationalism was rehabilitated by the end of the 1960s and became unassailable by the 1970s. (See the works of Cambel, Vietor, Purgat, and others.) Some Slovak historians go even beyond mere rehabilitation of postwar nationalism. Approving the legal measures as well as the illegal methods of persecution, they elevate postwar mass discrimination against the minorities to a respectable status be treating it as an organic part of "anti-Fascism."[63]

In the postwar drama of minority persecution, the survival of the Hungarians in Czechoslovakia had hung by a hair on five occasions.

The Hungarians were first threatened with destruction when it seemed that the Red Army's front, moving from north to south, would sweep them out of the country. The second danger of annihilation came at the time of Allied armistice negotiations with Hungary. Had the United States not vetoed the expulsion of the Hungarians as a condition of the armistice, the Hungarians of Slovakia might have shared the fate of the Sudeten Germans.

Potsdam signaled the third danger. The Czechoslovak request for the liquidation of the Hungarian minority by expulsion was shipwrecked, thanks again to an American veto. The fourth fateful threat was the Hungarian government's acceptance of the Potsdam decision on the expulsion of half a million Germans from Hungary, "to make room"—according to Czechoslovak plans—for several hundred thousand Hungarians from Slovakia. The fifth danger was the peace conference. Once again, the veto of the United States prevented the expulsion of the "final" two hundred thousand Hungarians, according to Czechoslovak plans, in addition to those hundred thousands who were supposed to be transferred according to other Czechoslovak-Hungarian agreements on "exchange" of populations.

It is safe to say that without the help of the United States, the Hungarian minority would not have survived in Slovakia.

CHAPTER 5

1946: THE YEAR OF THE PEACE CONFERENCE

Following the Prague meeting in December 1945, when the Czecho-slovak-Hungarian negotiations on population exchange had broken down, the anti-Hungarian measures in Slovakia did not abate. On the contrary. They became even more severe in order to force Hungary to resume nego-tiations. The tone of the Czechoslovak press too, became as rude as ever. Thus did for instance, *Nové Prúdy*, the Slovak Democratic Party periodi-cal, gave vent to Slovak nationalist rage against the Hungarian minority:

> It is enough for us [to wish them good riddance] that these people are Hungarian . . . they have destroyed our State, and continue to ruin our Republic. . . . We must free our land from mice and bed-bugs. . . . Let them go voluntarily to Hungary forever, where they will be turned into 'gentlemen', into that prototype of falsehood and Asian gypsyhood . . . . Let's sweep out the Hungarians from every-where even if they happen to be Communists or democrats.[1]

The mass organizations, too, were mobilized. They staged demonstra-tions to demand the expulsion of "Hungarians and Magyarones"–The latter, a pre-World War I term, a highly derogatory one, arousing hatred against the assimilated Hungarians of Slovak origins who betrayed their nation.

By this time, quite a few Hungarian anti-Fascists had acquired a so-call-ed "reliability certificate" which entitled them to citizenship. At the end of January, however, it was announced that no Hungarian would be allow-ed to vote at the upcoming elections in the spring of 1946. As the Bratis-lava *Pravda* explained: "At the meeting of the parties of the National Front in Prague it was decided that the Germans and the Hungarians would not have the right to vote; not even those whose reliability was recognized on the basis of their anti-Fascist activities and were granted Czechoslovak citizenship."[2] The decision became law on February 21, 1946. It explicitly limited the right to vote to citizens of Slav nationality. Germans and Hungarians, even if they had fought against Fascism, were excluded. Although the law discriminated *against* anti-Fascists, Slovak historiography still calls it an "anti-Fascist law."[3]

The Slovak press consistently criticized Hungary, and marshalled its arguments in favor of liquidation of the Hungarian minority. In early January 1946, the Bratislava Democratic Party paper *Čas* wrote: "In his official statement [Hungarian] Prime Minister Tildy said that democratic Hungary (democratic only in appearance) wishes to establish good neighborly relations with Czechoslovakia, but immediately added that Hungary was not responsible for the failure of such attempts. . . . He accused Czechoslovakia of confiscating the belongings of Hungarian citizens, of mass deportation of Hungarian citizens, of sending them to concentration camps merely because they happen to be Hungarian. [He accused] the Czechoslovak government of depriving the Hungarians of their rights, of their participation in cultural life. [He charged] that measures regulating property ownership and other decrees deprives the Hungarians of the very possibility of existence, and that the male population is deported *en masse* from the Hungarian areas. The Hungarian government, continued Tildy, has asked therefore for Allied intervention, and it is claimed that world public opinion has endorsed this step."

To this somewhat slanted summary of Tildy's speech, the Slovak paper *Čas* added the following, even more slanted, commentary:

> During the Prague negotiations Czechoslovakia extended its hand towards Hungary but the negotiations ended in failure because of the Hungarian delegation's attitude... It is claimed that the Czechoslovak government deprived the Hungarians of Slovakia of their political rights, of their cultural life, and limited their economic activities. The truth of course is that, while the Slovak National Council did deprive the Hungarians of citizenship, it exempted those who were able to prove their democratic thinking, their anti-Fascist behavior, and that they had taken part in the fight against the German occupation forces. Whose fault is it that there are so

few democrats among the Hungarian minority? Whose fault is it that only a small fraction of the Hungarian minority participated in the fight against the Germans either in the occupied or the un-occupied parts of Slovakia? This fact in itself proves that Czecho-slovakia's policy to rid herself of the Hungarian minority is correct . . . The cultural life of the Hungarians in Slovakia between 1918 and 1938 was down-right ideal. Whose fault is it that they did not like it, and yearned for something else?. . . The Hungarian popu-lation has to be resettled so that it would not become a tool for Hungarian aggression and revisionism. Hungarian revisionism is nothing but a wolf in sheep's clothing. . . . The Hungarian agricultural population in Slovakia is now being put to work in the framework of labor service in other areas of the Republic, where labor shortage prevails .

The "other" referred to by Čas are the Sudetenland of Bohemia, de-populated as a result of the Germans' expulsion then in progress. In late November 1945, some 12,000 Hungarian males were rounded up and taken for "labor service" from the solidly Hungarian southern regions of Slovakia to the depopulated Sudetenland. Within six weeks all Hun-harians escaped and returned home. But the affair created a deportation panic among the Hungarian population—not an unfounded one, as later events (the deportations taking place in 1946, described in Chapter 6) have proved it.

Continuing its commentary, Čas explained the November 1945 events this way:

This is not meant to be the forced dispersion of the Hungarian population, but a measure dictated by the necessity of reconstruc-ting Czechoslovakia economically. . . We must also mention the speech of László Rajk, a Communist member of the Hungarian Parliament. While declaring that chauvinism must be repressed in Hungary, Rajk also stressed that the Hungarian minorities [in the neighboring countries] have to be protected wherever they may be, if they are treated unjustly. Rajk stated that as far as treatment of minorities is concerned, the Hungarians are raising objections only against Czechoslovakia's policy, because Hungary cannot reconcile itself to rendering 600,000 Hungarians destitute. Rajk demanded rapid and effective measures for the protection of the Hungarians of Slovakia.

In conclusion, Čas outlined the actions Czechoslovakia should take in this matter: "It is up to us to convince the Great Powers that Hungary is a fire hazard whence fire may start anew and destroy the friendly balance among the peoples of the Carpathian Basin."[4]

The Hungarian Communist László Rajk soon found himself isolated on the Hungarian revolutionary left. The Hungarian Communists who returned from exile in the Soviet Union had been under the influence of the Russian Beria and the Czech Slánsky. They sided with Czechoslovakia *against* Hungary in the matter of Hungarian minorities. They attempted to pave the way for Hungary's acceptance of the Czechoslovak transfer demands.

Thus in the 1945 Christmas issue of the Hungarian Communist Party paper *Szabad Nép,* József Révai, former exile in Prague and Moscow, argued that a change in Hungarian foreign policy is necessary: "We Hungarians still believe that the world revolves around us. . . We must seek friendship with the neighboring states, first of all with the Slav countries . . . It is not enough to stake out the goals of our struggle against reaction in domestic affairs here at home. We must do the same in foreign affairs as well. The two are inseparable".

The Slovak Čas liked what Révai wrote, commented on it with satisfaction: "We Slovaks would like to see once and for all a complete break with Hungary's catastrophy policy and to see instead a concern for friendship with the neighbors to emerge." Yet Čas commented scornfully on Hungarian democracy: "Even though we recognize the beneficial activity of certain government leaders who wish to consolidate [Hungarian] democracy, this does not alter the fact that Hungary continues to be reactionary and Fascist, that the broad spectrum of the Hungarian population has to be reeducated in a democratic spirit."[5]

Clearly the self-appointed Slovak educators in democracy thought they can force Hungary to agree to compulsory population "exchange" and resettlement of the "remaining" Hungarians from Slovakia. They equated "democracy" with compliance with Slovak nationalistic demands. Hungary refused to oblige.

The Czechoslovak-Hungarian tug of war over "population exchange" elicited foreign comments too. Not surprisingly, in view of Czechoslovakia's wartime popularity in the Allied world, the Czechoslovak effort to change the multinational Czechoslovak state into a pure Slav nation-state found quite a few Western supporters. One of them was Ernest Davies, Labor member of the British Parliament. Reporting on his visit to Czechoslovakia, he was quoted by *Čas* as having said:

> I was surprised to see how well the Germans and Hungarians live in Slovakia, as I was able to find out at first hand. I spoke to people incaracerated in camps and I became convinced that they were incomparably better treated than if the situation were reversed. Their food is good, their lodgings are as well heated as my own apartment in London. . . . The rights of the Hungarian national minority were not curtailed beyond the closing of their schools. I had a chance to observe it myself when I attended a service in Hungarian at Szenc.[6] The members of the Hungarian minority live in their own homes, freely and without any restrictions. It is true that the Hungarians are worried about the uncertainty of their fate, what to expect after transfer to Hungary. But that is a matter for the Hungarian Government [to worry about]. I hope the United Nations organization will exert its influence to convince Hungary to agree to sign the population exchange agreement. Before I came to Slovakia, under the influence of propaganda of dubious value, I too had nebulous notions about the problems of the Hungarian minority. But now I was able to verify that the only solution to the minority question would be to exchange this [Hungarian] minority for the Slovaks of Hungary, because this minority has proven disloyal during the years of crisis, even though it enjoyed rights it could not have had in Hungary itself.[7]

Mr. Davies' source of information was not hard to guess. He had evidently been kept by his misinformers under the impression that there were 600,000 Slovaks in Hungary. Otherwise, he could not have found the idea of "exchange" with 600,000 Hungarians in Slovakia so attractive. Actually, the number of Hungarians in Slovakia was well over 600,000 while the number of Slovaks in Hungary was not much over 100,000.

Hungary's delaying tactics concerning negotiations with Czechoslovakia caused irritation in Czechoslovak government circles. The Czechoslovak strategy called for bilaterial agreement on the population exchange before the peace conference, so as to be able to propose there the transfer of the "remaining" 200,000 Hungarians. The Slovak government deputy, Kvetko, in charge of agricultural affairs, declared uncompromisingly on January 20th: "We definitely state that our attitude regarding the Hungarians and Hungary will not change: We know that whoever is in charge there, be it Mr. Tildy or Mr. Rákosi, they will never shed their revisionism or their old Saint Stephen's ideology. Their objective will always be the restitution of greater Hungary with the Slavs as their slaves."[8]

In the atmosphere of these weeks in Czechoslovakia, whoever expressed doubts about the advisability of the policy of expulsion was denounced as a Fascist enemy of democracy. And vice versa, whoever approved of the expulsion of the Hungarian minority was a true democrat.

Under growing Great Power pressure, euphemistically called "Great-Power advice,"[9] the Hungarian Government had no choice but to resume negotiations. The less than even-handed formula to be agreed upon was that as many Hungarians would be resettled from Slovakia *by force* as Slovaks from Hungary will sign up *voluntarily* for resettlement to Czechoslovakia. However, even before the actual signing of the Czechoslovak-Hungarian agreement, a Slovak official spokesman, J. Lichner, declared: "This is not the final solution of the question of the Hungarians in Slovakia, it is merely a first step . . . . Within the framework of the population exchange we count on the return of 150,000 Slovaks from Hungary and, on this occasion I express my satisfaction that the Hungarian Government has allowed us to freely propagate resettlement among the Slovaks on Hungarian territory."[10] (Actually, no more than about a half of the expected 150,000 signed up for resettlement.)

The agreement on population exchange was signed in Budapest on February 27, 1946. The agreement provoked astonishment in Hungary and panic among the Hungarians of Slovakia. On the other hand, in Czechoslovakia the agreement was hailed as a great political victory. Already a day before signing, on February 26, the Slovak National Council issued a victory proclamation beamed to the Slovaks of Hungary:

> The Slovak National Council solemnly stresses the fact that [by virtue of this agreement] a fragment of the Slovak nation living in Hungary is to return home, into the democratic Czechoslovak Republic, to territories which the Hungarians must leave. We hail this historical moment. Deeply moved, in the name of the entire nation we salute those Slovaks who until now had been torn apart from us.[11] [Later, the President of the Council, in his speech on this historic occasion, bluntly stated the aim of Slovak nationalism:] 'Sooner or later the Trianon borders must become ethnic borders as well. . . .'[12]

During the negotiations, the Hungarian Government insisted on the principle of parity, namely, that only as many Hungarians would be forced to leave for Hungary as Slovaks would volunteer to return to Slovakia. This was written into the population exchange agreement. This was a Hungarian success. However, the Hungarian Government failed to achieve another of its goals: restoration of citizenship to those Hungarians who would remain in Czechoslovakia. The Czechoslovak Government reserved its right to request at the forthcoming peace conference the expulsion of another 200,000 Hungarians who would "remain" in Slovakia after the population exchange. Clearly, the Czechoslovaks did not give up yet their objective to liquidating the *entire* Hungarian minority of Slovakia.

The exchange agreement gave the Czechoslovak Government the right to transfer an additional 1500 Hungarians who were declared as war criminals. Also the agreement entitled Czechoslovakia to send Hungary a Committee for Resettlement for a period of six weeks to propagate resettlement among Hungary's Slovaks. The members of the Committee could circulate freely, obtain information, and communicate with anyone they wished. Those Slovaks who volunteered to resettle had to file an application within three months, by May 27, 1946, with the Czechoslovak Resettlement Committee. The Hungarian Government had the right to attach a liaison unit to the Committee. As for the Hungarians of Slovakia, the Czechoslovak Government had six months, until August 27, 1946, the right to select the Hungarians to be resettled. Those selected would receive a so-called "white card," which also served as a guarantee against continuing discrimination. Finally, a joint commission of two Hungarians and two Czechoslovaks was to be entrusted with carrying out the population exchange procedures.

The Czechoslovak Resettlement Committee began its activities in Hungary under propitious economic and political conditions. Defeated, war-ravaged Hungary was in a much worse state than victorious, prosperous Czechoslovkia. The number of Slovak applicants for resettlement was correspondingly high. More than 90,000 Slovaks applied. Yet, later on only 59,774 actually decided to leave Hungary.[13]

The Czechoslovak Resettlement Committee took advantage of its guaranteed freedom of movement in Hungary for other purposes than carrying out the population exchange. It carried out a "census" of Slovaks living in Hungary and came up with an astonishingly high total of 481,946. The supposedly applied criterion for Slovak nationality was "mother tonuge" or "ethnic background."[14] The obvious objective, however, was to prove for propaganda purposes that there are more or less as many Slovaks in Hungary as there are Hungarians in Slovakia. In no time, the slogan, "half a million Slovaks in Hungary" came to be propagandized abroad, and treated as a scientific fact by scholars at home.

The Hungarian press took notice of the strange statistical item. A reporter of *Új Otthon* asked the secretary of the Czechoslovak Resettlement Committee did he really believe that the number of Slovaks living in Hungary was 481,946? He replied: "From the statistical point of view this is not a serious figure . . . I do not want to engage in a debate."[15]

Considering the conditions of exchange agreed upon (the principle of parity, that is) the number of Hungarians the Czechoslovaks have slated for exchange was entirely unrealistic. They compiled a list of 181,512 Hungarians designated for exchange, also a list of 106,398 Hungarian "major war criminals."[16] None of these figures fitted the principle of parity, or the additoin of "war criminals," limited to 1500 Hungarians, according to the exchange agreement.

In the agreement on population exchange with Hungary, the Czechoslovak Government stipulated to stop indiscriminate confiscation of Hungarian property in Slovakia. Pertinent directives were issued to this effect, but the public knew nothing about them. The press in Slovakia simply did not publish them. Moreover, the directives were ignored by the authorities themselves. Local national committees continued to issue confiscation orders. Not until November 16, 1946, did the Slovak Deputy for Internal Affairs issue a circular under number 37 873/9-IV4-1946 in which he scolded the national committees and ordered compliance with the directives.

Thus confiscations under way had to be halted and new procedures could be launched only against those persons of Hungarian nationality who committed offenses listed in earlier ordinances.

No order has ever been issued, however, to stop anti-Hungarian propaganda. Here is a sample of what the Slovaks in the year of the peace conference were told about their Hungarian neighbors:

> The Mongol tribes, the Huns, Avars, Tatars, Magyars elicited only repulsion and terror in Europe. Culturally none of these peoples ever created anything original . . . . The Hungarians base their history on stories, decorated with pretty lies. . . . They defended European culture [against the Turks] they say, though in reality they invited their relatives, the Turks. . . . To ensure lasting peace in Central Europe, the Hungarians would have to be sent back to their ancestral home between the Urals and the Black Sea, or even farther. . . . They never created anything serious in culture . . . those among them who did were considered renegades.[17]

Continued anti-Hungarian propaganda notwithstanding, in the spring of 1946 the population exchange agreement did bring some relaxation in hostile tensions between Hungary and Czechoslovakia. A new major crisis developed in the summer of 1946 when the Czechoslovak demand for further transfer of 200,000 Hungarians was rejected at the Paris peace conference. Already in May the Czechoslovak plan suffered a rebuff when the four-power foreign ministers conference in Paris discussed the conditions of the treaties to be concluded at the peace conference. Czechoslovakia had hoped that the plan for the expulsion of 200,000 Hungarians would be included among the proposals. It was not.

In the meantime, knowing full well that they would not be able to expel as many Hungarians as expected, neither prior to nor after the peace conference, the Czechoslovaks resorted to still another stratagem in their effort to reduce the number of Hungarians: they launched "re-Slovakization."

"Re-Slovakization" stood for a return to Slovak nationality of those who had beeen Slovaks at one time but, in the ethnic stirrings of the Carpathian Basin, either their ancestors or themselves had become Hungarian.

Re-Slovakization was supposed to have been voluntary, and even a matter of privilege. However, considering the methods employed it would be more accurate to describe it as forced assimilation. The Hungarian citizen was confronted with the choice: "Sign, or your life!" Signing meant civil rights, security, retention of belongings. Not signing meant homelessness, danger of persecution, economic bankruptcy.

This strange invention of instant assimilation was supported by a no less strange historical argument. Before Hungary fell victim of Ottoman-Turkish conquest in the 16th century, medieval "Southern Slovakia" had supposedly been completely Slovak; Hungarians fleeing from the Turks changed the ethnic composition of the area; oppressive Hungarian policies in the 19th century achieved further Magyarization. In other words, "re-Slovakization" was to compensate for Slovak losses and restore the ethnic status quo of the Middle Ages.

There is no historical evidence whatsoever to support this argument. Even Slovak historiography treats gingerly this theory. Avoiding to face the argument head on, they may say, as historian Samuel Cambel did, that a large portion of the Hungarian population strived "to become Slovak again"[18] by the means of re-Slovakization.

The re-Slovakization campaign began at the time of the spring census in 1946. All people who knew some Slovak were asked to indicate their "intention regarding their future nationality." By indicating their intention "to become again Slovaks," they could avoid all the consequences which threatened people of Hungarian nationality. By July, this "buying of souls" became a nation-wide propaganda campaign.

In the villages, both with mixed and purely Hungarian populations, the Slovenská Liga (a mass organization to promote Slovak nationalism) posted Hungarian language posters promising life of peace and material security as well as citizenship to those who were willing to "re-Slovakize." The posters said: "Think it over! Tomorrow you want to sleep in peace, or not?"

Despite the hourly drummings in the villages to call attention to the posters, the campaign at the beginning had only limited success, Yet, frightened and humiliated, more and more people started going to the town houses "to sign." At the end, panic prevailed and only a few stubborn villagers refused to sign up for re-Slovakization. Conflicts over signing created crises often within families. There was no one to advise

the simple folk. The intelligentsia was as confused and terrorized as the
people at large. Where the "educated" signed up, the entire village did
too. Where nobody took the initiative, more often than not, the entire
village remained Hungarian.

Since few towns since 1918, when Czechoslovakia came into existence,
remained immune to Slovakization, the pressure to re-Slovakize was even
greater in the cities than in the villages where Hungarian ethnic homo-
geneity survived in most places. Re-Slovakization thus proceeded smoothly
in urban areas. Also in mixed villages, or isolated Hungarian villages in
predominantly Slovak regions, the campaign to re-Slovakize was a success.
But in compact Hungarian rural areas there was resistance. For instance,
the county of Duna-Szerdahely (Dunajská Streda in Slovak) in the predominantly Hungarian Csallóköz region (Žitny Ostrov in Slovak) rejected
re-Slovakization almost completely.

The often heard objective of re-Slovakization had been that there
should be "no more than 200,000 Hungarians left" in Slovakia by the
time of the peace conference. The expulsion of these "remaining" Hungarians was to be achieved at the peace conference. The official ordinance
regarding re-Slovakization (No. 20,000-1-IV, 1946) was dated June 17,
1946. But the impact of re-Slovakization had been already felt before—
and long thereafter. As a matter of fact, the 1946 re-Slovakization campaign affected every census ever since. The dreaded Resettlement Bureau
was entrusted with the execution of re-Slovakization, re-Slovakization
in fact was described as "one of the significant activities of the Resettlement Bureau in Slovakia."[19]

According to the re-Slovakization ordinance, people registering for re-
Slovakization had to be classified into two groups. To the first group
belonged those who had already declared themselves Slovaks at the tiome
of the last prewar Czechoslovak census in 1930, but were "re-Hungarized
under pressure" following the boundary changes of the Vienna Award
of 1938. Such fluctuations in nationality were widespread among city
dwellers, in Bratislava (Pozsony in Hungarian), Košice (Kassa), Levica
(Léva), Lučenec (Losonc), Komárno (Komárom), Rimavská Sobota
(Rimaszombat), and Rožnava (Rozsnyó). Roughly half of the Hungarian
population in most of these cities belonged to the first group. However,
in Košice the ratio was as high as two-thirds, while in Komárno only a low
one-fifth. The second group, mostly village population, consisted of those

who had remained Hungarian in the census of 1930, but after decades or centuries, their Slovak "national consciousness" had now been supposedly "re-awakened."

It is claimed that 135,317 Hungarian families totalling 410,820 persons applied for re-Slovakization. In the fall of 1946, after "thorough scrutiny," 326,579 applicants were granted "the privilege" of declaring themselves Slovak.[20] The Hungarians who re-Slovakized were entitled to vote in the 1948 parliamentary elections, the rest of the Hungarians were not.

The statistical losses of the Hungarian population under forcible re-Slovakization were substantial. In the 1950 census, the Hungarian population of Czechoslovakia fell by almost 50 percent, to an all-time low of 369,505.[21] The true number of Hungarians, of course, has not changed, as attested by later census when re-Slovakization pressure had become less of a factor in statistics.[22]

Hungarian public opinion looked forward to the Paris peace conference, hopeful of an international solution of the question of the Hungarian minority of Slovakia. However, the Paris peace conference was a defeat for Hungary and for the one-in-four of all Hungarians living as national minorities in the neighboring states. Even the prewar system of protection of the rights of minorities was ditched by the Paris peace conference (lasting from July 29th to October 15th.) The only Hungarian success was the defeat of the Czechoslovak effort to get the approval of the transfer of the so-called "remaining" 200,000 Hungarians from Slovakia.

The speech on August 2nd by Czechoslovak Foreign Minister Jan Masaryk set the anti-minority tone of the conference: "It would be very difficult to persuade the Czechoslovak people to accept a return of the notion of minority protection, such as the treaties that were in effect between 1919 and 1938. Any Czechoslovak government which would attempt to enforce such treaties would probably be swept away by the ire of the people."[23] Foreign Minister Masaryk then went on denouncing the minorities as having been responsible for the Czechoslovak crisis that led to World War.

The question of the Hungarian minority in Czechoslovakia was raised on August 14th, when Hungarian Foreign Minister János Gyöngyösi, head of the Hungarian delegation, presented defeated Hungary's case before the assembly of victors. He began his speech on a note of hope in a fair solution: "The fact that we are allowed to have our say here, encourages us to hope that the peace negotiations this time are different from those that took place here more than 25 years ago."[24] The Hungarian foreign minister's hope in a different peacemaking than the one that produced the Treaty of Trianon had no foundation in reality whatsoever. Not unlike after World War I, in 1946 too, the peace settlement had been decided in advance. Not unlike in 1920, Hungary was expected to sign another dictated peace.

Ján Masaryk, secure in the company of victors, was surprised when the Hungarian foreign minister continued his speech by protesting against Czechoslovakia's mistreatment of the Hungarian minority, instead of showing "respect" to victorious Czechoslovakia as the Czechoslovak press expected him to do. The Hungarian Foreign Minister declared boldly:

> Hungarian democracy, born out of the chaos of war, found to its surprise, and to its chargrin, that thousands of Hungarians had been expelled from Czechoslovakia in a manner making a mockery of human rights, often on a few hours notice, with nothing but a few handbags. In Slovakia, 650,000 Hungarians were deprived of their civil rights, even of their basic human rights. Property of persons of Hungarian nationality was confiscated. Hungarians can engage neither in intellectual nor manual work. They have no rights whatever, cannot organize, cannot exercise their rights as citizens. The use of the Hungarian language is prohibited in public offices, in public places, often even in the churches; its public use is punishable. No periodical in Hungarian may be published in the Czechoslovak Republic. It is against the law to telephone or send telegraphs in Hungarian. No Hungarian may own a radio. There is no public instruction in Hungarian in any form. Even private tutoring is prohibited in Hungarian. Employees of Hungarian nationality have been dismissed both by the State and private firms without compensation. Payment of social security benefits has been stopped, disabled verterans, widows, orphans of the war receive no aid whatever. In spite of all these deplorable measures the Hungarian Government did everything in its power to improve relations between Czechoslovakia and Hungary. To this end, and despite its own hurt feelings, the Hungarian Government considered it its duty to enter

into direct negotiations to conclude the population exchange agreement, as recommended by the Great Powers.[25]

There were a few exaggerations in Gyöngyösi's speech. For instance, Hungarian workers in Slovakia did continue to find work in construction and mining; general confiscation of Hungarian property was not carried out; and, as a rule, Hungarian language in church services was not restricted. In any case, Gyöngyösi's statement had no international impact. Nobody believed it. Victorious Czechoslovakia's democratic prestige was safe against the accusations of Hungary, Hitler's defeated ally.

The following day, on August 15, Jan Masaryk replied. It was a nationalist propaganda speech. He emphasized the "betrayal" of the Hungarian minority, without bothering to mention the Slovak People's Party's role in the destruction of Czechoslovakia. He also said quite a few fuzzy half-truths and straight untruths which should have been promptly answered by the Hungarian delegation, but it was not. According to Masaryk: "Well before the war the leaders of the Hungarian minority had allied themselves with the Sudeten German traitor Henlein and, even worse, with Frank, the mass murderer at Lidice . . . . After South Slovakia had been unfairly awarded to Hungary by Germany and Italy, the Hungarians promptly occupied this territory and expelled tens of thousands of Slovaks and Czechs in a manner worthy of the Axis . . . . In the nice little town of Šurani [Nagysurány] Hungarian troops fired at the peasants as these were leaving church, simply because they were singing in Slovak."[26]

Most likely, Masaryk's denunciation of the leaders of the Hungarian minority made a deep impression. Yet the truth is, as I have said before, the only time János Esterházy, executive director of the United Hungarian Party, negotiated with K. H. Frank was in February 1938, following Frank's negotiations with the chairman of the Slovak People's Party, Ondrej Hlinka. Furthermore, to implicate the Hungarian minority with the wartime Nazi mass murders at Lidice, as Masaryk did, was simply dishonest. The Hungarian delegation should have promptly responded to these and other unfounded charges. But it did not.[27]

The Czechoslovak press back home was jubilant: "Gyöngyösi's words decreased the sympathy towards Hungary among its former supporters. Masaryk's speech on the other hand was regarded as a model of a reply to insults."[28]

The Czechoslovak press was particularly pleased by a report of the diplomatic correspondent of the British Reuter news agency: "The Hungarian hopes are dissolving at Paris. [According to the report by Reuter] Molotov had a long talk with the Hungarian foreign minister and explained that Hungary could not count on Soviet support in its attitude of blocking the expulsion of the Hungarian minority from Slovakia. . . .If the Hungarians did not know until now on which side the Soviet is standing—writes the diplomatic correspondent of Reuter—now they can rest assured that Molotov identifies himself with Prague regarding the Hungarians' deportation. The Hungarian hopes have vanished."[29]

On August 24, 1946, V. Clementis took part in the debate and brought up charges which have never been substantiated: "We could provide documentary evidence (photographs, reports) about the fate of tens of thousands of Czechs and Slovaks who were chased out of the southern areas of Slovakia by the Fascist units of Horthy's army."[30]

In September, the Czechoslovak demand for the transfer of the "remaining" 200,000 Hungarians was debated and decided upon.

On September 9, a statement was presented by the United States delegation to the Political and Territorial Commission on the subject of the transfer of the Hungarian population. The statement proposed the constitution of a sub-committee to examine all documents concerning the Czechoslovak amendments. In explaining this proposal, the American statement said in essence: the United States was convinced that the principle of forcible removal of civilian population should not be included in the peace treaty with Hungary. Instead, the American statement suggested border rectifications and bilateral agreements as better solutions "in mutual interest" of the minority question.

On September 16, Dr. Clementis spoke in support of the Czechoslovak amendment to the draft peace treaty with Hungary. The main point in his argument was the collective guilt of the Hungarian minority. He altered historical facts to suit his objectives and took episodes out of context by selective distortions. He kept silent about the part the Slovak nationalist movement played in Czechoslovakia's destruction, but exaggerated the Hungarian minority's role in it. Not unlike Ján Masaryk before him, Clementis too resorted to moral turpitude by mentioning in an entirely distorted context Esterházy's meeting with "Konrad Henlein and K. H. Frank, the ill-famed leaders of the Germans of Czechoslovakia before and after Munich." He accused the entire Hungarian minority of having, at the time of the Vienna Award of 1938, "hurled itself against the Czechs and the Slovaks."[31]

Not a word was heard from Dr. Clementis about the expulsion of some 120,000 Czechs from Tiso's Slovakia. But he recalled the recent "census" taken by the Czechoslovak Resettlement Bureau in Hungary and he claimed that "close to half a million" Slovaks lived in Hungary.[32] As I mentioned earlier, according to the Hungarian census of 1930, only 104,000 Slovaks lived in Hungary. This might have been less than the actual number of Slovaks—nationality statistics are never accurate in the Danube region. But the Hungarian census certainly was closer to the truth than the Clementis statistics.

Dr. Clementis also sharply criticized the attitude of the Hungarian Government regarding the execution of the population exchange agreement: "The Hungarian-Czechoslovak Mixed Commission, which should have worked out the details of the resettlement met for full fifty days, yet even the last meeting remained fruitless because of the obstruction of the Hungarian members."[33] For a change, this was true. Indeed, the Hungarians did everything in their power to delay any population transfer until the decision of the peace conference.

The principal argument Clementis resorted to in order to overcome Western opposition to the transfer of Hungarians from Czechoslovakia was the Potsdam decision directing Hungary to transfer the Germans. The Germans, he argued, are made to leave in order to make room for the 200,000 Hungarians from Slovakia. Then echoing once again Jan Masaryk's words, Clementis lashed out against any return to the prewar system of international protection of minorities: "If in spite of past experiences there are still some who hope that the happy days of treason under the cover of democracy and freedom may yet return, then permit me to say what the cruel lessons of the past compel me to say: Never again! In Czechoslovakia, there is no politician, not a single politically thinking person who even for a moment would consider the return to a minority policy whose failure has been so amply demonstrated by experience."[34]

Aladár Szegedy-Maszák, member of the Hungarian delegation, answered Clementis' statement: "I believe they [the Slovaks] now want to

achieve a two-fold aim: one, to make the world forget the role the Hitlerite Slovaks played in the disruption of the Czechoslovak Republic and
later in Slovakia under German protection. Two, they want to seize the
wealth of the industrious Hungarian peasantry of Slovakia. . . . Czechoslovakia now wants to force the revision of Potsdam. The reasons however,
which motivated the Potsdam decision have not changed. That is why we
firmly believe that the Paris conference will not favor further extension
[regarding population transfers] of the Potsdam decisions."[35]

The debate continued on September 20 with another speech by Clementis. He took issue with the Hungarian delegation's assertion that there
were 650,000 Hungarians in Slovakia. (Since then even Czechoslovak
sources have agreed with the figure.) He rejected the claim that the people's
tribunals and the charges against the Hungarians in Slovakia had gone to
excesses, then he questioned the Hungarian claim regarding re-Slovakization, denying that anybody had been compelled to surrender his nationality. (The rate of "re-Hungarization" since 1948 is sufficient proof in
itself that "re-Slovakization" in 1946 had taken place under duress and
terror.) Clementis also charged that in 1945 the Hungarian army had
taken active part in the suppression of the Slovak national uprising and
in the execution of Slovak partisans and patriots.[36] It is well-known, and
Clementis knew it, that Hungarian units did not take part.

On September 20, A. J. Vishinsky spoke on behalf of the Soviet delegation. He marshalled his arguments in support of the creation of a homogeneous Czechoslovak nation-state, adopting Masaryk's and Clementis'
charges against the Hungarian minority while disregarding the role of
Slovak Fascism. He said: "The Czechoslovak Government claims—and lists
unassailable facts—that in the days of the Munich tragedy the Hungarian
minority played a negative role by siding with the hangmen of the Czechoslovak people, Henlein and Frank, by rising against Czechoslovak independence, against the Czechoslovak state, against Czechoslovak freedom."
(Vishinsky seemed to have forgotten that it was always in the Hungarian
inhabited regions of Czechoslovakia that the Communist Party received
the largest number of votes.) Hinting at the anti-transfer statement of the
American delegation, he continued: "Indeed we are talking about forced
resettlement. Of course, this is a serious measure, but it seems unavoidable
in view of a series of events that led to it . . . . " Then he reiterated the
argument already mentioned by Clementis in his speech on September 16:

The Hungarian Government claims that it has no room for these people in Hungary. In reality is there room or isn't there? It is a well known fact that Hungary is expected to transfer into the American zone 500,000 Germans—and I am glad that Mr. Smith is present, because he knows the situation well on account of his military activities in Germany. This plan was approved by the [Allied] Control Commission in Germany; 500,000 Germans have to be transferred from Hungary to the American zone. The question arises, whether there would be room in Hungary for the transfer of 200,000 Hungarians from Czechoslovakia after the resettlement of 500,000 people from Hungary to Germany?[37]

Unmoved by Vishinsky's pro-Czechoslovak arguments, Bedell-Smith reiterated, on behalf of the United States delegation the negative American view of population transfers as a means of solving controversies between small nations:

For us forced resettlement (transfer) is worse than unpleasant, it is unacceptable. We cannot approve a theory which strives to forcefully resettle large masses of people from Czechoslovakia to Hungary a measure that could be carried out only against the will of both the Hungarian government and the Hungarian people.[38]

On September 23, the United Kingdom associated itself with the American view and declared that the transfer solution of the Hungarian minority question was unacceptable:

It would leave a very bad memory if the Czechoslovak delegation were to insist on chasing 200,000 Hungarians by force from their homes. . . . Mindful of the general interest, we don't believe that it would serve the cause of justice to include compulsory deportation into the text of this treaty . . . . The best solution for Hungary and Czechoslovakia would be to attempt to reach a direct accord.[39]

The proposed Czechoslovak amendment on the transfer of Hungarians was doomed. By suggesting a "direct accord," the British hinted at a compromise amendment. The road has been paved to a "Big Three" agreement to amend the text of the draft treaty by calling on Czechoslovakia and Hungary to settle their differences on the issue of transfer by direct negotiations. The compromise amendment became the much debated "Section 4/b" of the treaty of peace with Hungary which says: "Hungary will begin bilateral negotiations with Czechoslovakia regarding the solution of the problem of those Hungarians who not be transferred to Hungary on the basis of the population exchange agreement signed on February 27, 1946. If no accord is reached within six months of the coming into effect of this treaty Czechoslovakia will have the right to bring the matter up before the council of foreign ministers and request the council to help find a final solution."[40]

The debacle of the transfer plans at the peace conference has caused great disappointment in Czechslovakia. Undersecretary of State Clementis gave expression to it in the Prague parliament: "The public may judge for itself from the profuse text of the deliberations that, while the justice of our claims and objectives has been recognized, the sound and sensible conclusions have not been drawn."[41]

As reported in the Czechoslovak press, Foreign Minister Jan Masaryk commented even more bitterly on the Paris decision of the Hungarian case:

> [Jan Masaryk] expressed his disappointment over the attitude of the United States and Great Britain at the Paris peace conference for not supporting Czechoslovakia's just demands: the deportation of the Hungarian minority and border rectification. While declaring his regrets, he made comparisons with Munich, and added: 'It will be difficult to explain to our compatriots at home why our [Western] allies took this stand, whereas Russia and the Slav states supported us.' The minister hopes that the negotiations to be initiated with Hungary will bring a solution, hence the principle of expulsion of the 200,000 Hungarians is not abandoned. As he said: 'We are willing to go half way to meet Hungary, and discuss all necessary matters on the condition that it will be worth negotiating with democratic Hungary. But first we have to be convinced that a democratic spirit does exist in Hungary. Masaryk emphasized that Czechoslovakia will not accept any special status for the minorities, and the

children of Hungarians who remain in Czechoslovakia will have to attend Slovak schools. We have been very patient, but we paid dearly for it."[42]

Later on, Jan Masaryk explained what happened and why at the Paris peace conference, assuring his Slav compatriots that the Czechoslovak Government did everything in its power to gain international support for the expulsion of the Hungarians:

> At the peace conference, the matter that interested Czechoslovakia most was the Hungarian issue. The Czechoslovak proposals were dictated by the endeavor to solve once and for all the question which until now has rendered the peaceful coexistence between the two neighborly states impossible. . . . We have explained in detail the issues of resettlement and border rectification. . . . In spite of our repeated endeavors, we did not succeed in having the expulsion of the Hungarians included in the amended peace treaty. . . . By proposing the amendment, Czechoslovakia stressed before the world public opinion the seriousness of the problem from the point of view of European peace. The transfer proposal received the support of the Soviet Union, the delegations of the Ukrainian and Bielo-Russian Socialist Republics, and Yugoslavia. Poland [who also would have supported us] was not represented on the political and territorial committee dealing with Hungary. We also made use of France's approval of our first [expulsion] proposal.[43]

The Paris peace conference left the question of the Hungarians in Slovakia unresolved. And considering that the peace conference imposed no international obligations for the protection of national minorities, the threat to Hungarian minority's survival in Czechoslovakia (and elsewhere) has not been removed. The renewed threat appeared in the form of radical dispersion of the minority as a substitute for an "exchange" of "peaceful resettlement." The new plan of radical dispersal appeared the more realistic since after Paris nobody could hope that Hungary would accept a mass transfer of 200,000 Hungarians from Slovakia as a result of bilateral negotiations stipulated in the Treaty of Peace.

The Czechoslovak press campaign in fact soon shifted to the propagation of "internal measures" rather than bilateral negotiations to solve the Hungarian problems. The thesis of D. M. Krno's book "We Negotiated with Hungary," published shortly after the Paris peace conference, promoted the new effort. Discussing "internal measures," which became a euphemism for dispersal of the Hungarians from their homes in Southern Slovakia, Krno's book said: "While Hungary succeeded in shielding itself against the inclusion of transfer measures into the peace treaty, it received neither the right, nor the means to prevent the measures we deem necessary to eliminate once and for all the dangers of revisionism and irredentism from our border regions."[44]

After Paris, the situation was aggravated by the fact that article 4/b of the peace treaty, calling for direct negotiatins between Hungary and Czechoslovakia, could be interpreted by both parties according to their own interest. In Czechoslovakia it was argued that Hungary was obliged to undertake negotiations regarding the deportation of 200,000 Hungarians. Foreign Minister Masaryk made statements to this effect, although the text of the article merely obliged Hungary to negotiate regarding "the solution" of the problem, but not about "expulsion" of the Hungarian minority from Czechoslovakia.

Czechoslovakia certainly received a free hand in dealing with the Hungarian minority, and it was generally believed that in case of an internal dispersion of the minority she could count on the support of world public opinion. However, toward the end of the peace conference, the Czechoslovak press was also warning against the danger of delaying a radical solution, fearful that the world public opinion might shift to the Hungarian side: "The self-confidence of the Hungarians at Paris indicates that they created a good impression in the West. The future would soon decide whether Hungarian slyness or Czechoslovak justice wins. . . . If the victor becomes the loser at the time of peacemaking, this would sadly reflect on logic, on consistency, on right and on justice. Sin would triumph over virtue, injustice over righteousness."[45]

Czechoslovak apprehension increased after the peace conference. The Slovak *Nové Prúdy* wrote:

> The fact that some took the side of the Hungarians [at the peace conference] indicates that they were able to arouse sympathy abroad, whereas our position and behavior have been looked upon with critical eyes. Our impression in this matter is supported by

foreign press reports and also by the stand taken by the Austrialian delegate Ewatte, or by the delegate from New Zealand. . . . Here forces are at work against our interests. . . . It would be understandable that the Hungarians are defending themselves if their means of defense were not so offensive, as when they go as far as to call the entire Slovak nation collaborators and Fascists. It is difficult to understand whence the Hungarians have obtained such boldness, and how all this unpleasantness has come about. Our citizen, if he is reflecting over these matters, must frown while perusing foreign newspapers. Some Hungarian papers have gone so far as to advocate the solidarity of the progressive Hungarians and progressive Czechs against the reactionary Slovaks.[46]

Slovak commentators were incensed and disappointed that even the chairman of the Hungarian Communist Party, Mátyás Rákosi, took a stand against expulsion. Rákosi was quoted as having said: "Both as patriots and as Communits, we deem the compulsory expulsion of Hungarians from Slovakia incorrect and definitely harmful to the nations of the Danube Basin." Thus did one Slovak commentator vent his anger against Rákosi:

The Hungarian Communist Party does everything in its power to prevent the compulsory deportation of Hungarians. [Rákosi pledged that the Party] will devote greater attention to the interests of the Hungarian minorities beyond the borders, and will always speak up wherever and whenever the democratic rights of the Hungarians beyond the borders are being curtailed. Our answer to Mr. Rákosi regarding the deportation of the Hungarians is very simple: All [minority] Hungarians, who remain beyond the borders of Hungary in the neighboring states, become most harmful for the entire Hungarian nation the moment [Buda] Pest begins to care for them.[47]

Disappointment led to bitter outbursts. After Paris, it became obvious that, for the Slovaks, the population exchange and the demand for the expulsion of the "remaining" 200,000 Hungarians were a matter of nationalist minimum. The Slovaks have actually been hoping to gain more territory from Hungary. An article in the *Nové Prúdy* expressed the bitter mood of disappointment:

We must realize certain facts which not so long ago nobody among us would have believed. What happened to the plans we made at the time of the [Slovak national] uprising or the Košice program? How convinced we had been at that time that this war signifies the burial not only of German but also of Hungarian expansionism. We were told of a corridor linking [across Hungary] Czechoslovakia with Yugoslavia. We were whispering of [detaching from Hungary] Vác and Miskolc in order to connect central [mountainous] Slovakia with Košice [in the east] by way [of plainlands] of the South. Then retreat was sounded. We were left with our pre-Munich borders. And the next stage was already a defensive one. We had to fend off the bites of Hungarian appetite.[48]

The Czech press did not pay much attention to the development of the Hungarian affair. It reconciled itself to the lack of success at Paris with short and objective comments. Only *Obzory,* organ of the Czech People's Party, wrote a relatively longer report, not shying away even from quoting "Hungarian satisfaction" with "achieved successes."[49]

Meanwhile, in Southern Slovakia, among the Hungarian population the atmosphere was growing tense. The Hungarians had over-estimated the results achieved at Paris. They became ever more aware of the ominous sharpening of Slovak nationalist propaganda. Insignificant local incidents were blown up out of proportion in the Slovak press: "Every day we receive news about the misdeeds of the Hungarians. It seems we have reached a point where the so-called Hungarian blue-blood is continually boiling, and us Slovaks can no longer feel at home because our safety is constantly endangered. The Hungarians who are still living in our southern borderlands have indulged in some detestable acts. The Hungarians of Pozsonypüspöki have gone so far in their impertinence that the portrait of the President of the Republic has become the target of beer mug shootings. Those who honor [their] crown of St. Stephen have turned [our] sympbolic Partisan statue into an object of derision. While tearing [our] flags off the houses, they sing the [Hungarian] national anthem of our eternal enemy. . . ."[50]

According to another story in the Bratislava *Pravda:* "How far will the impertinence of the Hungarians go? Hungarian chauvinists and terrorists have committed excesses in the county of Verebély. In the village of

Baracska, persons of Hungarian nationality have it so good that they have completely forgotten that the Hungarian chauvinist regime of terror is no longer in charge. One day, they started shooting in the streets with military rifles that had been hidden illegally and singing Hungarian songs. . . . The shots were aimed at the houses of peaceful Slovak settlers. . . . [51]

The dark days of November in 1946 have foreshadowed grave events which were to follow. Anti-Hungarian Slovak nationalist sentiments have been growing threateningly. To the Slovaks the Hungarian problem was no longer a matter of population exchange, or direct negotiations with Hungary, or re-Slovakization. The new wave of dissatisfaction called for "internal regulations." General Dr. M. Ferjenčik, the Slovak deputy in charge of internal affairs, declared in the predominantely Hungarian town of Érsekújvar (Nové Zámky) on November 17, 1946, two days before the beginning of the first deportations:

> While we want to bring home from abroad every Slovak soul, Hungary has obstructed the return of Hungarians to their country. We know why. But precisely because we do know, it only strengthens our resolution to put an end once and for all to all threats and revisionist attempts directed against our country. [52]

General Ferjenčik's veiled hint sounded like a declaration of war. Two days later the Hungarians had learned what he meant. The deportation of the Hungarian population to the Czech lands had already been prepared in detail. The decision had been taken to "solve" the Hungarian question by a radical dispersion of the population. The Hungarian minority found itself at the edge of the precipice.

CHAPTER 6

THE DEPORTATIONS

The failure of the transfer solution of the Hungarian question had a disheartening effect on the Czechoslovak public opinion. There were signs too that the less radical nationalist circles in the country were getting tired of the constant tension fuelled by the Hungarian issue. But the radical nationalist elements were not ready to admit defeat. Obsessed by Slav prejudices against the Hungarians, they were determined to wipe out the Hungarian ethnic character of Southern Slovakia.

The hard line advocates of the ethnically homogeneous Czechoslovak nation-state were encouraged by the lack of interest the Great Powers had shown at the Paris Peace Conference in international minority protection. Unlike the peace treaties after the First World War, the new treaties did not obligate multiethnic states to respect the rights of ethnic minorities. This was hailed by the victorious nations of Central and Eastern Europe as a triumph of the homogeneous nation-state. The free hand granted to the victors against the vanquished tempted the Slovak nationalists to use force against the Hungarian minority. They decided to solve the Hungarian problem by internal dispersion under the guise of so-called "domestic measures."

At the beginning of November 1946, an ominous tone spread all over the Slovak nationalist press: "In case we cannot reach agreement with Hungary, our government and the parliament will find the means with which to solve once and for all the problem of the Hungarian minority, if necessary by merely domestic means. In any case Slovakia and its southern borderlands can only be Slovak and nothing else."[1]

For some time after the Paris Peace Conference, neither the Czechoslovak nor the Hungarian side showed eagerness to open direct negotiations as envisaged by the treaty of peace between the two countries. Most likely, the motivation for hesitation on the Czechoslovak side was the conviction that internal dispersion under "domestic measures" offered better chances for a radical solution than international negotiations of any sort. The Hungarians, on the other hand, regarded delay in opening direct negotiations as salutary from their point of view. Their hope was that delay may cool down the hot temper of Czechoslovak nationalism. Evidently, neither the Hungarian government nor the Hungarian minority had been aware of the behind-the-scene Czechoslovak preparations for internal dispersion.

As we now know, tentative plans for the tragic 99 day episode of the winter deportations in 1946-47 had actually been laid already in the summer of 1946. According to the Slovak historian Samuel Cambel:

> In Bratislava on August 6-7, 1946, at a joint meeting of the central authorities and the local Slovak national organizations it was decided that, in order to ensure the necessary manpower [for economic reconstruction] force would be used against the Hungarian population of South Slovakia pursuant to the provisions of Presidential decree 88/1945 [on universal labor service]. It was on this basis that the compulsory labor service of the Hungarian population of South Slovakia was decreed [in November 1946], the intention being that by the same token the [ethnic] structure of South Slovakia's population would be altered. The recruitment campaign did not apply to Hungarians under investigation for treason or cooperation with the Germans. . . , nor to those who had been selected for expulsion within the framework of the population exchange agreement. . . . [2]

Historian Cambel thus frankly revealed the early plans for internal dispersion. The exemptions from deportation also revealed the social thrust of the intended measures. As it is well known, the Hungarians selected as "war criminals" (in excess of 100,000) were mostly intellectuals and well-to-do peasants, while the Hungarians selected for exchange (another 100,000) were also well off farmers. The strategy of the final solution was clear. Expulsion would take care of the intelligentsia and of the kulaks, whose land would be made available for Slovak colonization, while the deportation would disperse the "remaining" Hungarians, belonging mostly to the agrarian proletariat.

Indoctrination of the Czechoslovak public opinion for supporting the new wave of anti-Hungarian measures began in late October. Dr. J. Lettrich, chairman of the Slovak National Council, declared before departing for a good-will tour of the United States: "The brotherly Czech nation and the government devote much greater attention to the German problem. Two and a half million Germans are already across the border, while so far, not even five percent of the Hungarians have been expelled from Slovakia. The problem of replacing the missing workers and employees in the Czech borderlands and in Czech industry arises following the departure of the Germans, and the situation is also serious in agriculture. The matter concerns us [Slovaks] insofar as they expect us to fill the gap caused by the departure of German manpower in the Sudeten area. We must deal with this because it is primarily a Slovak national concern . . . ."[3]

It should be noted that Czech willingness to cooperate with the Slovaks in the matter of the Hungarians' deportation to the Czech lands was not always unanimous. President Beneš himself counselled caution as this press release by ČTK, the official Czechoslovak new agency indicates: "The delegation of the Slovak Resettlement Bureau calls on President Beneš. The President of the Republic received the delegation of the Slovak Resettlement Bureau and of the National Reconstruction Foundation, which briefed the President regarding the possibilities for the solution of the Hungarian problem of Slovakia. In the course of the conversation they discussed the question of resettlement of the Hungarians. The President emphasized that the Hungarian issue was not merely an internal Slovak matter, but a concern of the State as a whole and it even has international implications, which have to be clarified."[4]

Beneš's counsel of caution evidently refered to the fact that dispersion would bypass international agreements and the deportation project would imply that Czechoslovakia no longer wished to avail itself of direct negotiations envisaged by the peace treaty, nor believed that the population exchange was urgent. Apart from that, Beneš, did nothing to stop the Slovak plans against the Hungarian minority. Moreover, Czech scruples —whether motivated by international concern, class or humanistic considerations—conveniently disappeared once deportations began. The fact that the Minister of Agriculture in the central government was the strongly nationalist Slovak Julius Ďuriš contributed to a speedy decision on the deportations. In Bratislava, the Slovak National Council, and the Board of Representatives (the highest government authority in Slovakia) unanimously approved the measure.

As the deportations began, Minister Ďuriš declared: "We will. . .employ Hungarians on Bohemian lands. We will bring about order by ourselves since it cannot be done on the basis of mutual accord between Czechoslovakia and Hungary, because Hungary is sabotaging the population exchange; and we will carry all this out even if international forums do not approve."[5]

When Minister Ďuriš spoke, the sate of siege already had been lasting for four days in the solidly Hungarian populated Western Csallóköz (an island between the two branches of the Danube). The 99 days drama began in the early hours of November 19, 1946, and it lasted until February 25, 1947. It surprised both the affected population and government circles in Hungary, for after Paris, Hungarian public opinion expected relaxation of tensions and a return to reason.

The deportation operations were carried out according to detailed plans. Military units closed in on one or two villages ata time and then ordered the selected families to get ready for evacuation with their belongings. Those to be deported were informed that they must leave their homes for good. Their real estate, their domestic animals, their agricultural equipment would be confiscated. There was not right of appeal. Family members had to leave regardless of age or sex. The designated families were transported by military trucks to the nearest railroad station whence they were dispatched to Bohemia under close guard. There was no relief even on the coldest days, although the winter that year was particularly severe. There was a cold wave all over Europe.[6]

The family sentenced to deportation was handed a flyer in Hungarian titled "Instructions." Its standard text read as follows:

Instructions

According to the two-year plan for reconstruction, enacted by law 129/1946, we want to carry out the reconstruction and reorganization of Czechoslovakia, thus to ensure the livelihood of the people of the Republic and raise the standard of living of the nation. In accordance with decree 88/1945 of the President of the Republic [on universal labor service], and in order to carry out this [two-year] plan, the labor force necessary for the economic life may be displaced to areas and into occupations where there is a lack of manpower.

Each family will unconditionally and immediately receive adequate housing at its new place of work. A job assignment, food tickets and other coupons covering daily needs, also a remuneration commensuate with the category of work.

Since these persons will receive all the necessities of life at their new place of work, they may not take with them large quantities of cereal and flour. They are, however, authorized to take along the following articles and food items: 10 kgs. of cooking and bread flour per person, 3 kgs. of beans or peas, 1/4 kg. of poppy seeds, 20 kgs. of potatoes, 5 kgs. of vegetables; furthermore, any amount of home-made jams, preserves and homegrown fruits. For seed a maximum of 15 kgs. of corn, rye or oats per fowl. Lard and smoked meat to the extent of one slaughter. If this unit is not at the person's disposal, 1 kg. of lard, and 2 kgs. of meat per person. Furthermore, a family may take along any quantity of poultry, but no more than its stock as of December 31, 1946. No one may bring along or alienate (sell) horses, cattle of any kind (bulls, cows, calves), or pigs. Furthermore, every family may take along a complete set of furniture, all their clothing, and all those effects which are not part of the equipment inventory: agricultural machines, fireplaces, ovens, etc.

The families thus recruited into the work program will receive all the necessities of life at their new places of designation just like any other Czechoslovak citizen. The right of citizenship will be settled and the immovable property left behind will be duly compensated for on location and will not be confiscated.

The not particularly humane details of the deportations have been related by several Hungarian writers living in Slovakia (László Dobos, Viktor Egri, József Mács, Gyula Duba). We know from their reports that those condemned to deportations received "Instructions" which varied according to time and place. Gyula Duba, in his book on these events, had mentioned "Instructions" which did not include compensation for the confiscated property, but limited labor service to only one year.[7]

Gyula Duba, living as he still does in Slovakia, could only intimate what has to be pointed out here more clearly: the role of Hungarian collaborators. Hand-picked officials of Hungarian nationality assisting at the deportations cannot be excused even if we assume that they allowed some persons to get away. They should not have accepted the assignment in the preparation and execution of the deportations. From reading the decree on universal labor service 88/1945, they should have realized that deportation was an abuse of power; they had the opportunity to take a stand, even to protest. How can one blame Slovaks for having done nothing, when persons of Hungarian nationality collaborated in these nationalist abuses of power?

After November 19 panic broke out in the entire Csallóköz. A mass of refugees attempted to cross the Danube into Hungary. On the Hungarian side, propaganda against the deportations began immediately. On the Czechoslovak side, the operations were kept as quiet as possible. Yet it was not possible to keep the matter secret. The Hungarian press turned the affair into a European scandal.

Slovak historians (Zvara, Purgat, Cambel and others) still refer to the Hungarians' deportations as "recruitment," the official term used at the time of the deportations. But this term is unacceptable. The "recruited" as well as their families were forced to leave their homes without any promise of an opportunity to return, and their wealth was confiscated. The terminology of the Presidential decree 88/1945 is not applicable. In the case of the Hungarians, the decree merely was a legal pretext. The decree did declare universal draft for labor service. It did not, however, authorize confiscation of belongings nor the deportation of family members. The action against the Hungarian persons as well as the confiscation of their belongings was illegal. The action violated Czechoslovak laws in general, and it was in conflict with the Czechoslovak-Hungarian population exchange agreement as well. We must deal in greater detail with the story of the Presidential decree 88/1945, because the decree is still being cited in every historical work published in Czechoslovakia to cover up the illegal assault.

The Presidential decree 88/1945 empowered the government to draft men between the ages of 16 and 55 and women between the ages of 18 and 45 for labor service. The decree also lists the conditions for exemption.

The drafted person could serve a maximum of one year. In the case of the Hungarians, however, no heed was paid to age-limit or time limit. Moreover, every attempt was made to make the action against the Hungarians appear as legal is defeated by the practice of collective confiscation of belongings, which in the Presidential decree, is nowhere mentioned. Unfortunately, some Slovak historians are not bothered by these facts.

For instance, J. Purgat intentionally broadens the Presidential decree to include deportation and confiscation. He simply declares: "It followed from the universal labor service decree 88/1945 that the belongings of the Hungarians were confiscated, and they were deported to Bohemia and Moravia."[8] The fact of the matter is that Presidential decree 88/1945, rather than authorizing confiscation of property and deportation of entire families explicitly called for special assistance to family members of those drafted for labor service.[9] Other Slovak authors, J. Zvara and S. Cambel describe the events of those tragic 99 days as a rather pleasant labor service, not bothering even to mention confiscation of property and deportation of family members. It should be noted, however, that, in contrast to Slovak historiography, some Czech historians do call a spade a spade: They speak of "the Slovakization of the Hungarian minority," and denounce the actions by which Hungarians from South Slovakia had been "incorrectly recruited and transported to Bohemia."[10]

No better than the accounts of the Slovak historians was the information dispensed by the Slovak press on the deportation of the Hungarians. For a while, the Czechoslovak press kept silent altogether. The deportations began on November 19, but the first report in the papers appeared only ten days later. The Bratislava *Čas* reported on November 19:

> The expulsion of the Hungarians from Parkan [Párkány] and its vicinty began in the commune of Nana [Nána] on November 25. Seventy-five families were removed on this day from this relatively small commune. The deportation went smoothly, thirty families reported voluntarily. Thirty-five military trucks were provided for the transportation of the belongings to the railroad station and each of these was escorted by six soldiers and two security agents. Four trucks were made available to each of the families, and even more if need be according to the amount of belongings, while relatives and

neighbors could share the transportation facilities. The deportations continued on November 26 adn 27, this time from Parkan itself. The process went likewise smoothly. The Hungarians from the area of Parkan were resettled in Plzeň, Kladno, Pardubice, and the environs of other cities in northern Bohemia, where they will be assigned to work according to their experience and ability. The railroad cars are heated, and a military kitchen contingent accompany the deported to the point of their destination. The first transport left Parkan Wednesday evening at 7:00 pm on November 17.[11]

Among many other aspects, this news story failed to explain why thirty "volunteer" families from Nána needed the "escort" of eight armed men per truck to oversee their willingness to leave their homes.

With the first Slovak press reports on the deportations, also the press war between Hungary and Czechoslovakia had begun. Hungarian Foreign Minister, János Gyöngyösi, lodged vigorous protests against the "acts of inhumanity" taking place in Czechoslovakia. In turn, the Bratislava *Čas* on November 26 took issue with the Hungarian protest under the following front page headline: "The Hungarians do not cease to incite against Czechoslovakia. Czechoslovak reply to Hungarian Foreign Minister Gyönggösi. The propaganda of lies does not delude our Hungarians." An official report by the Slovak Press Agency that followed offered the Czechoslovak version of what was going on in the solidly Hungarian populated regions of Southerrt Slovakia:

As is known, on October 28, 1946, the National Assembly of the Czechoslovak Republic solemnly enacted the law [129/1946] regarding the two-year plan for the reconstruction of the Republic. From the beginning it seemed probable that, in order to carry out this plan of reconstruction, well organized and sizable labor forces would become necessary. The Presidential decree 88/1945 on universal labor service, approved by the National Assembly, intends to realize this objective. Article One of the decree states that every man and woman capable of work may be enlisted for performing urgent tasks of general interest. Since there is manpower shortage in the Czech provinces, it was necessary to apply the decree 88/1945 to the area of the entire Republic for the recruitment of labor, and to extend it to all strata of society, regardless of nationality. 180,000 Slovaks went to work in Bohemia within the framework of the recruitment of manpower. Of course, the citizens of Hungarian nationality cannot be exempted from the application of this law, and the Presidential decree regarding labor service applies to them as well. It should be noted that the recruitment for labor took place precisely according to the letters of the law, and in a humane and social manner. The citizens will be transported from the gathering points to their new workplaces in railroad coaches with their packages shipped in covered freight cars. They receive hot and cold meals during the journey. In some unavoidable cases, members of the family, first of all relatives and children living in a common household, accompany the workers. This takes place with the agreement of the family members; their wishes are taken into consideration, with the intention to ensure family togetherness and the care of family members. The children will be provided with milk along the way. The workers thus recruited will be working under favorable conditions; Hungarians will receive the same pay as the Slovaks. In addition to payment in kind the workers will receive monthly wages between 1800 and 2200 crowns, a sum which far surpasses the average monthly wage of the workers in Hungary. The decree regarding the recruitment of labor force is applied to the whole country, including the areas inhabited by Hungarians. It is carried out in an orderly manner and meets with understanding on the part of the Hungarian inhabitants of the country.

The official version was totally misleading. It described the situation of the deported Hungarians as no different from that of the Slovaks called up for labor service, which was a lie.

A follow-up story in the same issue of *Čas* dealt with the international aspects of the case and condemns the Hungarian protests in sharp terms:

The Hungarian radio broadcasts rumors to the effect that the recruitment campaign had resorted to inhuman methods. Even official government organs—as can be learned from Foreign Minister Gyöngyösi's speech—are spreading misleading information and describe the recruitment procedures in a distorted manner. At the same time, the Hungarian media are conducting a crude propaganda campaign against the recruitment of manpower [in Czechoslovakia] inciting the Hungarian population to provocative acts. The scare rumors spread by the Hungarians are inventions of ill will and do not correspond to reality in any way. In the commune of Gutor disorders erupted among the Hungarians when *agents provocateurs* began to spread rumors that people would be taken to Siberia. Some families fled to Hungary. But ten families, upon finding out that it was only a matter of labor service in the Czech lands, sent a messenger over to the Slovak side with the word that they wished to return voluntarily and subject themselves to the labor service law rather than remain in Hungary. The distortion of the true nature of things and the continued slanders against the Czechoslovak Republic certainly do not serve the cause of peaceful settlement of disagreements between Hungary and Czechoslovakia. The Hungarian government, crudely and intentionally disregarding its treaty obligations, refuses to carry out the population exchange agreement, persecutes and oppresses the Slovaks of Hungary, particularly those who have signed up for resettlement, and incites systematically against our State, in order to blacken our reputation before world public opinion. . . . Those who know Hungarian propaganda could easily fit the present campaign against Czechoslovakia among the memories of past slanders which distorted the truth, spread lies about Czechoslovakia where peace, order and exemplary democracy prevails, where, instead of unscrupulous propaganda, every effort is concentrated on constructive work.[12]

Three days later, without comment, *Čas* reported on November 29: "Hungary sent a note to the foreign ministers of the four Great Powers in New York, as well as to the Czechoslovak Government, protesting against the alleged persecution of the Hungarians in Slovakia. The note lists a whole series of incidents which allegedly took place last week."[13]

The right-wing Hungarian nationalist press, in its zeal to stir up sentiments against Czechoslovakia, carried exaggerated stories about the deplorable events taking place on the other side of the Danube. The Slovak press, eager to discredit Hungarian propaganda, readily quoted such articles, like the one published in *Kossuth Népe* which stated: "The terrorist groups of the Hlinka Guard deport thousands of Hungarians to their unknown fate. Diplomatic measures and articles which appeared in the Hungarian and world press have not contributed to a mitigation of the misfortune of tens of thousands of Hungarians. The Slovak agencies accelerate the deportation of the Hungarians, for they fear intervention on the part of the Great Powers. Many Hungarians have met their death in the waves of the Danube. The Slovak soldiers scan the waters of the Danube with searchlights. As soon as they spot a Hungarian refugee they wildly open fire with their machine guns . . . . Human fantasy cannot conceive of all the horrors happening in southern Slovakia . . . ."[14]

While the Hungarian right was exaggerating the events in Czechoslovakia, the Hungarian left did the opposite by condoning the Czechoslovak measures. In the confusion of propaganda, quite a few Hungarian progressives failed to recognize the true situation, and let themselves be misled. This, too, was welcome news for the Slovak press. Thus *Práca* reported from Budapest: "In *Népszava,* the daily of the Hungarian Social Democratic Party, the editor-in-chief Zoltán Horváth, writes an article in which he rejects the Hungarian press attacks against Czechoslovakia. Horváth was a member of a delegation of Hungarian Social Democrats who participated in a congress of Social Democrats held in Prague. The Hungarian journalist had a chance to freely visit Southern Slovakia and could see how baseless are the Hungarian press reports according to which the Czechoslovak authorities persecute the Hungarians living in Czechoslovakia. Editor-in-chief Horváth could see it for himself that no deportations of any kind had taken place, that there was no persecution, but simply recruitment and truly for labor service. This duty for labor service is valid for the Hungarians of Czechoslovakia no less than it is for the Slovaks themselves."[15]

It remains a mystery how the Slovak hosts managed to convince the visiting Zoltán Horváth that resettlement of Hungarians and confiscation of their belongings was in harmony with labor service obligation.

The Bratislava *Pravda* quoted a similar Hungarian point of view from the Communist *Szabad Nép:* "The Hungarian Communists condemn the propaganda campaign directed against Czechoslovakia under the title 'disturbers of the peace.' The newspaper *Szabad Nép* objects to the irresponsible way the Hungarian press writes about Czechoslovakia. It points out that right wing elements are exploiting the momentary difficulties of the

Hungarians of Slovakia, formenting thus additional tensions between Czechoslovakia and Hungary. The newspaper wounders what effect it has abroad when Hungarian papers denounce the Czechoslovakia of Beneš, Gottwald and Široký for allegedly doing the same thing which Goering and Ribbentrop had been condemned for. *Szabad Nép* warns that the *Manchester Guardian* has already accused the Hungarian press of conducting a propaganda of lies."[16]

The Hungarian press did exaggerate. On the other hand, it was the protest of the Hungarian press which placed the issue of the Hungarians in Czechoslovakia into the focus of international attention. And it was the pressure of world public opinion which eventually forced Czechoslovakia to stop the deportation of the Hungarians.

As for the press war between the two countries: the Czechoslovak press certainly exaggerated no less in its efforts to defend and conceal the deportations than did the Hungarian press in its efforts to attack and denounce them. A good illustration of Slovak reporting on this subject was the news story datelined from Budapest in the 1946 Christmas issue of *Čas* comparing the minority policies of the two countries:

> The Hungarian papers swarm with sharp and inconsiderate attacks against Czechoslovakia because of the labor service performed by Hungarians from Slovakia in Bohemia. They raise a hue and cry around the whole world, and sent out diplomatic circulars asking that the Powers take the Hungarians of Slovakia under their wings and help prevent the use of force against them. The articles in the Hungarian press appear under fantastic headlines: Manhunt in Csallóköz, and the like. Those who are misled by these articles must believe that the most reactionary regime rules Czechoslovakia, or one at least of the wild West variety. . . . And what is the situation in Hungary? Here the Slovaks who have signed up for repatriation have been fired from their jobs, they have been cut from all sources of income. Thus in Békéscsaba alone more than 200 civil servants are without work and pay since July. . . . Can there be a greater terror and lawlessness than to take away the bread of the people, their livelihood, and to prevent them from going where they can make a living? Is there a person or statesman who would understand this? Especially since this is happening in a country which

pretends to be democratic! How would Mr. Minister Gyöngyösi justify such heinous injustice?[17]

The question has often been raised: Why did millions of Slovaks and Czechs accept every nationalist excess against the Hungarian minority without any dissent whatsoever?

For one thing, one must remember that there were very few Slovaks who were not implicated in one way or another in the affairs of the Fascist Tiso Slovakia. Since the anti-Hungarian policy had been paraded as an anti-Fascist policy, any dissent with it might have easily been labed as "Fascist," an accusation which at that time might have carried with it, if not the threat of prison, but at least existential bankruptcy. And then, too, even those who did have a so-called anti-Fascist or revolutionary record could not so easily turn against the policy of nationalist fanatics either. After all, that policy had been ushered in by the victors whose deeds were immune to criticism.

Not even the Czech writers could find an answer to this dilemma. They invariably approved of the Presidential decrees and of other measures devised against the Hungarian minority. From Budapest, the Hungarian Writers' Association asked the Czech writers to denounced the offenses committed against the Hungarians. The Czech reply was evasive:

> The Czech Writers' Association reassured the Hungarian Writers' Association that they feel at one with their faith in humanity and world solidarity. But, if the offenses mentioned refer to the Hungarian population living in Southern Slovakia, the Czech Writers' Association must note that the Hungarian press campaign in connection with the labor service in South Slovakia has been denounced as unwarranted and has been criticized recently in the Hungarian press itself. The Czech Writers' Association assures the Hungarian writers that the Hungarians of Southern Slovakia are treated decently and humanely within the letter of the Czechoslovak laws and decrees.[18]

What could one expect from the simple citizen, if there wasn't a spark of courage even in the Association of Writers? Actually, I know of only two written dissents: A protest from the Catholic church, and a criticism by a political party. The Slovak *Katolické Noviny* expressed at least once its astonishment at the deportation of Hungarians—and was promptly rebuked for it as being "un-national." The Slovak Catholic paper wrote: "The resettlement of the Hungarians of Slovakia is tantamount to the deprivation of rights of the Hungarian people."[19] The other written evidence of outspoken dissent against the deportations came from Jaroslav Fabok, secretary of the Slovak Democratic Party. He declared at Želiezovce (Zseliz) on January 21, 1947: "We will not tolerate that the inhabitants of Hungarian nationality be resettled . . . ."[20] This was all.

It must be added, however, that the Slovak people observing the events had noticeably been filled with anxiety. The unusual roughness astounded the public. But what one could hear was only the voice of Slovak nationalist fanatics running amok. The Slovak population at large was scared and silent.

In the last days of January 1947, the Hungarian Foreign Minister, János Gyöngyösi met in secret at Bratislava with Ján Masaryk's Deputysecretary of State Vladimir Clementis. The news of the secret meeting was leaked to Associated Press in Bratislava, which prompted Foreign Minister Gyöngyösi to call a press conference upon his return to Budapest and inform the public of his meeting with Dr. Clementis.

The Associated Press report and the Gyöngyösi press conference revealed that the Hungarian-Czechoslovak meeting at Bratislava to resolve the crisis created by the deportations and other unresolved issues had ended in failure. The Czechoslovak press reported at great length the press conference of the Hungarian Foreign Minister, but also expressed indignation over the failure to be informed from domestic sources: "What is the advantage of being informed about matters of direct relevance by foreign press agencies?—asked *Nové Prúdy.*[21] Another paper, *Práca*, published a lengthy and polemical report on Gyöngyösi's press conference under the headlines: "The Hungarian Foreign Minister continues to distort the facts. Hungary wishes to bring up the matter of resettlement at the United Nations." The news report itself stressed that the failure of the Bratislava meeting was caused by Hungary's "recalcitrant stand." The paper also informed the public of an exchange of notes between the two countries:

Gyöngyösi read the text of the diplomatic note which our [Czecho-slovak] Government had sent to Hungary on January 7, 1947. . . . The note explains that we hope for a continuation of the dialogue with Hungary, and would like to interpret the original agreement on population exchange in such a manner that the persons already [forcibly] resettled and those who already left [voluntarily] as re-fugees should not be included in the count of those to be resettled in the future. Our government also hopes that the Hungarian govern-ment would grant a 30 day extension for the registration of the Czechs and Slovaks in Hungary [for resettlement to Czechoslovakia], and that the exchange be concluded by December 31, 1947. The Hungarian reply remitted on January 14 stated that those proposals constitute changes of substance in the agreement signed on February 27, 1946. As long as the dispersion of the Hungarians [in Czecho-slovakia] continues, the Hungarian Government considers any kind of an accord as useless.

The *Práca* report continued with an account of the Gyöngyösi press conference on the controversial Bratislava meeting:

Gyöngyösi referred to the fact that the meeting was meant to be secret but was betrayed by circles in Bratislava. He denied that he demanded cessation of the labor service in Czechoslovakia, but he insisted that the workers not be compelled to abandon their homes under the guise of labor service . . . . To the question, whether Hun-gary had carried out the population exchange agreement, he [Gyöng-gösi] answered that the actual resettlement according to the terms of the agreement had not even begun because neither party had studied and arranged the proposal for exchange. As far as the Brat-islava meeting was concerned, he declared that the meeting took place on his initiative . . . [and] that the Great Powers will be in-formed. . . . [According to Gyöngyösi], the Czechoslovak Govern-ment wishes to replace the earlier agreement with a newer one, even more favorable to itself. After the signing of the peace treaty Hun-gary intends to bring up the matter at the United Nations.[22]

Following the miscarried Bratislava meeting, the Hungarian Government had sent a note to the Great Powers informing them of the dispersion and persecution of the Hungarians of Slovakia. The Slovak press responded with a threat: "If Hungarian propaganda assumes that it can camouflage its own responsibility by unjust charges and systematic interference in our internal affairs, then it will soon be cured from this error."[23]

Slovak anger had been further heightened by Cardinal Mindszenty's radiogram to the King of England and to President Truman. Said the first page headlines of the February 8, 1947 issue of the Bratislava Čas: "General Hungarian offensive against Czechoslovakia. Both Gyöngyösi and Mindszenty complain about us." Yet the report itself led one to believe that even Czechoslovak circles were worried about the developments:

> The Hungarian Cardinal Mindszenty . . . urges intervention against the policy of the Czechoslovak Government, in order to stop the persecution of the Hungarians. The radiogram contends that the Hungarians in Czechoslovakia had suffered the most cruel oppression during the past two years. On the grounds of collective guilt for the war they have been deprived of all human and civil rights, even though these rights are guaranteed by the Charter of the United Nations which Czechoslovakia flouts. Under the disguise of general labor service . . . Czechoslovak authorities, assisted by armed forces, deport farmers and their families, whose estates range between 10 to 100 hectares, including the sick, children and women. There are also priests among the deported. These people are taken to places more than 600 kilometers away from their homes. Mindszenty urges rapid intervention on behalf of these Hungarians. He sent a similar telegram to the Vatican requesting that the Holy See intervene with the Czechoslovak Government. . . .

The Čas report then turned to the protest note sent by Hungarian Foreign Minister Gyöngyösi to the representatives of the Great Powers in Budapest:

> [The note] describes the situation of the Hungarians in Czechoslovakia, and points out those international guarantees which might serve to solve the problem of the Hungarian minority. The Hungarian

Government requests the friendly help of the Allied Great Powers in resolving the continually deteriorating Czechoslovak-Hungarian relations, caused by the problen of Hungarians deprived of all rights. According to the note the Hungarian Government is convinced that as long as the Hungarian question is not solved by bilateral negotiations, there can be no improvement in the situation of the Hungarians of Czechoslovakia; establishment of diplomatic relations among the nations of Central Europe remains likewise an impossibility. Finally the Hungarian Government requests the Great Powers to assert the decisions of the Paris [peace] conference in the matter of the Hungarians of Czechoslovakia.

While reporting at great length the Hungarian complaints, the Slovak press was also anxious to repeat some Hungarian leftist opinions and some more recent foreign views which found no fault in the Czechoslovak treatment of the Hungarian minority. The February 9 issue of *Práca* wrote: "Even the representatives of the Hungarian people, for instance Kisházy and Horváth, who in December visited the Hungarian workers [deported to Bohemia] , could see it for themselves that the Hungarians are provided with everything the same way the Czech or Slovak workers are . . . . In January, it was an Englishman from London, Johnson, who visited the Hungarian workers. He spoke to them, and delcared afterward that his general impressions were very favorable."[24]

On February 10, 1947, the Treaty of Paris between Czechoslovakia and Hungary was signed in Paris. On the same day, the Slovak National Council and the Board of Representatives in Bratislava issued a communiqué expression hope that the population exchange between the two countries will soon start so that "100,000 Slovaks could return home" from Hungary. It also made reference to the fate of the Hungarians of Slovakia: "By authority of the peace treaty, and for the sake of building a lasting peace, we wish that the question of the remaining Hungarians living intermingled with Slovak elements in the southeastern borderlands of our country should be solved once and for all."[25]

In the meantime, deportations of the Hungarians from the Slovak southeastern borderlands continued to the Czech northwestern borderlands, despite renewed unusual cold waves all over Europe. Also further legislative measures against the national minorities kept coming from Prague. On

February 14, 1947, the National Assembly approved a law regarding the confiscation of property. The Slovak press thought the law was long overdue. Commented *Práca* the next day: "The law has great significance regarding Slovakia as well, because it makes it possible to solve the economic issue of the Hungarian minority in South Slovakia where there continues to be many stores, industries, or estates in operation which should have been in the hands of Slovak settlers a long time ago."[26]

The press war, too, continued full force between Hungary and Czechoslovakia. On February 13, *Čas* reported that "Czechoslovakia rejects and denies the Hungarian falsehoods. Our correspondent in Budapest informs us that General Dastich, the Czechoslovak liaison at the Allied Control Commission in Budapest, handed two notes of protest in the name of the Czechoslovak Government to the Hungarian Foreign Ministry. The first note rejects the attempts of the Hungarian Minister of Foreign Affairs to interfere in the internal affairs of Czechoslovakia in connection with the execution of Presidential decree 88/1945 regarding universal labor service obligations. The second note points out the systematic disregard on the part of Hungary of the population exchange agreement concluded between Czechoslovakia and Hungary . . . . "

However, Hungary did not stay idle either. On the occasion of signing the Treaty of Peace with Czechoslovakia, Hungary handed a note to the president of the peace conference in Paris. The note expressed the Hungarian nation's dissatisfaction with the unjust peace. The Czechoslovak press duly noticed that the Hungarian protest is expressing dissatisfaction in particular with the situation of the Hungarians in Czechoslovakia. *Čas* reported on February 13, 1947:

> The [Hungarian] protest declares that the exclusion of legal guarantees [for the protection of minorities] from the peace treaty allowed for the cruel persecution of the Hungarians in Czechoslovakia. The Czechoslovak Government outlawed the Hungarian minority, and has displaced tens of thousands of Hungarians under the cover of universal labor service, carrying away the population in the dead of winter under the most inhumane conditions. All this contradicts the spirit of the United Nations. The Hungarian Government requests that the peace conference intervene to ensure the rights of the Hungarian minority. Hungarian Foreign Minister Gyöngyösi made similar statements in the course of his conversations with the editor of the Swiss *Neue Zürcher Zeitung.*[27]

The Czechoslovak Foreign Minister Jan Masaryk, too, made a statement in Paris on the occasion of signing the peace treaty. He expressed his hopes that the question of the dispersion of the Hungarian minority in Czechoslovakia could be solved by direct negotiations between Hungary and Czechoslovakia. He added:

> When I return to Prague I hope I will have the opportunity to examine the situation, and to arrive at a sensible agreement. I don't know how we are dealing with the Hungarian population. It is possible that errors have been committed. If indeed this was the case, I will be the first one to recognize and attempt to rectify it.

Masaryk's statement was a step in the right direction inasmuch that, implicitly, it admitted the possibility of a critical re-evaluation of the policy of dispersal introduced against the Hungarian minority. However, he also questioned the Hungarian contention that the Hungarians had been dealt with roughly in Czechoslovakia. He declared: "We are a small, peace-loving nation, and the whole world knows us for our humanistic policies. The attempt to make us appear as slaveholders is unreasonable to say the least."[28]

To prove that there are influential people in the world who disagree with the Hungarian point of view, the same issue of *Čas,* covering the signing of the Treaty of Peace between Czechoslovakia and Hungary, published this report from London: "Labor MP John Haire handed an inquiry to the British Foreign Office asking whether the British Government knows about the deportations of Hungarians in Czechoslovakia. In reply Christopher Mayher, Secretary of the Foreign Office answered: 'The resettlement of Czechoslovak citizens within the borders of the State is not in contradiction with article 5 of the Peace Treaty concluded with Hungary'."[29]

Another Czechoslovak paper, however, felt disgruntled about a pro-Hungarian stand of American Slovaks in the matter of the deportations. *Práca* took issue with F. Hrobák's statement in the *New York Times:* "He takes the side of the Hungarians against us. He reproaches Czechoslovakia that they use allegedly barbarian methods to chase the Hungarians from places where they had been living for centuries . . . Andrej J. Valušek defended us vis-à-vis the insults of Hrobák."[30]

The deportation of Hungarians from Southern Slovakia came to a sudden end on February 25, 1947. The decisin to stop the deportations had come, most likely as a result of the unfavorable publicity in the West and under pressure of the Great Powers, the United States in particular. The deportations came to a halt at a time when the eastward moving action to disperse the Hungarian population had just reached Tornalja. Thus, the Hungarians in the eastern counties of Southern Slovakia from Rožňava (Rozsnyó) to Veľké Kapušany (Nagykapos) were spared the experience of being deported to Bohemia. On balance the deportations, not unlike the population exchange and re-Slovakization, did not achieve its goal. But the memory of the 99 days left an indelible mark on all Hungarians of Slovakia, including those who were not directly victims.

It was no secret that the deportations had a twofold objective. Its aim was to weaken the Hungarian ethnic element in Slovakia on the one hand, and to force the execution of the population exchange agreement with Hungary, on the other. In that sense, the action was successful on both counts.

Jozef Dickal, writing in *Nové Prúdy,* summed up the success of the action this way: "The Hungarian authorities had to be forced to put an end to their delaying tactics and to seriously begin the execution of the population exchange. This took place thanks to the resettlement of the Hungarians from South Slovakia into the Bohemian borderlands." The author was less satisfied with the work ethic of the Hungarian deportees: "How did the Hungarian workforce function in Bohemia? Not very well. Although the Hungarians were provided with everything in the Czech lands, and nobody expected unusual productivity on their part (women and children were not expected to work), still they shunned the assigned work and, whenever possible, filter back to their birthplace. In this they are often successful. However, the Hungarians who filter back do not return to their own homes, for these have in the meantime been assigned to Slovaks from abroad. Thus, they hide at their friends or relatives who have not yet been deported."[31]

The great élan with which the deportations were carried out came to a halt after 99 days, without further commentary. After the Communist seizure of power in February 1948, the victims were able to sue for the recovery of their confiscated properties. These suits continued for years. However, in most cases the dust of time covered the losses caused by confiscation. The conditions were never really ripe for compensation: "In South Slovakia, in the middle of 1949, there were more than 10,000 un-solved cases of confiscation affecting mostly small [landholding] peasants of Hungarian nationality."[32]

All in all, according to Czechoslovak sources, 44,129 Hungarians were transferred from the borderlands of South Slovakia and settled in the Czech lands. They left behind 4,000 buildings, 25,000 hectares of land numbering 11,764 plots.[33] By this count, the average individual plot of the deported Hungarians would have consisted of 2.12 hectares. But quite a few were much larger, those of the so-called kulaks. In any case, these figures show that most of the deported peasants were rather small Hun-garian landholders, attached to the land they worked on, since time im-memorial, with their own hands.

CHAPTER 7

1947: THE YEAR OF THE POPULATION EXCHANGE

The abrupt ending of deportations in February 1947, created a new situation of uncertainty in the postwar struggle for survival of the Hungarian minority in Czechoslovakia. However, no one doubted that the price for the unexpected reprieve would have to be paid somewhere else. Yet there was hope, too, as always, even in a hopeless situation.

Slovak nationalist hysteria had shown by 1947 signs of running out of steam. The impact of international moral censure of Slovak persecution of the Hungarians, too, had slowly been felt. Also the Yugoslav example of following a policy of reconciliation with the Hungarians could not have passed unnoticed. Hungarian rule over South Slovakia during the wartime years and the relatively tolerant Hungarian policy toward the Slovak national minority of that territory could not be compared to the military and political brutalities committed during the war in the Hungarian-occupied Voivodina province of Yugoslavia; yet, Tito's regime, after a brief reign of terror, followed no such policy of retribution as Czechoslovakia did against the Hungarian national minority. The Czechoslovak press responded to signs of rapprochement between Yugoslavia and Hungary with a mixture of embarrassment and irritation. For instance, *Obzory*, organ of the Czech People's Party wrote in January 1947:

> We criticized Yugoslavia because it did not coordinate its policies with ours vis-à-vis Hungary, although Hungary's aggressive tone against the democratic Czechoslovak Republic has not ceased to this day. We also pointed out that Hungarian-Yugoslav flirting has repercussions in the West, which is being exploited against us. In vain are we the nation of Masaryk, we are being denounced for dealing more brutally with the Hungarian minority than Tito's Yugoslavia, a country not exactly renowned for coddling its citizens . . . . The

173

Russian-language *Novaja Vengrija,* published in Budapest, carried a statement by [Hungarian] Foreign Minister János Gyöngyösi in connection with the Hungarian-Yugoslav agreement on population exchange and river traffic. . . . The framework of this accord makes provisions for a voluntary exchange of 40,000 people, under no pressure of force whatsoever. Maybe the Hungarians are hoping—not entirely without reason—that this measure adopted by Yugoslavia will become a model for other Slav states, such as Czechoslovakia.[1]

At the same time, the Czechoslovak press also voiced its disappointment over the failure to mobilize all the American Slovaks in support of the measures directed against the Hungarian minority. According to the Slovak paper, *Rol'nícka Nedel'a,* among the Slovaks in America "only the left supports the [anti-minority] Košice government program [of Czechoslovakia."[2]

In Czechoslovakia, too, the popular fever favoring deportations of national minorities was diminishing, if only because by the end of 1946 the deportation of the Germans had practically ended. Thus, in the wake of forcing the implementation of the principle of the homogeneous Slav "nation-state," new tasks of rebuilding confronted both the public and the leaders of the nation. First of all, there was the problem of settling the lands left vacant by deportations; to place, that is, under Slav control the former Sudeten German industry now struggling with a lack of manpower. Also, it became a necessity to make the public forget as soon as possible the aftermath of radical solutions by expulsion, which was not always pleasant to Czech observers. *Obzory* quoted a German broadcast from Berlin on the post-expulsion situation of the Sudeten Germans, sounding far from pleasant to Czech ears:

With the last two transports, which arrived in the Soviet zone of occupation on November 30, 1946, the resettlement of the Germans from Czechoslovakia is completed. Of the 2,900,000 Germans one million arrived in the Soviet zone . . . . Along with the forcibly resettled came 45,000 German anti-Fascists, who although they received authorization to remain in Czechoslovakia, prefered to leave bringing their belongings along. These resettlers will become the initiators and founders of new branches of industry; moreover, they will solidify the anti-Fascist character of the society, both in industry and administration.[3]

In the wake of efforts to liquidate the Hungarian minority, the Hungarians seemed not quite out of place in Czechoslovakia. Yet no one was willing to take the responsibility for drawing sensible conclusions from the absurdity of the situation. Neither individuals nor organizations had the courage to propose new solutions. Only privately could one hear ironic remarks regarding the handling of the Hungarian issue resulting in a dead end.

There were some who still insisted that efforts at a total expulsion of the Hungarians should be continued. The Government, however, opted for going ahead with the execution of limited expulsions as provided by the population exchange agreement and the peace treaty. Almost simultaneously with the ending of deportations, the press began a propaganda campaign in favor of carrying out without delay the population exchanges between Hungarian and Czechoslovakia. And the tone of this propaganda was as hostile as ever against Hungary and the Hungarians. Setting the ultra-chauvinist tone of the campaign, *Práca,* the Slovak daily of the trade unions, wrote in late February 1947: "In Paris they signed the peace treaty with Hungary, but this treaty does not at all compel Hungary to carry out the population exchange agreement. . . . Is it possible that even after signing the peace treaty with Hungary, hundreds of our compatriots [in Hungary] should die of hunger, because of the cold winter, or from the bullets of Hungarian gendarmes, only because they applied for transfer [to Slovakia] ?"[4]

Thus the press tried to sustain the anti-Hungarian nationalist mood by stories about the death of hundreds of Slovaks in Hungary and about volleys fired at the Slovaks by Hungarian gendarmes. At the same time, the Slovak press expected the Hungarian peasants of Slovakia to cultivate their lands conscientiously, to produce even uder the most hopeless conditions. In the third year of total lawlessness, the agriculture of the Hungarian-populated regions had become completely paralyzed. In the spring of 1947, the former rich wheatfields of Southern Slovakia presented the sorry spectacle of fields laying fallow. The Bratislava *Pravda* discussed the bankrupt state of agriculture in the Hungarian regions of Slovakia:

Last week, members of the Slovak National Council visited the counties of Szepsi and Királyhelmec. . . . The farmers of Hungarian nationality, as could be readily ascertained, had made no preparations for sowing. They use no fertilizer, the wheat has been ground and eaten long ago, there is nothing left to sow in the spring. The catastrophic lack of seed is accompanied by new difficulties. . . the estates confiscated from the Hungarians have not yet been distributed. . . the Hungarian farmers of South Slovakia do not care to cultivate the productive lands, hence the proposal of the Minister of Agriculture is perfectly justified, that the owners of the non-productive lands be severely punished.[5]

The Hungarian Government was eager to ease the plight of the Hungarian minority in Czechoslovakia. Uppermost in the mind of Hungarian Foreign Minister Gyöngyösi was the fate of the Hungarians deported to the Czech lands. He arrived in Prague in mid-March 1947, to discuss the matter with Czechoslovak State Secretary Clementis. According to information leaked out to the press, the meeting led nowhere. Gyöngyösi proposed that the Hungarians mobilized for labor service be allowed to return home. The Czechoslovaks termed this "interference in domestic affairs," and negotiations with the Hungarians were broken off.[6]

Later in March, a 30-member Hungarian government delegation, headed by Special Envoy and Minister Plenipotentiary Pál Sebestyén, arrived in Bratislava in an attempt to find a way out of a deadlocked situation. It was announced that Foreign Minister Gyöngyösi would arrive later. The negotiations with the Czechoslovak Government delegation headed by State Secretary Clementis, began on March 24 in nearby Pudmerice, in the castle of the Slovak Writers' Association.[7] The results of the conference came to be known as the Bratislava Agreement.

The Hungarian delegation found itself in a difficult position with its hands tied by agreements for the exchange of populations, while threatened by the possibility of resumed deportations. Surrender was the only choice it had to end the deadlock. No official communiqué was issued on the Bratislava Agreement. The events that followed indicated however that the Hungarians consented to begin the population exchange as soon as possible, regardless of the predicament of other Hungarians, in particular of the deportees, or of certain moot issues, such as the matter of masses of Hungarians indiscriminately pronounced "war criminals" by the Slovak Peoples' Courts.

At the Pudmerice meeting, the Czechoslovak delegation was unwilling to discuss as a matter of principle the fate of those Hungarians who were not included in the population exchange agreement. In particular, they consistently characterized the Hungarian appraisal of the deportations as "interference in internal affairs." The press eagerly supported this point of view. According to *Práca:* "The Hungarians again include proposals whereby they interfere in our internal affairs, although they know full well in Budapest that we cannot discuss the mobilization of Slovakia's Hungarian population for labor service." The paper also underlined Czechoslovakia's right to became a "nation-state," stressing that "there will be no minorities among us and we will sign no accord for their defense."[8]

The execution of population exchange between Czechoslovakia and Hungary began shortly after the Bratislava Agreement in late March. But the atmosphere between the two nations remaied as hostile as ever. It is worth quoting to this effect a speech Andrej Žiak, a Slovak deputy, delivered around this time in the National Assembly:

> The pure Slav character of our Republic is at least as important to the Slovaks as it is to the Czechs. Total Slav character, however, can only be achieved with the total expulsion of the Hungarians from Slovakia, just as we had done it with the Germans. The question arises [in this matter] whether our foreign policy had not failed to take the necessary steps even before the termination of the war. Whether everything had been done on the part of our government to encourage the Great Powers to solve the Hungarian problem at the Potsdam conference. . . . Our government is willing to observe all agreements in the spirit of justice and honor. However, due to their character and to the morality of their diplomacy, the Hungarians are incapable of keeping their word, they have no honor. Thus, due to the despicable character of our negotiating partners, our brothers in Hungary are perishing and dying. . . . The real face of the false Hungarian has revealed itself. Taking advantage of the international political conjunture, the Hungarians have deliberately obstructed the execution of the agreement. . . . Our blood curdles in our veins, we clench our fists, when we think of it, that for a year now the democratic Czechoslovak Republic has been held in

check by a country which had been defeated unconditionally as a
German satellite, a country which is the prototype of feudalism,
gentryism and political baseness.[9]

The backing down of the Hungarian Government at the Pudmerice meeting signalled the end of the Hungarian policy of procrastination. The Hungarian surrender became common knowledge by the beginning of April.
It also became obvious from a complete reorganization of the Hungarian
Resettlement Committee in Budapest. The Slovak press, hailed the turn of
events with satisfaction: "The end of the career of Mr. Jócsik" [Lajos
Jócsik, Hungarian State Secretary in charge of resettlement], thus did the
headline of the Bratislava *Čas* inform the public of the expected new
course. "He [Jócsik] wanted to prevent the success of the Hungarian-
Czechoslovak negotiations. . . . According to *Kossuth Népe* the cause of
his resignation was that his office was impotent from the start and was
unable to fulfill the basic requirements for the resettlement of Hungarians
from Slovakia."

Čas went on denouncing Mr. Jócsik, (incidentally, a well-known Hungarian progressive intellectual in interwar Czechoslovakia): "The agency of
Jócsik carried out its public activities with official support from the highest circles of government since July of last year. This was the agency which
rejected the applications of Slovaks asking for resettlement from Hungary.
The Czechoslovak Government protested several times against the practices of this agency but without any results. The employees of Jócsik continued to persecute our brothers; moreover, they became even more aggressive. It was clear that the Hungarians do not want to carry out the
population exchange agreeement, but use all sorts of excuses for making
it imperative."[10]

A final agreement on the execution of the population exchange—according to a *Čas* report dated May 29, 1947—was completed and signed
by Clementis and Gyöngyösi at the end of May at Trenčianská Teplice.
Although the Trenčianská Teplice document was merely a technical
matter, the *Čas* report tried to arouse sanguine expectations as if the
question of expelling a further 200,000 Hungarians—a claim Czechoslovakia was pressing unsuccessfully at the Paris peace conference—had also
been resolved. Said the *Čas* report: "They also agreed to continue negotiations on the matter of a further 200,000 Hungarians, following ratification

of the peace treaty by the national assemblies of both countries." The Slovak paper concealed the fact that the peace treaty relegated the Czechoslovak claim to bilaterial negotiations without any obligation on Hungary's part to endorese the plan of expelling an additional 200,000 Hungarians from Czechoslovakia.

The Czechoslovak press, however, was right when hinting at a change in the Hungarian policy toward the Hungarian minorities. *Československý Východ* was right in saying: "Foreign Minister Gyöngyösi had to change his course. Otherwise the Czechoslovak-Hungarian negotiations. . .would have remained impossible. Even so the negotiations proceeded haltingly, and there was a danger that they might collapse again. Still, it was possible to clear the most serious obstacles. The activities of the [Hungarian] Social Democrats [on the verge of being absorbed into the Communist Party] contributed most to this success. . . "[11]

Ever since the end of World War II, Hungary's concern for the Hungarian minorities in the neighboring states has been branded as "irredentism," a term which the Danubian victors over defeated Hungary turned into a synonym of "Fascism." This new concept was fully accepted by the postwar Hungarian Communist regime following the collapse of the Coalition Government in the spring of 1947. It became a guiding principle in dealing with Hungarian minorities, and it remains basically valid to this day. Essentially it is a surrender to the nationalism of the neighboring states by supporting, through passive cooperation, the forcible assimilation of the Hungarian minorities, presently amounting to over one-fourth of the entire Hungarian nation.

In the context of Hungarian-Slovak relations, "irredentism" has been a constant charge of the Czechoslovak press against János Gyöngyösi, Foreign Minister of the Hungarian Coalition Government. He was specifically charged with "a renewal of Hungarian irredentism" during the last stages of Hungarian-Slovak negotiations on population exchange in the spring of 1947. The target of Slovak press attack was Gyöngyösi's statement to Swiss journalists in which he said:

The circumstance that the peace treaty contains no measures for the protection of the rights of the Hungarian population in Czechoslovakia or in Rumania is most painful for Hungary. Since more than one-fourth of the Hungarian nation lives in the neighboring states, it is the obligation of the government to ensure basic human rights and true civil equality for these minorities. It should be in the best interest of the neighboring states to arrive at the true cooperaion which the Hungarian government is striving for . . . . The fact that the peace treaty make it possible for Hungary to join the United Nations is an encouraging sign. We must hope that this circumstance will eventually lead to a mitigation of the provisions of the peace treaty.

In Slovak eyes, even this conciliatory statement by the Hungarian Foreign Minister, emphasizing merely human rights of the Hungarian minorities, and not Hungary's territorial claims, served as a proof of sinful "endeavors of irredentism."[12]

The actual resettlement of the Hungarians from Czechoslovakia to Hungary, according to the March Bratislava Agreement, began in early April 1947. The Slovak press sounded triumphant:

The preparations for the expulsion of the Hungarians began on April 8, 1947. 45 Hungarian families had been selected for resettlement from Nagymácséd, and 7 from Nagyfödémes in the county of Galánta; and a further 12 families from Tergenye in the county of Léva. On Friday, in the evening of the 11th, the first transport was ready to leave. Two trains were available; the first one numbered 7236, left on April 12 in the wee hours of the morning. Everyone was relieved: Finally!"[13]

Thus began the expulsion legally, on the basis of an agreement between the countries. By June 11, 177 Hungarians were forcibly resettled from their thousand-year old homes.[14] The Slovak press, however, was not satisfied with the speed and scope of expulsions. *Národná Obroda* urged mass expulsions with confiscations of all "war criminals," who "participated in the expulsion of several thousand Slovaks from Southern Slovakia [after the Vienna Award of 1938 which transferred that territory to Hungary] into truncated Slovakia."[15] As I noted earlier, the number of Slovaks expelled under the Horthy regime from the territories awarded to Hungary in 1938 did not exceed 5,000. On the other hand, the number of minority

Hungarians indiscriminately pronounced "war criminals" by the Slovak People's courts fluctuated around 100,000.

Paradixocally, the mass migrations forcibly imposed by victorious Czechoslovakia both on Hungarians (expelled from Slovakia to Hungary) and Slovaks (resettled from Hungary to Slovakia) has met with less than universal satisfaction among the Czechoslovaks. Thus, the Slovak press took notice of a "whispering campaign" which denounced the Slovaks resettled from Hungary to Slovakia as being "basically also Hungarians or adventurers."[16]

Before long, more and more reports reflecting disillusionment with the population exchange appeared in the Czechoslovak press. *Čas* censured "the greediness of certain resettled Slovaks who, while they arrived almost completely penniless, came up right away with impossible demands."[17] *Náš Národ* published an even more sweeping criticism:

> The further the resettlement action proceeds, the more the initial impetus loses its strength. Many of the settlers are dissatisfied and overly demanding, although their demands are unjustified. . . . It is inadmissible that a year after a person has applied for Slovak nationality he still continues to speak Hungarian and shows no inclination to learn the Slovak language. It is amazing that not only as far as language is concerned, but as regards their feelings as well, the settlers continue to live under the spell of Budapest. They are Slovaks on paper only. Such persons do not fulfill our expectations, and will not consolidate the southern areas, but will remain harmful or destructive elements. . . .[18]

The mixed Slovak reactions to the population exchange were noted in the Czech press as well:

> A source of pain for present-day Slovakia is the so-called returnees from Hungary . . . . Unfortunately, about most of them, it cannot be said that they are Slovaks. The Slovaks themselves are not pleased with them, either from an ethnic or from a moral point of view. These are people mostly without Slovak national consciousness, often they do not even know the [Slovak] language. For instance, the miners who came to Handlová from Hungary demanded Hungarain schools for their children. . . .[19]

The critical tone of the press was exaggerated. It was wrong to assume that the majority of the resettlers were Hungarians, or persons of dubious morality. Mostly the intellectual resettlers lacked command of the Slovak language, and had something to hide as far as their political background was concerned. On the other hand, from the Slovak point of view, the exchange action did achieve some of its nationalistic ends. It helped to convert quite a few formerly completely Hungarian villages into ethnically mixed communities in Southern Slovakia. Of course, the recently resettled Slovaks were unable to assimilate old Hungarian village communities. As a rule, most villages transformed by the population exchange did not alter their ethnic composition in the expected way, not even in the next thirty years. In a few cases, in fact, the changes were in favor of the Hungarians, the Slovak setters having been assimilated by the Hungarian majority.

It is worth quoting the following from a detailed Slovak report on the transferred Slovaks in their new environment:

> At the beginning of December, I visited resettled Slovaks in Deáki and Pered, in the county of Vágsellye . . . . Deáki received 700 re-settlers and Pered the same . . . . If only the villages had a more Slovak character. I heard a father, to quote his son: father, when are we moving under the Tatra mountains to our Slovak villages? All that we hear is Hungarian. The street is full of it. At the same time, the settlers also wished to emphasize that they are willing to bear patiently the initial difficulties. They are unhappy only about having to speak Hungarian even at home, because often their stubborn Hungarian fellow citizens speak to them in Hungarian in a downright provocative tone . . . . Some of the villagers even said that they do not feel personally quite safe.[20]

The fact of the matter is that the forcible transfers brought about a series of crises in the villages, and later errors aggravated the situation. No wonder that mutual prejudice is still the living legacy of 1947, the year of the population exchange—and more.

The year 1947 witnessed not only the realization of the population exchange, but also brought to fruition the so-called re-Slovakization action.

Since early spring 1947, the press had been urging prompt processing of re-Slovakization requests. The administration, however, proceeded haltingly. Applicants were kept in suspense and the chaos grew as time passed.

A memorandum prepared by the local branch of the Matica Slovenská and of the Slovenská Liga, the two institutions in charge of the re-Slovakization campaign, complained in May 1947: "Liberated Southern Slovakia is full of Hungarianized Slovaks, and of Slovaks whose national consciousness has not yet been aroused. Their fate cannot be indifferent to us. . . ." The memorandum also complained of the harmful economic consequences of re-Slovakization in some communities: "Economic life has reached the stage of bankruptcy. The damages reported informally are enormous. . . and the moral consequences are even more serious. The re-Slovakized person is ridiculed, threatened, treated as a traitor. He does not wish to frequent Hungarians, and does not dare to come among us [Slovaks] . . . we have forced uncertainty upon him and feelings of a lower order, we have jeopardized his rights to his property."[21]

Re-Slovakization of Hungarians, unexpectedly, also aggravated Czech-Slovak relations. And there the impact of re-Slovakization had been most immediately felt, in cities like Baňská Bystrica, Gelnica, Poprad, Prešov, Spišská Nová Ves, Žilina. In solidly or significantly Hungarian populated areas, however, the re-Slovakization campaign had met with more problems than its promoters had been able to solve. And, despite the re-Slovakization the Hungarian character of the cities did not change perceptibly, not to speak of the countryside. From Levice (Léva) in the West to Košice (Kassa) in the East, the sound of Hungarian along the ethnic borderline kept irritating the Slovak chauvinistic sensitivity.

Slovakization of Hungarians, which mean to serve the government program of turning Czechoslovakia into a pure Slav state, paradixocally, aggravated the not overly fraternal relations between Czechs and Slovaks. In some places, re-Slovakization committees had been impotent, the Slovaks complained, because Czechs were chosen to preside over them. And Czechs, supposedly, had not been sufficiently prejudiced against the Hungarian population, nor could they have been sufficiently familiar with the confused ethnic situation in Slovakia. The Slovak paper *Čas* was urging the transfer of the re-Slovakization administration entirely under the jurisdiction of the Slovak National Council in Bratislava.[22] *Práca* objected to the appointment of a Czech as chairman of the re-Slovakization committee.[23] *Nové Prúdy* expressed scepticism in the entire business of re-Slovakization. The papers said: "Re-Slovakization is a matter of re-education, and re-education cannot take place overnight, not even in a month, it cannot be carried out by means of decisions and ordinances."[24]

The main difficulty with re-Slovakization was that the "re-Slovakized" Hungarians did not take the forcible change of nationality seriously. The senselessness of the action had become an open secret. There was no way of forcing hundreds of thousands of "re-Slovakized" Hungarians to forget their language and culture overnight. A Slovak writer had good reason to dispair over the situation in the "re-Slovakized" Hungarian town of Érsekújvár (Nové Zámky): "80% of the Hungarian population of Nové Zámky re-Slovakized . . . . On the other hand, the fact remains that one can barely hear Slovak spoken in Nové Zámky. You will never find these 80% Slovaks. Only a few government employees speak Slovak here and there. What happened to the re-Slovakized persons?"[25]

The once fanatic confidence of the Slovaks in "re-Slovakization" of the Hungarians had been broken. The passive resistance of the Hungarians had solidified. Economic circumstances too, had been working against the success of Slovakization, whether by means of re-Slovakization or resettlement. Many a Slovak settler, seeing that his survival was in jeopardy in a Hungarian environment, was to consider leaving, although *Čas* warned: "This would be a great mistake and has to be prevented!"[26]

In 1947, despite failures of the Slovakization efforts, the people of the disintegrating society of the Hungarian minority were searching in vain for encouraging signs which might end their plight.

The countries of Eastern Europe had already been shaped into a solid Soviet bloc. In world perspective, the growing tensions of the cold war were determining the relative positions of both large and small nations. In Slovakia, however, it was as if time had come to a standstill. Officially, an anachronistic parochial nationalism of the Slovaks ruled seemingly insuperable. The Slovak nationalists in power obstinately refused to take cognizance of the existence of the Hungarians which prevented them from turning the country into a purely Slovak nation-state. All Hungarian initiatives at reconciliation have met with brusque official Slovak refusal. Any suggestion that citizenship rights to the Hungarian minority should be restored was treated as being tantamount to treason against the Czechoslovak Republic. Neither the obvious fiasco of re-Slovakization, nor the partial success of the population exchange could bring the rulers of the country to their senses. Not to speak of the dismal consequences of the deportation of Hungarians to the Czech lands, creating conditions of serf-dom reminiscent of a wretched past when peasants could not own land but were tied to it like cattle and forced to cultivate it for the benefit of feudal lords.

In the heat of the Slovakization campaign, even the position of the Hungarians with a revolutionary record became critical. The concept of a "reliable Hungarian" vanished in Czechoslovakia. A person of Hungarian nationality could not be granted citizenship or enjoy any political right of any kind even if he had fought with arms against Fascism during the war. The official nationalist temper of the country was such that it ex-pected every anti-Fascist to "re-Slovakize" without exception. Thus there remained but two alternatives: To give up one's nationality, or to leave voluntarily for Hungary. Those who did not re-Slovakize and stayed (like the well-known Hungarian anti-Fascist writer, Zoltán Fábry) automati-cally ostracized themselves, they became undesirable aliens, even if they had been granted exemption from the Presidential decrees in 1945, issued against the minorities. The Slovak National Council in Bratislava kept warning the population that every applicant for citizenship had to be accompanied by a "certificate of nationality," to make sure that no per-son of German or Hungarian nationality would receive civil rights.[27]

No wonder, the Slovak nationalist leadership had been watching ner-vously, and with anger, the "Slav brother" Yugoslavia where, after initial barbaric reprisals, the integration of the Hungarian minority into a federal state had begun already in 1946. When in the fall of 1947, following the Communist take-over in Hungary, the first postwar visit to Belgrade of the Hungarian Prime Minister Dinnyés was to take place, the Slovak press noted bitterly: "The Slav brothers in Yugoslavia are negotiating with the Hungarians, with that Hungary which has caused us so much trouble in settling the nationalities issue in Slovakia. The Yugoslavs probably con-sider the Hungarian Communists as honorary Slavs, just like the Nazis had made an exception of them a few years ago by regarding them as honor-ary Aryans [a favorite Czechoslovak slight, referring to the Hungarians' non-Aryan Asiatic origins]."[28]

An earlier visit that year (in 1947) to Prague of the Hungarian Com-munist Mátyás Rákosi, by then the real power behind the Budapest regime, had left no friendly memories behind either. Rákosi, namely, insisted on the restoration of the rights of the Hungarian minority, which elicited irritated comments in the Czechoslovak press:

> In one respect Hungary today is identical with the former regime, its views regarding the minorities have not changed. Although Czechoslovakia is a nation-state of the Czechs and the Slovaks, the Hungarian Communist government today continues to advocate the views of Gyöngyösi [Foreign Minister of the Coalition Government], namely that the Hungarians of Czechoslovakia have to be granted minority rights. This will be the hardest nut to crack in the Czechoslovak-Hungarian negotiations . . . . [29]

Following the Communist take-over in Hungary, the Hungarian Social Democratic press anticipated improvement in the situation of the Hungarian minority in Czechoslovakia. One such report was promptly denied as unfounded in Prague: "Some of our press organs spread the news [based on reports of the Budapest *Népszava*] to the effect that Hungarian schools will reopen in Czechoslovakia on September 1, 1947. . . . Hungarian schools were not discussed either in the Cabinet, or in the National Assembly, and their reinstallation was never even considered. On the contrary, our entire policy is aimed at bringing about by mutual agreement a total population exchange [between Czechoslovakia and Hungary] . . . . Representatives of the Czechoslovak and Hungarian Social Democratic parties have discussed in that sense this issue recently."[30]

It was not exactly "in that sense" (namely, "total" exchange) that the Hungarian Socialists have been trying to influence Czechoslovak policy toward the Hungarian minority. Their efforts, however, were of no avail. The ruling Czechoslovak élite remained as hostile against the Hungarians toward the end of 1947 as it had always been since the end of the war.

For the Hungarian school-age children, the third "empty year" started on September 1, 1947. General illiteracy was spreading. Since the war, about 100,000 Hungarian school-age children could not attend school. In desperation, some Hungarian parents began to urge to founding of Slovak schools in Hungarian regions. As one anonymous letter written put it in the Bratislava *Čas:* "Let us have Slovak schools! Masses of children do not

not go to the school in Czallóköz [Žitny Ostrov once a purely Hungarian island of the Danube] . . . . children of ten and even older cannot write or read! Who will be responsible for these illiterates?"[31]

Some Slovak nationalists, on the other hand, were convinced that they were winning the battle against the Hungarians. In a lengthy demographic and historical essay, Juraj Palkovič came to the conclusion that only a fragment of the former Hungarian minority is left, and soon all Hungarians will be assimilated: "It is not possible to determine the present number of Hungarians in Czechoslovakia, but after the conclusion of re-Slovakization and the carrying out of the population exchange not many Hungarians will remain, barely a third of their numbers in 1930."[32] Palkovič discounted the Hungarians deported to Bohemia, considered the 300,000 re-Slovakized persons as Slovaks, and thus arrived at 200,000 Hungarians "remaining," who could be easily assimilated.

Palkovič's computer was tilling too soon the bell for the death of the Hungarian minority in Czechoslovakia. Even at the time Palkovič was predicting the liquidation of the Hungarians, other Slovak observers were less optimistic about the Slovakization of the Hungarian regions of Slovakia: "A large part of the population cannot speak proper Slovak. . . little has been done for this [Hungarian populated] area until the present. There are no Slovak books in the villages, and thus we have to appeal to the Delegate in Charge of Schools and bring his attention to the fact that in two years he has not taken any advantage of the opportunities for Slovakizing this area."[33]

In retrospect, the Slovakization effort under the postwar regime came to be regarded as harmful to Socialism by Communist commentators. It is worth quoting the remarks of a recent observer, Dr. F. Tomek:

> The fact that the question of the Hungarian workers remained unsolved also had its [harmful] consequences. According to the ground rules of the labor unions, they [Hungarians] could not become members, even though in certain places they constituted the majority of the workforce. The officers of the Slovak Labor Union Council attempted to solve the problem on January 22, 1947, by proposing the right of membership in labor unions in Slovakia for the actually employed German and Hungarian workers, since these workers were fully participating in the effort for the reconstruction

of the country, and most had not committed offenses against the Slovak and Czech nations. Unfortunately, the Central Council of the Labor Union adopted a negative stance, and weakened the struggle of the working class in Slovakia by 80,000 Hungarian workers.[34]

Even before the Communist take-over in Czechoslovakia, in February 1948, there were a few people who had the courage to criticize publicly the senseless and reactionary Slovak nationalist policy. The Minister of Interior in the Prague government characterized the representatives of the Slovak Democratic Party as "L'udák-Fascist elements."[35]

Toward the end of the postwar coalition regime, the Czech press occasionally struck a realistic tone in the matter of the nationalities problem. In August 1947, the Czech National Socialist *Dněšek* raised the question: what should be done with the remaining Germans? It approved of the mitigation of the discriminatory measures, and advocated civil rights for the remaining 150,000 Germans.[36] As for the Hungarians, the Czech Social Democratic *Cíl* encouraged a Czechoslovak-Hungarian rapprochement, and by the end of 1947 demanded economic cooperation between the two neighbors.[37]

In contrast, the Czech People's Party, representing the "democratic" opposition to the Communists, supported uncompromisingly the anti-Hungarian Slovak nationalist policy, as this excerpt from its weekly, *Obzory,* illustrates:

The principle of the expulsion of 200,000 Hungarians was not included in the peace treaty, thus we must deal with a strong Hungarian minority. Even if it is not dangerous now, it may become dangerous tomorrow. We have had sad experiences in the past and we cannot rely on the promises of the Hungarians that in the future they will respect the laws of the Republic. The Hungarian government already considers the demands of the Hungarian minority [for civil rights] as part of its own program. This attitude was confirmed by the summer visit of the leadership of the Hungarian Communist Party. . . .But let us await the facts. The Republic is a nation-state, we do not recognize national minorities. Should Yugoslavia guarantee rights to its minorities, it would do this because it

is not a nation-state. Our Parliament spoke to the Hungarians in un-
mistakable terms.[38]

The commentator in the *Obzory* was referring to the debate in the National Assembly on the ratification of the peace treaty with Hungary during which the Slovak representatives, both of the left and of the right,
Laco Novomeský and Fedor Hodža, resolutely professed their faith in the
homogeneous Slav nation-state.[39] Nor did the paper fail to reject the
eventual "new directions in the policy of the KSČ [Czechoslovak Communist Party] :

> The patriots of the KSČ are gradually burying the principle of the
> nation-state. . . . The first secretary of the Hungarian Communist
> Party [Mátyás Rákosi] declared at a rally that during his visit to
> Prague, where he arrived at the invitation of the KSČ, he discussed
> the minority rights rights of the Hungarians with postive results. . . .
> We must ask the gentlemen of the KSČ whether they have indeed
> dropped the principle of the nation-state. . . . The question is much
> too serious for the *Rudé Právo* [organ of the KSČ] to pass over it
> in silence.[40]

The Constitutional Assembly elected in 1946 was not able to draft a
new Czechoslovak constitution because of conflicting views among the
coalition parties. The Communist Prime Minister Klement Gottwald did
present a draft to the National Assembly as early as July 8, 1946, and the
draft definitely stated that the Czechoslovak Republic is the national
state of the Czechs and the Slovaks. Press comments emphasized this
point by adding: "The expulsion of the Germans and the Hungarians,
the Czechization and Slovakization of the border lands will be assured
by constitutional guarantees, so that in the future only the Czech and
Slovak nations may decide in matters of state or public life. The civil
rights of other Slav nations and the non-Slav Germans and Hungarians
will be respected."[41]
All through 1947, the Coalition Government of Czechoslovakia still
solidly and unanimously professed the fundamental principle of expulsion with regard to the Hungarian minority. The Communist Party, too,
as a member of the coalition, had not ceased to advocate that principle.

The Communists, in fact, explicitly denied in the spring of 1947 reports of a rapprochement between the Czechoslovak and the Hungarian parties, or any plans for changes in the new constitution.[42]

Yet a conflict between the Czech Communist and the Slovak nationalist points of view became increasingly noticeable by the summer of 1947 over the handling of the Hungarian question. In June, following the collapse of the Coalition Government of Ferenc Nagy in Hungary, the Czech Communist paper *Tvorba* pointed out that the road of Hungarian evolution is determined not by the press campaigns of the "reactionary" Hungarians, but by the "democratic" Hungarians.[43] *Tvorba* also looked forward with confidence toward the upcoming Hungarian elections: "They [the elections] will bring about a new situation in Hungary, and they will decide whether Hungary's road will lead to a people's democracy and socialism, or whether the power or reaction and bourgeois democracy will be revived."[44]

The Czech Communist leadership seemed to be well aware of the dead end the mishandling of the Hungarian issue in Slovakia had led to. The "leftward" turn of the political trend in Hungary, following the Communist takeover in June 1947, came to be regarded by the Czech Communists as a convenient opportunity for settling the Hungarian question in Czechoslovakia by different means. The Slovaks, however, whether of the right or of the left, resisted conciliatory moves. In three years since the end of the war, there was only one conciliatroy gesture of Slovak cultural policy toward the Hungarian minority: Communists in Hungarian-populated Komárom (Komárno), at the end of 1947, issued a Hungarian-language calendar. However, even that had been rapidly withdrawn from circulation by the Communists because of attacks by their bourgeois coalition partners. The Slovak National Council wanted to carry over intact the anti-Hungarian "liberation platform" of 1945 into 1948, without party distinctions, insisting on the principle of the pure Slav nation-state. This chauvinistic principle, depriving the Hungarians of all their civil rights, also demanded that no schools should be opened in Slovakia for the Hungarian national minority in 1948.

Thus, as the new year arrived, once again the Hungarian children entering school age, were condemned to illiteracy in "democratic" Czechoslovakia, for the third straight year, in the middle of Europe, at the dawn of the Atomic Age.

CHAPTER 8

THE PEOPLE'S COURTS IN ACTION

It is frightening but true that not even the horrors of the Second World War were able to teach mankind to protect itself against the recurrences of barbarism. The theory and practice of aggression survives. Conflicts between nations and races, more often than not, are still being resolved by ancient methods of violence. The Second World War did engender the desire to bring order into the chaos of international affairs. Agreements had been signed for the protection of human rights and for the punishment of war crimes. The charter of the Nuremberg military tribunal was drafted and certain countries adopted its principles of retribution into their legal codes. However, the meaning and objectives of this politically motivated justice in the aftermath of the war differed considerably from country to country.

In Czechoslovakia, the explicit task of the people's courts was to punish so-called war crimes. Roughly speaking, there were three types of war crimes, rather arbitrarily, recongized by Czechoslovak laws: acts motivated by Fascist ideology; disloyalty to the Czechoslovak state either before or during the war; collaboration with the enemy under occupation. The peculiarity of the Czechoslovak people's courts persecuting war criminals was that they meted out justice according to different judicial standards, and assessed the individual cases according to different ideology, depending on whether the accused was Czech, Slovak, German, or Hungarian. The German and Hungarian population was collectively deprived of civil rights already by the Presidential decrees of 1945, therefore it could not realistically be expected that they would receive fair trials. Yet the political corruption of the people's courts led to such distortions of justice, especially against the Hungarian minority of Slovakia that it surprised even those who expected the worst.

The people's courts in Slovakia did not conceal their bias. Their manifest purpose was to scare the Hungarian population and force it to flee the country. In other words, the people's courts in action, by different means, continued the government's expulsion policy. The scare tactics of the people's courts was directed in particular against the intelligentsia as a part of the liquidation strategy against the Hungarian minority. According to Slovak calculations, if the better educated Hungarians were forced to flee, the people left behind would find it hard to organize themselves as a distinct ethnic group. The people's courts were thus assigned an important role in the final solution of the Hungarian question in postwar "democratic" Czechoslovakia.

Stretching and exaggerating the concept of war crimes against the Hungarians to no end, it looked as if the Hungarian minority in Slovakia had been burdened with war crimes more heavily than any other people of Europe; as if this fragment of the Hungarian nation, half a million or so strong, had been one of the principle causes and culprits of the Second World War. Later generations of Hungarians and non-Hungarians, unfamiliar with the facts, might conclude from the records of the people's courts that the Hungarian minority of Slovakia had sunk already before the Second World War to such a low point of morality that, when Munich and war came, they were ready to commit the most abject crimes—in brief, that the Hungarians of Slovakia were a band of criminals. The supposedly scholarly monograph on the people's courts written by the Slovak historian Anton Rašla would only further confirm such an impression.[1]

Law 33/1945, establising and regulating the activities of the people's courts in Slovakia, was promulgated on May 15, 1945, shortly after the promulgation of the Košice government program in liberated Czechoslovakia. The two were linked by both letter and spirit. The Košice program has laid the foundation for the theory of the Hungarian minority's collective guilt against the Republic. The people's courts in action were to furnish the evidence for that theory. The law of retribution enabled the people's courts to deal more strictly with the Hungarians, since almost any organized Hungarian activity in Slovakia could be declared as "Fascist" and thus automatically serve as an evidence of any type of war crime, in particular in its vaguest form: collaboration with the enemy.

Charges of war crimes were meant to provide moral justification for the general policy aimed against the Hungarians: expulsion. When the

Potsdam conference failed to authorize Czechoslovakia to follow a policy of expulsion against the Hungarian minority, the greater became the effort of the people's courts to furnish moral justification for such a policy. The law made the work of the courts easy by putting the Hungarian State under the Horthy regime on an equal footing with the Hitlerite Third Reich. The overwhelming majority of Czechoslovakia's Hungarian minority lived during the war in Horthy Hungary; that fact alone could be easily manipulated to produce some sort of evidence of a war crime. Since one of the principal trademarks of the Slovak law, similar to the Nuremberg charter, was the principle of retroactivity, nothing was easier than to prove that a Hungarian living under the Horthy regime committed a war crime against Czechoslovakia.

A network of local people's courts began to operate shortly after Slovakia's liberation. Major war criminals were prosecuted by the county people's courts, and the top ones by the National Court in Bratislava. The greatest number of cases had been dealt with by 1946, although quite a few cases dragged on until the summer of 1947.

The first summary of the activities of the people's courts was published in March 1948 by the Slovak Secretary of Justice, Dr. Julius Viktory. According to this first account, only 19 percent of those condemned as war criminals were Slovaks.[2] However, according to Rašla's monograph, quoted above and published in 1969, the final percentage of Slovaks was 28.9 percent (2295 persons). The Hungarians took the lead with 59.74 percent (4812 persons); Germans and others made up the rest, 11.77 percent (950 persons).[3] In 1946, there were 2.7 million Slovaks, 600,000 Hungarians, and 158,000 Germans living in Slovakia. Taking the size of various nationalities, the statistical ratio is as follows: 0.085 percent of the Slovaks were sentenced for war crimes, as compared to 0.8 percent of the Hungarians and 0.5 percent of the Germans. In other words, the people's courts dealt ten times more severely with the Hungarians, but only about twice as severely with the Germans. It is worth noting that the Czechs were more severe against their own people than the Slovaks. The people's courts in the Czech lands found 0.16 percent of the Czechs guilty (13,284 persons),[4] which is twice as many as the corresponding number of Slovaks found guilty by the people's courts in Slovakia.

The severe punishment of Hungarians in Slovakia can also be measured by comparison with the war crime trials in Hungary. There only 0.17

percent of the population (17,699 persons) were sentenced[5] (about the same ratio as Czechs in the Czech lands). The Hungarian minority of Slovakia would thus appear to have been five times as "Fascist" as the Hungarians in Hungary proper. Also, the Hungarians of Slovakia fare far worse than the Sudeten Germans did in the Czech lands. The Czech people's courts sentenced only 0.4 percent (about 14,000 persons) of the Sudenten Germans, which in percentages is about half of the Hungarians condemned by the Slovaks.[6]

Thanks to the Slovak "anti-Fascist" zeal, the Hungarian minority of Czechoslovakia, with 0.8 percent, had set a European record in producing war criminals. Yet the Slovak press still kept urging stricter measures against the Hungarians and as late as 1968, the Slovak historian J. Purgat bemoans the fact that the activity of the people's courts against the Hungarians was not sufficiently effective: "Even though the data are not yet complete, nevertheless they indicate that the activities of the people's courts were inadequate, especially in the areas inhabited by the Hungarians."[7]

It is characteristic of postwar conditions in Slovakia that anti-Hungarian attitudes could be invoked as a mitigating circumstance by Slovak war criminals. Šaňo Mach, Tiso's Minister of Interior, in his war crime trial, defended his approval of the deportation of Jews by saying that he considered the Jews as "90 percent Hungarians," which was termed a "more profound" argument.[8] Šaňo Mach escaped the death sentence.

The Slovak Secretary of Justice, Dr. J. Viktory, squarely admitted the pro-Slovak bias of the people's courts: "I was not guided exclusively by the laws. . . . Had I been guided exclusively by the principles of the retribution decrees, we would have had to jail most [Slovak] civil or public servants for decades, and dismiss the rest without exception as collaborators, if only because they served the Fascist regime."[9]

The same spirit of leniency had been shown by the people's courts in action toward members of the National Assembly of Tiso's Slovakia. They were either exonerated or sentenced to but a few months in jail. However, the only openly anti-Fascist member of that Assembly, the Hungarian Deputy János Esterházy, head of the Hungarian Party, was condemned to death as a traitor. In fact, any member of the Hungarian Party could be charged with treason whereas Slovaks even with leading roles in the Hlinka

Party were left unmolested. The courts were given a free hand in deciding what was treason and what was not, which political act should be considered Fascist and which should not. The courts had the right to declare, without even having to supply evidence, that the accused Hungarian was "an enemy" of the Czech and Slovak nation. What deeds determined this qualifiction, never was spelled out with any precision. Ethnic discrimination could prevail unchallenged because of the vague language of the law.

Law 33/1945 on the people's courts in Slovakia defined treason as any act that "significantly promoted the military-political or economic interests of Nazi Germany or Horthy's Hungary." Tiso's Fascist Slovakia, a creation of Hitler, was not placed on equal footing with Nazi Germany. But in Southern Slovakia, those Hungarians who did not "resist" under the Horthy regime since they supported the "Hungarian occupation" by their daily work, could be tried as traitors. This double standard of the courts was supported by the theory of Czechoslovakia's "legal continuity" during the war.[10] In line with this theory, the entire Hungarian population of Southern Slovakia could be charged indiscriminately with treason.

Another Slovak legal definition of war criminals was of no help either to protect the Hungarians against arbitrary persecutions. It spoke of those "who had aided the Fascist occupation force and the traitors at home in any form whatsoever." Since "Fascist occupation" meant Hungarian administration in the territories returned to Hungary in 1938, any Hungarian who had anything to do with that administration could be found guilty. By the same token, any Slovak could have been found guilty of aiding the "traitors at home"—namely the Tiso administration of independent Slovakia. However, the people's courts served as much as a shield for the Slovaks as they were used as a weapon against the Hungarians.

Finally, the law defined treason as activities directed against the Czechoslovak Republic from May 21, 1938 (date of partial mobilization following Hitler's annexation of Austria) to October 28, 1945 (liberated Czechoslovakia's first national holiday commemorating the founding of the Republic in 1918). The starting date of this period in particular could have been applicable to Slovak prewar activities in destroying Czechoslovakia with Hitler's assistance. Yet the people's courts, not unlike Czechoslovak historians, have always adhered to the theory that the principal cause of Czechoslovakia's disintegration had been the collaboration between the Sudeten Germans and the Hungarian minority.

Historical evidences brought to light by the Slovaks themselves during the trials of the Slovak war criminals contradict the deliberate falsifications, yet the views of the falsifiers are left unchallenged.

Concerning the controversial question of whose collaboration with whom had been the principal cause of Czechoslovakia's downfall in 1938, it may be worth quoting the following passage from the prosecution's charges at the Tiso trial in 1947:

> The leaders of Hlinka's Slovak People's Party openly stated that they did not consider autonomy as an end goal; for some time, Dr. Tiso has stressed that the People's Party was aiming at full sovereignty of the [Slovak] nation . . . . Thus the German plan relied on Hlinka's Slovak People's Party and its autonomist program, especially on the separatist and radical wing of this Party. Czechoslovakia could have resisted a German attack, it had an excellent army, which was demonstrated by the mobilization of May 1938, when the Germans did not dare to launch an attack against the country . . . . The cause of the destruction of Czechoslovakia was not its inability to defend itself, but the disintegration within brought about by Hlinka's Slovak People's Party and his collaboration with the Germans.[11]

On the other hand, the defense at the Tiso trial cited the theory—also evoked by the Czechoslovak delegation at the peace conference—according to which the disintegration of the Republic was caused by the collaboration of the Sudeten Germans and the Hungarian minority. Significantly, the jury at the Tiso trial rejected this point of view. Tiso was found guilty, sentenced to death, and executed.

The Tiso trial had also touched on the expulsion of the Czechs from Slovakia under the Tiso regime—a most sensitive issue since it contradicts the claim of Czech-Slovak national unity as well as the wartime theory of Czechoslovakia's legal continuity. The court, showing great resourcefulness in protecting Czechoslovak interests, blamed the expulsion of Czechs personally on Dr. Ferdinand Ďurčanský, Minister of Foreign Affairs in Tiso's Slovakia.[12] What a fine example of double standards! The expulsion of five thousand Slovaks from Southern Slovakia under the Horthy regime served to support the charges of Hungarian collective guilt, but the expulsion of twenty times more Czechs from Slovakia under the Tiso regime was blamed on one single person.

The Tiso trial also brought to light some interesting evidences touching on the Vienna Award which returned Southern Slovakia to Hungary on the basis of the controversial ethnic principle. It was revealed that at a Cabinet meeting on October 25, 1938, the Prague Government at Tiso's advice, accepted the Hungarian territorial claims against Czechoslovakia "to the same extent as later determined by the adjudication of Germany and Italy." [13] This evidence certainly puts the so-called "Vienna boundary" into somewhat different light than the views denouncing it as an utterly unjust "Fascist" violation of democratic Czechoslovakia's territorial integrity.

In the same context, the minutes of the Prague Cabinet meeting of November 4, 1938, also deserve attention: "Minister of Foreign Affairs Chvalkovský expressed his appreciation for the attitude of the Slovak Government's ministers [present] at Vienna [during the German-Italian arbitration proceedings on Slovakia's frontiers]. By accepting the Polish demands, they cleared the way for an agreement with Poland without resorting to [German-Italian] adjudication." The Same minutes point out that Užhorod became part of Hungary because the Jews of that area sided with the Hungarians. [14]

The people's courts in Slovakia were unfair to the Hungarians and lenient to the Slovaks. Their unfairness to the Hungarians did not bother the Slovak sense of justice but the leniency to the Slovaks occasionally did. Thus M. Ferjenčik, head of the Department in charge of Internal Affairs in Slovakia, honestly admitted:

> The people's courts which should have been a significant factor in the purification process, did not live up to expectations, and did not fulfill their tasks; all this was the logical outcome of our overpoliticized internal conditions. . . . In general it can be said that the justice provided by the people's courts was very complex and difficult to understand. If we add the reciprocal concessions made by the [political] parties—the deals, that is, which overlooked certain things on one side in return for similar favors from the other side— it will become pretty clear how this purification process actually

worked and how it might have worked for the benefit of our State
and our public life.[15]

The leniency of the Slovak people's courts toward the Slovaks was noticed and disapproved by the Czech press, both Communist and bourgeois.
Wrote one Czech paper: "Slovakia, in fact, had been completely inter-
woven with Fascism under the Tiso regime . . . [today] the lower political
leadership in Slovakia includes persons who would have been condemned
for collaboration in Bohemia. The problem of Slovak collaboration is intri-
cate and presents no clear solution."[16]

Czechs and Slovaks showed the same insensitivity, however, in one
respect. They failed to notice the unfairness of the people's courts to the
Hungarians. If anything, the anti-Hungarian activities of the people's courts
were held to be unsatisfactory. The juries were blamed for handling the
Hungarian cases only half-heartedly, often on the assumption that the
Hungarian minority will be expelled anyway. *Národná Obroda* deplored
that even Communist Hungarians were protecting Hungarian "traitors."[17]
The Czech Communist *Tvorba,* however, strongly denounced the Slovak
judiciary for its leniency toward Slovak Fascists.

The attention of the Czech public focused on the Slovak question
only in the spring of 1946 [at the time of the elections]. All of a
sudden it assumed primary importance, requiring quick and decisive solutions. The [Fascist] L'udáks—thought by the Czechs to
have been liquidated long ago—sided openly and totally with the
Democratic Party during the election campaign, resorting to L'udák
methods to the fullest. It turned out that, with a few exceptions,
all former members of parliament of the HSLS [Hlinková Slovenská L:udová Strana—Hlinka's Slovak People's Party] were at liberty,
that all important officials of the Hlinka Guard and of the Party
were free to move about in Slovakia—what is more, that many of
them still occupied posts in central offices, on the [Slovak] national
committees at the county level, in the army, in the security agencies, at the universities, in the schools. These destroyers of the Republic, thought to be sitting behind bars, continue to work and interfere in the public affairs of Slovakia and of the Republic . . . . In
the editorial offices of *Čas* and of the other papers of the Democratic

Party there are twelve newsmen who had worked formerly for Hlinka's *Slovák* or *Gardista*.[18]

In reply to Czech criticism, Dr. Juraj Šujan, the Slovak State Attorney of the famous Tuka trial of 1929, published a critical survey of the Slovak people's courts:

> Forty percent of the total [145] cases was not tried by the [Bratislava] National Court, and some of these were major cases. . . . What is the reason? Why even some of the most important cases were not tried by the National Court? After the Tiso trial . . . [conflict] had arisen between the presidency of the National Court and the presidency of the Slovak National Council. [It was rumored that the cause of conflict was the Slovak National Council's effort to save Tiso's life.] The leadership of the Slovak National Council dismissed Dr. Daxner, President of the National Court. Dr. Daxner refused to leave his office, and while he had the backing of the [Czechoslovak] Government, the leadership of the Slovak National Council stuck to its decision. This . . . [conflict] continued to the end [of the existence of the National Court].[19]

Dr. Šujan then listed the biased acquittals and mild sentences. However, in a follow-up study of the people's courts, Dr. Šujan himself came to the biased conclusion that actually the Hungarians bear the main responsibility for the very existence of Slovak Fascism:

> It seems that we did not fully understand the significance of the people's courts. We did not appreciate fully the fact that the task of this judicial process was to consolidate our politically still not fully mature and gravely ill [Slovak] nation. For, as a result of long [Hungarian] oppression, our nation was dragged into a policy of collaboration with Hitler by Hungarians, Magyarons [Hungarized Slovaks] and irresponsible persons.[20]

The effort to blame the Hungarians for the misdeeds of Slovak Fascism was, of course, nothing new. It was voiced during the peace conference in Paris. It was present at the Tiso trial in Bratislava. The defense attorney,

Dr. Grečo, tried to prove that Tiso and his Slovaks were actually not responsible for Czechoslovakia's destruction. For, in Dr. Grečo's words:
"The causes of Czechoslovakia's disintegration were pan-German expansionism and Hungarian revisionism."[21] In such an atmosphere it was il-
lusionary indeed to expect any measure of fairness from the Slovak
people's courts toward the Hungarians.

The trial of János Esterházy, head of the Hungarian Party in Tiso's
Slovakia, was one of the most glaring examples of the double standards
practiced by the Slovak people's courts against the Hungarians.

Postwar Czechoslovak policy regarded the Hungarian Party in Tiso
Slovakia as the legal successor of the United Hungarian Party in prewar
Czechoslovakia. The intention was to burden Esterházy and his Party with
responsibility for the destruction of Czechoslovakia and with charges of
collaboration with the Sudeten Germans and Nazi Germany. The Hungarian Party's critical attitude toward the Fascist Tiso regime was never recognized. In particular, its opposition to the Slovak Fascist artocities that got
under way in 1942 was kept under silence. János Esterházy was the only
member in the Slovak Parliament who voted against the deportation of
the Jews in 1942. At the time of the Slovak uprising in 1944, Esterházy
was in Hungary. He was arrested by the Hungarian Fascist Arrow Cross
regime after October 15, 1944, because he refused to allow the Hungarian
Party of Slovakia to be affiliated with Arrow Cross organization. Following his release, he returned to Bratislava and announced his resignation
as head of the Party which—or, rather the little that was left of it—came
by then under the control of a handful of local pro-Nazis.

Pursued by the Gestapo, Esterházy went into hiding in Slovakia. He
chose to stay with his people, rejecting exile. After Slovakia's liberation,
captured by the Russians, he was taken to the Soviet Union as a "war
criminal." So say the Slovak sources, which also purport to know that
"in the Soviet Union half of his sentence was remitted and he was able to
return to Slovakia by 1948."[22] Meanwhile, in 1947, the National Court
in Bratislava sentenced Esterházy to death in his absence. Upon his return
from the Soviet Union, his death sentence was commuted to life in prison.
He died in 1957 in a prison hospital.

"In contumaciam," János Esterházy was sentenced to death by hanging
on September 16, 1947, by the National Court in Bratislava. The correspondent of *Čas* filed this report on the verdict:

The main trial of János Esterházy, deputy of the former Slovak National Assembly, took place before the National Court in Bratislava
on Tuesday under the presidency of K. Bedrna. The whereabouts of
the accused are unknown, he is probably in the Soviet Union. He
was charged with crimes for the destruction of the [Czechoslovak]
Republic, as well as for his activities as leader of the Hungarian Party
and its Deputy in the National Assembly of the Slovak State. Dr. M
Čikvonova, the defense attorney appointed by the State, moved that
the trial be adjourned, considering that the accused was not present,
and to make it possible to prepare the material for defense. After deliberations, the Court rejected the motion of the defense. After the
presentation of the evidence the Court reached a verdict *in contumaciam,* according to which the accused János Esterházy was condemned to death by hanging, furthermore to the loss of his rights
as citizen and to the confiscation of his property.[23]

The later commutation of János Esterházy's death sentence to life im-
prisonment should be regarded as fortunate. His execution would have
been one of the most shameful acts of postwar Czechoslovak policy a-
gainst the Hungarian minority. Even some contemporary Slovak historians admitted Esterházy's anti-Fascist record. Moreover, even Communist
historiography in Hungary, the country most eager of the Soviet bloc to
be critical of its own nationals, has occasionally ranked Count János
Esterházy among "opponents of the Germans and the Arrow Cross."[24]
The Esterházy trial has stirred up spontaneous indigation among Hungarians everywhere, overpowering the scattered voices of official Hungarian Communist approval. Esterházy's anti-Fascist stand, his person, has
never been rehabilitated. However, the facts of his political activity in
opposition to the Tiso regime in Slovakia was at least publicly recorded
in the memoires of Zoltán Fábry, the distinguished Hungarian Communist writer, a witness and victim of the tragedy of the Hungarian minority
in Czechoslovakia:

> When Fascism had triumphed, János Esterházy and his party, the
> Hungarian Party of Slovakia, did not collaborate; thus the Hungar-
> ian minority of Slovakia became the sole collective carrier of anti-
> Hitlerism in this country. But who knows about this? . . . . He
> [Esterházy] held out to the last moment though his cause was lost.

He did not flee, he did not evacute. He faced without fear the judgment he expected . . . . What had to happen to a Hungarian count,
and to his 'nation of gentlemen,' that he should be waiting for the
Russians to come? That he should be rooting for them, even if they
should be the harbingers of an avalanche which would eventually
bury him?[25]

The Hungarians of the territories returned to Hungary in 1938—and re-
annexed by Czechoslovakia after the war—found themselves even in a
worse situation than the Hungarians who remained in Tiso's Slovakia. The
so-called "support of the Fascist occupying forces" section of the Slovak
retribution law was the easiest to apply against these Hungarians. They
could be accused of "loyalty to the Horthy regime." The "Fascist-nation"
theory could reap among them a rich harvest of "war criminals" by pro-
nouncing them just guilty of "passivity."

I have called attention several times to the complex psychological causes
of the apathy of the Hungarian masses during the last stages of the war.
But to the Slovak historian, this was simply evidence of the "Fascist integration almost of the entire Hungarian society."[26]

Serious researchers and eye witnesses know that, after 1941, the Hungarian Fascist Arrow Cross organization in "occupied" Southern Slovakia
fell apart and lost mass support. Decline began with Hitler's attack on the
Soviet Union already in 1941. Disintegration became complete by 1944.
Under the impact of military developments on the eastern front of the
war, branches of the Arrow Cross in some regions stopped their activities
already in late 1941.[27] In Eastern Slovakia, according to a Slovak research-
er, active Arrow Cross members in the Hungarian-populated regions drop-
ped from 2,000 in 1941 to 200 in 1944.[28] These figures could hardly support the Slovak thesis of almost total "Fascist integration" of the Hungarian society.

Yet Slovak historiography consistently treats the postwar policy of
discrimination against the Hungarians as an "anti-Fascist" accomplish-
ment. Manifestly reactionary and inhumane nationalist actions against
the Hungarians are described as "progressive and revolutionary." Furthermore, Slovak historians maintain that the policy toward the Hungarians in
liberated Czechoslovakia was more democratic than the policy of the
Horthy regime had been toward the Slovaks. For, "the regime of the

people's democracy of Slovakia never behaved as roughly towards the Hungarians as did the Horthy regime vis-a-vis the Slovaks in occupied areas."[29]

One particularly favorite theme of Slovak historiography is the alleged "mass" expulsion of Slovaks from "occupied" Southern Slovakia under the Horthy regime. We have dealt with this myth, proving how groundless it is. As we have shown, the "mass" expulsion amounted to no more than 5000 Slovaks. Yet, Slovak historiography still keeps silent about the 81,000 Czechs and Slovaks who left Southern Slovakia before the Hungarian "occupation forces" arrived. They lump the 81,000 together with the 5000—or, rather, arbitrarily quote astronomical figures about "mass" expulsions as if they were solid statistics. Why? Most likely, because it is necessary to maintain such myths in order to support the "Fascist-nation" theory against the Hungarians, in order to vindicate the collective deprival of the Hungarians' civil rights, in order to justify the entire policy of retribution.

Myths and lies are the ugly legacy of war. Unfortunately, they are being spread long after the war, deliberately and consistently. For instance, Dr. Daniel Okáli, head of the Slovak Government Department in charge of postwar resettlement, in 1968 was talking of the expulsion of "hundreds of thousands" of Czechs and Slovaks from "occupied" Southern Slovakia.[30] Nor did he sober up by 1969, when he asserted that "one-third" of Slovakia had been attached to Hungary in 1938, that the Hungarians evicted "hundreds of thousands" of Slovaks and Czechs from their homes, and that further "hundreds of thousands" of Slovaks were inducted into the armies of Horthy and used as cannon fodder.[31]

The mood of reprisals in the aftermath of a war may be regarded as understandable. However, under no circumstances should lies born in that postwar mood be treated forever as historical facts, as it became common practice in Slovak historiography.

In Czech lands the spontaneous desire for vengeance against the Germans was much more blood-thirsty than the anti-Hungarian mood in Slovakia. The Slovak public, in fact, as I have shown in my earlier chapters, had to be manipulated from above in order to burst out in an unprecedented fury of anti-Hungarian emotions. Yet, unlike in Slovakia, the political trials in the Czech lands were much less dominated by vindictiveness.

So much so that the Czech people's courts came under criticism for their lack of understanding of the purpose of "political justice":

> The new Republic basically adopted the pre-Munich judicial system of the Republic. It became obvious that some of the judges do not understand the requirement of the times and hand down sentences which are incomprehensible to our citizens. . . . If we compare our political trials with those in other countries, with France or the Soviet Union . . . we can see that our judicial system leaves a lot to be desired. The purpose of a political trial is different from the trial of a common felony; in a political suit we are passing judgement not over a single culprit but over a movement and an ideology from which the actions of the accused stem.[32]

There was no ground for similar complaints regarding Slovak "political justice." The trials of Hungarians took place in an atmosphere of political prejudice. The sentences depended on nationality, on political party or movement; unlike the Czech practice, the Slovak people's courts in action were overpoliticized. Also, the basic purpose of the People's courts in Slovakia differed from its purpose in the Czech lands. In the Czech land, *after* the expulsion of the Germans, the prosecution was directed mainly against the Czech traitors, whereas in Slovakia it was aimed all the way against the Hungarian minority and *in support* of its expulsion.

The divergence between the administration of Czech and Slovak justice was apparent to the Minister of Justice, a Czech. However, he sought the explanation of this divergence in the "divergent laws" governing retribution in the Czech and Slovak parts of the country. In Slovakia, the Slovak National Council reserved the right of considerable autonomy for itself: "The leading officials of the Ministry of Justice were unwilling to defend the independence of the judge . . . . Since the [Daxner] affair of the President of the National Court in Bratislava, judicial independence was indeed threatened."[33]

The Communist deputies in the National Assembly were generally dissatisfied with the activities of the People's courts in Slovakia, but only because of Slovak leniency toward their own Fascists: "How can it be that the traitors are running free, that leading figures of the Fascist regime not only were not punished, but occupy important positions in the national economy or in the State administration and use their positions of power to become centers of underground anti-State L'udák activities?"[34]

The administration of justice by the people's courts was corrupt. However, corruption also enabled quite a few Hungarians to escape sentences the corrupt courts meted out against them. Corrupt practices of the peopl's courts followed from the very role they were assigned to play in the Government's efforts to expel the Hungarian minority from Czechoslovakia.

Thus, many Hungarians, sometimes even those condemned to as much as ten years for "war crimes" were allowed to go free if they pledged to leave the country. Often, after sentencing, the Hungarians were discreetly told that their sentences would be carried out only if they refused to move to Hungary. I myself was witness to such an incident in 1947. Of course, in order to force a condemned Hungarian to flee to Hungary, it was necessary to reach harsh verdicts. Nobody surrendered his home to avoid a few months in jail. This has never been written about, yet only in the context of the expulsion policy can the people's courts' actions against the Hungarians be properly understood.

The corrupt system enabled still another mode of escape. In view of the large number of Hungarians convicted, it was impossible to find room for them in the prisons. Therefore, those condemned to shorter times, one or two years, usually were sent to labor camps. There, within a few months, the guards told them not to return "necessarily" after next Sunday's furlough.

Much as nationalist propaganda from above was disseminating hatred against the Hungarians, relations among Slovakia's peoples of mixed nationality did not always correspond to the chauvinist spirit of official policy. And, despite the hate propaganda, unlike in the German populated regions of the Czech lands, no lynchings ever occurred in the Hungarian populated regions of Slovakia following liberation from Nazi occupation.

CHAPTER 9

1948: END OF THE NIGHTMARE

The winter of 1947-1948 was a turning point in Czechoslovakia's postwar history and in that of the Hungarian minority's as well. In February 1948, the Coalition Government, the last of its kind in the Soviet orbit, collapsed. On February 25, President Beneš appointed a new government headed by Prime Minister Gottwald, which marked the end of the coalition era and brought the country under the exclusive control of the Communist Party. With the takeover by the Party of the working class, Czechoslovakia joined the ranks of the people's democracies in Eastern Europe.

The political change was swift and immediate. The change in the status of the Hungarian minority was gradual. The nightmare that began with Czechoslovakia's liberation in 1945 did not end abruptly with the Communist takeover in 1948. There were a few straws in the wind suggesting the approaching democratization of Czechoslovak policy toward the Hungarian minority. Sporadically, new ways of thinking made their appearance in the Communist press, new attitudes were in the making, mainly in the Czech lands. Slovakia, however, remained in the grips of a policy of intransigent hostility toward the Hungarian minority. In fact, before the February takeover, there was no indication in Czechoslovak ruling circles of any real willingness to reassess the policy of total liquidation, there was no sign of a search for new ways of peacefully coexisting with hundreds of thousands of Hungarians in Slovakia.

Preparations for the May general elections went on in January 1948, according to the discriminatory measures adopted since 1945 against the national minorities. Only persons of Slav nationality could register. Hungarians and Germans were denied the right to vote, even if they were granted Czechoslovak citizenship on the grounds of their anti-Fascist record. The only exception were the so-called "re-Slovakized" Hungarians, provided they received already their certificates of Slovak nationality.[1]

Dr. Jozef Lettrich, President of the Slovak National Council and head of the Democratic Party, stubbornly defended the Slovak nationalist policy, declaring that "expulsion, resettlement, re-Slovakization is the new way of solving the Hungarian problem in Slovakia."[2] The Slovak press too continued its anti-Hungarian propaganda in the same vein, giving vent, however, to disappointments with the progress of the policy of Slovakization. Concern and anger was expressed in particular over the suspension of the population exchange between Hungary and Czechoslovakia. Also, a new type of complaint was spreading which ever since became a favorite propaganda slogan of postwar Slovak chauvinism. Instead of Slovakization of Southern Slovakia, so ran the complaint, a "Magyarization" of the resettled Slovaks is taking place because of the still predominantly Hungarian environment. The case of Gúta (Kolárovo, as the Slovaks renamed it) in the Csallóköz (Žitný Ostrov) was given wide publicity. There 2000 Hungarians had been expelled and 2100 Slovaks from Hungary settled in their place. The Slovak settlers made no dent in the Hungarian character of the community, while resettled Slovaks from Hungary, who did not even speak Hungarian before, now supposedly were well on their way to becoming "Magyarized" in Gúta.

Commenting on the suspension of population exchange since November, the Slovak press during the winter of 1947-1948 began to report rumors to the effect that the minority rights of the Hungarians in Czechoslovakia might be restored. The source of these rumors was the supposedly changing attitude of the Communist Party in matters of minority rights and, also, the pending alignment of Czechoslovakia's policy with that of the people's democracies in Eastern Europe. Such rumors in the midst of intensifying crisis in the coalition regime, besieged by the Communists, could not be taken lightly. It became increasingly evident that the extreme nationalist stand against the Hungarian minority was not in line anymore with Communist policy.

The ultra-nationalist Slovak Democratic Party, the principal antagonist of the Communists in Slovakia, was forced to take notice of the changing political climate when at its Congress on January 25 included the following ambiguous but conciliatory sentence in its resolution: "We hope that every problem of the remaining Germans and Hungarians will be solved on the basis of humanity, law and democracy."[3]

Meanwhile the press of the Democratic Party was following the new political course with anguish. *Nové Prúdy* was irritated that the Hungarians expelled from Czechoslovakia were allowed to organize themselves in Hungary "on the model of the [expelled] Sudeten Germans" in West Germany. The periodical was also indignant about other matters:

> Hungary consistently disregards the population exchange agreement. We must ask, who is responsible for the systematic violations of the agreement, and who is responsible for the continued [Hungarian] revisionist propaganda against Czechoslovakia. He is none other than [Mátyás Rákosi] the First Secretary of the Hungarian Communist Party. . . . Since June 1947, when Rákosi became the power behind the regime in Hungary, there was no change [in Hungary's attitude toward Czechoslovakia]. As far as the revisionist propaganda is concerned it was in fact Rákosi himself who during a conversation in Prague, in the presence of Gottwald and Slánsky, declared that the simplest way to reach reconciliation between Czechoslovakia and Hungary would be to transfer South Slovakia to Hungary. . . . It should be also noted that Št[efan]. Bašt'ovanský [a Communist] from Slovakia who, in Warsaw took part in September 1947 at the [founding] conference of the Cominform does not differ at all from the Hungarian Rákosi.[4]

Thus was the Slovak anti-Communist charge of "treason" born in 1948 out of nationalist anger over the Communist Party's change of policy toward the Hungarian minority.

With the deepening of political crisis in February 1948 the hope was rapidly vanishing that the Coalition Government between the bourgeois parties and the Communists could be maintained. The Slovak Democratic Party, the chief antagonist of the Communists in Slovakia, as well as the principal exponent of the anti-Hungarian policy, adjusted in ambiguous terms its platform in late January, by pledging "democratic" solutions. The Party press, however, kept its chauvinist anti-Hungarian tone to the very end. The last issue of the Democratic Party *Nové Prúdy* appeared on February 22 in the midst of the showdown between the bourgeois parties and the Communists. It was the paper's swan song in praise of the intolerant

Slav nation-state policy which was about to come to an end with the Communist takeover. The paper's editorial reaffirmed its faith in aggressive Slovakization as the only guarantee of solving the Hungarian question.[5]

The Slovak Democratic Party press was not alone in finding it hard to give up the policy of liquidating the Hungarian minority. *Sloboda,* the paper of the Liberty Party (*Strana Slobody*), warned in late January that "the Hungarian danger is still present. . . ." and advocated a resolute continuation of the Slovakization policy. Characteristics of the chauvinistic Slovak temper was the notorious "Hungarian calendar affair" in early February. *Čas* indignantly attacked the Slovak Communist Party for publishing a Hungarian calendar in the Hungarian town of Komárom (Komárno)' "Where are you, old Slovak fighters of Komárno? Can't you discipline your Hungarians and their profit hunter Slovak accomplices? Today a calendar, tomorrow a textbook, and the day after tomorrow: Everything back! [A reference to the Hungarian revisionist slogan of the post-Munich times]".[6]

Obzory expressed similar ill forebodings by quoting at great length from a *New York Times* report on the Slovak-Hungarian conflict. "It was hardly possible that after the expulsion of three million Germans the Slovaks should not attempt to get rid of the Hungarian minority," said the quote from *The New York Times.* But the newspaper also spoke of an impending "normalization" of relations between Hungary and Czechoslovakia, which would mean the granting of minority rights to the Hungarians on the model of People's Democratic Yugoslavia and Rumania.[7] Then less than a week before the Communist takeover on February 22, the Czechoslovak press carried a statement of the Hungarian Minister of Foreign Affairs Gyöngyösi, expressing his hopes that "the accords concluded with Rumania and Yugoslavia will also have favorable impact on the northern neighbor [Czechoslovakia], and that the sorry situation of the Hungarians living there will be resolved in the spirit of democracy and equality."[8]

Only the Communist press in the Czech lands struck occasionally a new revolutionary tone disrespectful of nationalist shibboleths on the eve of the Communist takeover. In early February, *Tvorba* published a re-examination of the Munich crisis omitting entirely the until then compulsory argument blaming the German and Hungarian minorities for Czechoslovakia's disintegration. *Tvorba's* analysis stressed the class aspect: "Munich was no bolt from the blue! It was a direct and logical consequence of this [class interest] policy. But times are changing. . . . Now the working people are at the helm of the Republic. They have removed from leadership the big industrialists and large landowners, the principal accomplices of the Munich tragedy."[9]

The takeover by the working class in February 1948 brought about a new situation regarding the prospects of solving Czechoslovakia's nationalities problem. The view of official historiography, however, as if the Communist takeover of February 1948 would have solved everything at once, is wrong. As far as the Hungarian question was concerned, the search for new ways did not come until the Berlin crisis and the Stalin-Tito break. Only the seriousness of the international situation resulting from these crises in the summer of 1948 started to fulfill the February promise of change.

In the spring of 1948, the policy of discrimination against the Hungarian minority still continued unabated. In April, I myself saw an announcement of the Slovak National Committee in Revúca warning the population that anyone who would hear Hungarian spoken should report it immediately to the security organs. Many Slovaks felt in fact that with the February Communist takeover, the hour had struck for tougher measures. They thought that everything that could not be carried out against the Hungarians under the coalition regime would be carried out now.

In early March, the Slovak Communist Party daily *Pravda* published a statement by the Slovenská Liga, reflecting the ultra-nationalist Slovak expectations following the February events:

> The Slovenská Liga salutes the victory of the people's democracy in Czechoslovakia because it sees in this victory the final triumph of those national ideals for which the Slovenská Liga is fighting. On this occasion the Slovenská Liga proposes to achieve the following goals:
> 1. South Slovakia has to be cleared of all elements hostile to the Slovak, Czech, and all other Slav nations, especially of the reactionary Hungarian intelligentsia.
> 2. The Slovak language has to be introduced consistently and uncompromisingly into private and public life, its use has to be guaranteed in the official life, in business, and in the churches.[10]

The anti-Hungarian tone of the Slovak press did not change after the February change of the Prague regime. Also the forcible transfer of the Hungarians was resumed according to the Czechoslovak-Hungarian population exchange agreement. In general, the Slovakization of the Hungarian populated regions of Southern Slovakia went on as before. And the new constitution of the Republic made public in May made no mention of national minority rights. The new constitution followed the ideology of the 1945 Košice program of the homogeneous Slav nation-state, stressing that Czechoslovakia is exclusively the state of the Czechs and Slovaks:

> Now we have decided that our liberated country will become a nation-state, which will rid itself of all alien elements, and will live in friendship with the fraternal community of Slav states and with all peace-loving nations."

The new constitution was duly described abroad as nationalist, and criticized (by one French paper at least) for not including protection for the Hungarian and German minorities.[11] The elections that followed on May 30 deserved the same criticism: only Czechs and Slovaks were allowed to go to the urns.

In June, President Beneš resigned and thus one of the principal architects of the anti-Hungarian policy disappeared from the political scene. His departure was expected to have a favorable effect on the evolution of the nationalities policy under the new regime. Hungarian public opinion in fact always considered the policy of discrimination as the personal work of President Beneš. The lifting of discriminatory measures, however, had to wait still a little longer.

Only the forcible population exchange between Czechoslovakia and Hungary was stopped in the summer of 1948, while discrimination in general against the Hungarians in Slovakia did not relent. Administrative actions and judicial decisions against the Hungarians continued to be executed according to Beneš's dreaded Presidential decrees issued in 1945.

Real change in Czechoslovak policy toward the Hungarian minority did not come until after the double crisis precipitated by the Berlin blockade and by the Stalin-Tito break. Need for closing of ranks among the people's democracies under Soviet guidance in this crisis situation resulted in a radical revision of Czechoslovakia's minority policy.

Discrimination against the Hungarian minority legally ended in the fall when on October 12, 1948, the Czechoslovak Government restored citizenship to the Hungarians by virtue of Law 245/1948. Commenting on the Law, Antonín Zápotocký, the new Prime Minister, (succeeding Gottwald who, in turn, succeeded Beneš in the presidency of the Republic) said: "It will strengthen the good-neighborly and friendly relations with the Hungarian People's Democracy, it will serve the interests of the Czechoslovak Republic and peace in general."[12]

Law 245 itself, it should be pointed out, did not guarantee specifically minority rights, it restored citizenship to the minorities, nothing else. Only the gradual development of Socialist cultural institutions and participation in revolutionary popular self-government did in due course open the road to regaining minority rights.

In the late fall of 1948, the authorities were flooded by Hungarian minority problems, including the two most painful ones: 1. The national illiteracy of the Hungarian minority resulting from almost four years of closed schools and from the almost total expulsion of the intelligentsia capable of cultural leadership. 2. The future of the Hungarians deported to the Czech lands.

A new Hungarian school system did finally open in the fall of 1948, but in most cases only on paper. There were no Hungarian teachers available—and not enough Hungarian pupils either, since many frightened parents did not dare to enroll their children. As for the deported persons, their return created chaotic conditions that lasted for years. In general, the blows of four years of persecution left wounds among the Hungarians which decades could not heal.

The complex problem of the Hungarian deportees was tackled by the Ministry of Agriculture and by the Ministry of Welfare, which jointly issued an appeal in November 1948, saying:

Many among you have already gotten accustomed to the new environment and prefer to stay. The Ministry of Agriculture wants to meet your wishes, and will allocate land and lodgings in the Czech provinces. Those who want to remain in the Czech provinces may immediately present their application to the office of the National Agricultural Foundation. Those agricultural workers who do not

intend to settle permanently either as farmers or as industrial workers in the Czech provinces may return to Slovakia between January
1, 1949 and April 30, 1949. The return of the Hungarian workers
will take place in large groups, and the State will defray the cost of
travel. Those who, for serious reasons, cannot return to their former
holdings may settle elsewhere in groups, where they will receive the
equivalent [of their former holdings] or even more land . . . . The
success of repatriation procedures requires that nobody should return to Slovakia before the appointed time, without the approval or
instruction of the competent authorities . . . . Any hasty return may
result in unpleasant consequences, because it would violate the laws
regulating the execution of the economic plans, also the laws regulating labor service, and thus entail strict punishment.[13]

Endless legal battles and bitter conflicts regarding property rights followed the return of the Hungarians from Bohemia. The return of belongings confiscated from some ten thousand families and compensation for
damages did not go as smoothly as the official repatriation proceedings
envisaged with feigned benevolence. The planned organized transports
could not accomplish much. The Hungarian deportees did not wait as
ordered, despite the threat of punishment. They left on their own within
weeks and demanded the return of their former properties from the Slovak settlers. Practically nobody was willing to accept different lands as a
compensation. The resulting chaos was mitigated only by the decision of
some twenty-five percent of the deportees who chose not to return but
preferred to take advantage of economic opportunities in the Czech lands,
depopulated by the expulsion of the Sudeten Germans.[14]
    One of the problems aggravating the repatriation process was the Slovak
refusal to admit any wrongdoing to the Hungarians. The deportations, it
was claimed, had nothing to do with anti-Hungarian policy. In Slovak
Marxist view, the deportations served social justice. According to that interpretation—also expounded by the Slovak-controlled Hungarian-language
press—this is what happened:

    The Government took up the cause of the little man. It was prim-
    arily a social measure not a Hungarian-Slovak issue. It is our firm
    conviction, that the Czechoslovak people's democracy will overcome

the difficulties and will lend a helping hand to the Hungarians returning from Bohemia. We cannot do this, however, at the expense of the little Slovak, the Slovak smallholder, the Slovak worker. . . . The problem cannot be solved by sharpening nationalist antagonism but only on the basis of class solidarity. . . . Those who were unable to recover their former homes, [often] refuse to be housed in large apartments. . . and prefer to lodge with their poor relatives who are short of space. . . . Some hesitate to accept eight or ten acres, and insist on their own [former] two and a half acres. . . . If someone wants to be a farmer he should accept the land offered to him and get to work, even if he cannot return to his former home—let him not sink into sentimental nostalgia and long for his own little hut. We cannot make any progress this way, even if we do understand such conservative sentimentalism.[15]

Such hypocritical interpretations improved neither the lot of the repatriated Hungarian agrarian proletariat nor the Slovak-Hungarian proletarian brotherhood. The repatriated Hungarian peasants ultimately found their way to economic recovery in the agrarian cooperatives set up by the Government under the Communist policy of collectivization.

The cultural recovery of the Hungarian minority posed even greater problems than the economic rehabilitation. What was left of the Hungarian intelligentsia was weak both in numbers and in levels of education. Under such poor leadership the reconstruction of culture from scratch was a slow and arduous process. The four-year ban on Hungarian culture, the illiteracy forced upon the school-age children had left its marks even after thirty years—not to speak of the psychological effects of intimidation which had affected generations.

The inferiority complex feeding on the memories of persecution, its debilitating moral and spiritual consequences are still a threat to the survival of the Hungarian minority in Czechoslovakia. The failure of four years of Czechoslovak policy to liquidate the Hungarian minority by expulsion and dispersal did not necessarily end the perils of extinction.

EPILOGUE

THE NATIONALIST MYTHS LIVE ON

The Communist takeover, in February 1948, confronted Slovak historiography with a dilemma. Marxist historical analysis has become mandatory under the new regime but Slovak historians could not bring themselves to a Marxist reassessment fo Czechoslovak policy toward the Hungarian minority. The chasm between Marxist ideology of class struggle and the nationalist ideology of the Košice program that inspired the policy of discrimination against the Hungarian minority was obvious. To admit that, however, would have entailed parting with nationalist myths. This the Slovak historians had no heart to do. Thus, while paying lip service to scientific Marxism, they went on cultivating their emotional anti-Hungarian nationalism.

During the Stalinist 1950s, Slovak historians resolved their dilemma of how to interpret the "Hungarian question" by keeping silent about it. The silence had lasted essentially until 1965. In that year, with "liberalization" picking up momentum in Czechoslovakia, Juraj Zvara published a study on the postwar "solution" of the Hungarian question. Zvara tried to work out a compromise between the nationalist view, so dear to the heart of Slovak historiography, and the Marxist ideology reigning officially supreme in a Communist society. He admitted that some anti-Marxist "mistakes" had been committed in the course of postwar "solution" of the Hungarian question, but he also excused and justified them by so-called Slovak "rightful self-defense nationalism."[1]

Actually, by different means, Zvara only continued the well-established tradition of double morality and double standards in Slovak thinking on the Hungarian question. However, even the little self-criticism implied in Zvara's Marxist reinterpretation—the admission of some Slovak "mistakes"

215

—was too much for the nationalist mythmakers. Disguising themselves as Marxists who knew more about Marxism than Zvara, they corrected what they thought were Zvara's mistakes.

In the February 1967 issue of *Historický Časopis,* representative periodical of Slovak historiography, Zvara came under sharp Marxist attack by Maria Lavová.[2] She denounced Zvara's study as a "pamphlet," smacking of political opportunism. She blamed Zvara for being insufficiently informed about the history of the "solution" of the Hungarian question. Above all, in Lavová's caustic criticism, Zvara was not familiar enough with the Marxist dialectical theory of "rightful self-defense nationalism." For, as Lavová summed up her own Marxist dialectical thesis on this matter: ". . . if one may speak of nationalism on the Slovak side, it was a defensive nationalism which was but a reaction to extreme Hungarian chauvinism."[3]

To justify Slovak "defensive nationalism" as a reaction to "Hungarian chauvinism," Lavová relied on facts which were of very dubious provenance indeed, based on hearsay, rumors, or simply inventions of anti-Hungarian propaganda of the 1940s. Prominent among them were the "terrible sufferings" of the Slovak people under recent Hungarian rule; in particular the expulsion of Slovaks, following Hungarian re-possession of South Slovakia in 1938, ranging from "tens of thousands" to "hundreds of thousands." We have dealt with these propaganda items in our earlier chapters, while discussing the Slovak postwar efforts to brand the Hungarians as a "Fascist nation."

In addition to her effort to whitewash Slovak nationalism, as a "defensive reaction" to Hungarian chauvinism, Lavová also eagerly defended the record of the Slovak Communist party. She attacked Zvara for not identifying properly the "bourgeois nationalists" who had been bearers of "alien ideology" in the Party at the time of the postwar "solution" of the Hungarian question.[4] She also claimed that the Party, since then, has condemned these bourgeois bearers of "alien" nationalist ideology. Lavová made several vague hints at a link existing between the condemnation by the Party of Slovak "bourgeois nationalism" and postwar Czechoslovak policy of discrimination against the Hungarian minority. In order to set the record straight on that score, the following facts should be borne in mind.

At the Ninth Congress of the Slovak Communist Party in 1951, which dealt with bourgeois nationalism, the two principal speakers on this issue,

Štefan Bašt'ovanský and Karol Bacílek, had made no condemning references whatsoever to the policy of discrimination against the Hungarian
minority.[5] And, in 1950, at the trials of leading Slovak Communists accused of "bourgeois nationalism," the charges connected with the "Hungarian question" emphasized explicit only State relations between Czechoslovakia and Hungary rather than discriminations against the Hungarian
minority. Let me quote a pertinent passage from the state Prosecutor's
speech: ". . . the accused strived for the undermining of Czechoslovak-
Hungarian mutual relations, according to instructions received from
Clementis, as demonstrated . . . especially by the activities of the accused
Okáli during the solution of the question of citizens of Hungarian nationality in Slovakia. Okáli used the office of the Czechoslovak Resettlement
Committee for hostile activities against the Hungarian State."[6]

In the context of the trials of the bourgeois nationalists it is quite
clear that what was meant by the "Hungarian question" was never the
policy of discrimination against the Hungarian minority but, rather, the
execution of the Czechoslovak-Hungarian agreement on population exchange. Nor should it be left unmentioned that, when "liberalization"
prompted the Party to rehabilitate Clementis and his "bourgeois nationalist" colleagues, the lawlessness suffered by the Hungarian minority has
never been mentioned among the condemned "illegalities" of the past.
And neither the Party nor the Government has ever denounced the extreme chauvinist Košice program of 1945 that served as the fountainhead
of all aspects of the policy of discrimination against the Hungarians. In
fact, the text of the Košice program, painstakingly annotated and docu-
mented, has been reissued as recently as 1977—presumably with both
Party and Government approval—by the Slovak Pedagogical Publishing
House for use in Slovakia's schools.

Ever since the Zvara-Lavová debate on the interpretation of the Hungarian question, the theory of Slovak "defensive nationalism" as a reaction
to "Hungarian chauvinism," alongside with all the flimsy "documentation"
supporting that theory, has been integrated into contemporary Slovak
historiography. Although pretended to be Marxist, it is an unmistakably
nationalist interpretation, pure and simple. As we pointed out several
times in this study, after a brief respite in the "liberal" 1960s, Slovak
historical thinking entrenched itself more solidly than ever in the prejudices of a monolithic nationalism.[7]

A particularly favorite topic of Slovak historians, eager to prove "Hungarian chauvinism" as a justification of Slovak "defensive nationalism," is the "brutal oppression" of the Slovaks under the Horthy regime. We have shown, and repeat once again for the sake of truth, and not in defense of the Horthy regime: During the Second World War, the persecution of Slovaks in Southern Slovakia under Hungarian administration affected at most three percent of the Slovak minority population. The remaining 97 percent did not live under worse general conditions than the Hungarian majority, with only one major exception: Slovaks were at a disadvantage regarding the availability of Slovak-language education. There is no way, however we look at it, to draw a comparison between the situation of the Slovak minority in wartime Hungary and that of the Hungarian minority in postwar Czechoslovakia. During the four years of lawlessness, 97 percent of the Hungarians in Slovakia were deprived of all rights, and only some 3 percent were pardoned of criminal charges under the theory of collective national guilt; and even those 3 percent suffered, as did the 97 percent, total cultural deprivation.

The rise from the depths of the 1940s took a long time. The first decisive stop on the arduous road to recovery from the humiliations suffered by Hungarians during four years of lawlessness had been the recognition of the Hungarian minority's civil rights in the fall of 1948, following the February takeover by the Communist Party. In 1954, the Party invalidated the re-Slovakization program, thus restoring a measure of objectivity to the nationality statistics in Czechoslovakia. While according to the census of 1950 there were still only 369,000 Hungarians counted, the census of 1960 found again some half a million Hungarians in Czechoslovakia. (According to the Czechoslovak census of 1980, there are 579,600 Hungarians, which comes close to the prewar official figure of 634,000.) Still another step toward rehabilitation came during the liberal "thaw" of the 1960s, when in 1963 "discriminations" in general had been condemned with the other so-called "illegalities" of the 1950s. Slovak thinking on the "Hungarian question," however, shows no change. The nationalist myths of the 1940s live one. They are kept alive by Slovak historiography and translated into a policy against the Hungarian minority by the authorities of the Slovak Socialist Republic, an equal state, since January 1, 1969, with that of the Czechs, within federated Czechoslovakia.

NOTES

Introduction

1. Zoltán Fábry, "A vádlott megszólal," (The accused speaks up), in *Stószi délelőttök* (Forenoons at Stósz), Bratislava, 1968. Supplementary note by the author of the English Version: A caveat is in order concerning the text of the quotations. For the sake of precision, it would have been desirable to check Dr. Janics's sources in the original. This, unfortunately, could not be done within the limits of the project that produced this adaptation. Almost all quotations in the English Version went through at least two translations (from Czech or Slovak into Hungarian, and then from Hungarian into English), and some even three (whenever Dr. Janics quoted from Czech or Slovak sources that had already been translated from another language). Accuracy could have suffered in the course of these multiple translations. Whenever in doubt as to correct wording, I tried to reproduce the correct sense. The English rephrasing, I trust, has never falsified the original meaning of the quoted text as a whole—*S.B.*

Chapter 1

1. Cf. Emery Reves, *Anatomie míru* (Czech translation of "The anatomy of peace"), Prague, 1947.
2. Cf. M. Gilbert, *Nuremberg Diary,* Oxford University Press, 1947.
3. L. Holotik, ed., *Prispevky k dejinám fašizmu v Československu a v Mad'arsku* (Contributions to the history of Fascism in Czechoslovakia and Hungary), Bratislava, 1969, p. 178. (L. Lipscher's contribution).
4. József Sebestyén, *Hodža Milán útja* (Milan Hodža's Road), Bratislava, 1938, p. 170.
5. Edgár Balogh, *Hétpróba* (Test of strength), Budapest, 1975, p. 158.
6. Ibid., 234.

7. *Irodalmi Szemle*, (Bratislava) September, 1967, p. 835.

8. Quoted by R. Freund, *Chráňte Československo* (Defend Czechoslovakia) Prague, 1938, p. 126.

9. Cf. R. W. Seton-Watson, *Nové Slovensko* (The New Slovakia), Prague, 1924, pp. 112-118.

10. Sándor Balogh in *Századok*, 1970/71, p. 196.

11. Samuel Cambel, *Slovenská agrárna otázka* (The agrarian question in Slovakia 1944-1948) Bratislava, 1972. (See more on this topic in the last section of this chapter and in Epilogue—*S.B.*)

12. Dr. Bohuslav Ečer, *Norimberský soud* (The Nuremberg Tribunal), Prague, 1946, p. 155.

13. Igor Daxner, *L'udáctvo pred národným súdom* (The L'udáks before the People's Court 1945-47) Bratislava, 1961, p. 142.

14. Ibid., p. 143.

15. Loránt Tilkovszky, *Južné Slovensko v rokoch 1938-1945* (South Slovakia in the years 1938-45), Bratislava, 1972, p. 20.

16. Loránt Tilkovszky, *Revízió és nemzetiségpolitika Magyarországon, 1938-1941* (Revisionism and nationalities policy in Hungary) Budapest, 1967, p. 20.

17. For the speeches delivered at the peace conference, see Chapter 4.

18. *Stav a úkoly výzkumu národnostní otázky v Československu* (The state and tasks of investigation of the nationalities question in Czechoslovakia) 1975, p. 73. (Issued by the Silesian Institute of the Czechoslovak Academy of Sciences for internal use. Contains the material of the conference held at Trinec on September 23 and 24, 1974.)

19. *A Wilhelmstrasse és Magyarország* (Wilhemstrasse and Hungary) Budapest, 1963, p. 258.

20. L. Lipscher's contribution in Holotik, op. cit., p. 177.

21. Ibid.

22. Dr. Ivan Dérer, *Slovenský vývoj a l'udácka zrada* (The Slovak events and the betrayal of the L'udáks) Prague, 1946, p. 249.

23. Editorial in *Felvidéki Magyar Hírlap*, "Tévedések és hazugságok" (Mistakes and lies), February 19, 1939, p. 7.

24. *A Wilhelmstrasse és Magyarország*, p. 260.

25. Cf. Loránt Tilkovszky, op. cit., p. 17.

26. Igor Daxner, op. cit., p. 52.

27. *Historický Časopis* (Bratislava), 1969/3, p. 352.

28. Ibid.

29. *Čas,* September 18, 1947.

30. Zoltán Fábry, *Stószi délelőttök* (Forenoons at Stósz) Bratislava, 1968, p. 371.

31. *Nové Slovo* (Bratislava), August 21, 1969.

32. Martin Vietor, *Dejiny okupácie južného Slovenska* (The history of the occupation of South Slovakia) Bratislava, 1968, p. 348.

33. Ibid., p. 191.

34. Juraj Purgat, *Od Trianonu po Košice* (From Trianon to Košice) Bratislava, 1979, p. 93.

35. *Střední a jihovýchodní Evropa ve válce a v revoluci 1939-1945* (Central and Eastern Europe in the war and revolution, 1939-1945) Prague, 1969, p. 444. (Essay by R. Hoffman.)

36. *Kulturný Život* (Bratislava) (Article by Zora Jesenská.) January 13, 1967.

37. Vilém Prečan, *Slovenské národné povstanie* (The Slovak national uprising) Bratislava, 1965, p. 186.

38. Holotík, op. cit., p. 313. (Article by Juraj Fabian.)

39. Juraj Fabian, *Svatoštefanské tiene* (Shadows of St. Stephen), Bratislava, 9166, p. 107.

40. Ferenc Z. Nagy, *Ahogy én láttam* (The way I saw it) Budapest, 1965, p. 157.

41. Endre Kovács, *Magyar-lengyel kapcsolatok a két világháború között* (Hungarian-Polish relations between the two wars) Budapest, 1971, p. 338.

42. Zsuzsa Boros, "Német fogságból menekült francia hadifoglyok Magyarországon a második világháború alatt" (French POW's escaped from German camps in Hungary during World War II), *Történelmi Szemle* (Budapest), 1973, Nos. 3-4, p. 434.

43. *Tiszatáj,* November 27, 1975. (A review of J. R. Nowak's book.)

44. Loránt Tilkovszky, *Revízió és nemzetiségpolitika,* p. 75.

45. *Bulletin of the State Planning and Statistical Office* (Bratislava), October 1, 1946, p. 101. See also, Dr. Ján Svetoň, *Slováci v Mad'arsku* (Slovaks in Hungary) Bratislava, 1942, p. 59. The author states that the number of people of Slovak nationality who left voluntarily was 50,000. Thus, the number of Czechs must have been 31,000 (out of a total of 81,000).

46. Dr. Vladimír Kuna, ed., *Almanach oslobodeného juhu* (Almanach of the liberated South) Nitra, 1946, p. 125.

47. Tilkovszky, op. cit., p. 94.
48. Vladimír Srb, *Demografická příručka 1966* (Demographic handbook 1966) Prague, 1967, p. 46.
49. Igor Daxner, op. cit., p. 73.
50. Ibid.
51. Vladimír Clementis, *Odkazy z Londýna* (Messages from London) Bratislava, 1942, p. 42.
52. In particular the following works belong to this category: Authors' Collective, *Dejinná križovatka* (Historical crossroads) Bratislava, 1964; Juraj Zvara, *A magyar nemzetiségi kérdés megoldása Szlovákiában* (The solution of the Hungarian nationality question in Slovakia) Bratislava, 1965; Samuel Cambel, *Revolučný rok 1945* (Revolutionary year 1945) Bratislava, 1965; Authors' Collective, *Príspevky k dejinám východného Slovenska* (Contributions to the history of Eastern Slovakia) Bratislava, 1965; Ján Jablonický, *Slovensko na prelome* (Breakthrough in Slovakia) Bratislava, 1965.
53. Vietor, op. cit., in note 32; Cambel, op. cit., in note 11.

Chapter 2

1. The initial unfriendly Western attitude toward the exiles is strongly emphasized by Czechoslovak interpretations: "The road was long from the formation of the Czechoslovak National Committee in Paris, on October 17, 1939, to its transformation into a Provisional Czechoslovak Government; it reflected the unfavorable position taken by the Western Powers toward the restoration of the Czechoslovak Republic." In Otáhalová-Červinková, ed., *Dokumenty z historie československej politiky 1939-1943* (Documents from the history of Czechoslovak policy) Prague, 1966, p. 10. Hereafter referred to as *Dokumenty*.
2. The Soviet Union was the first to recognize the London Czechoslovak government-in-exile on July 18, 1941, following Hitler's invasion. The recognition by the United Kingdom followed on July 30, 1941.
3. Dr. Edvard Beneš, *Šest let v exílu* (Six years in exile) Prague, 1947, p. 97. (Beneš's letter to his American cousin, Vojta Beneš.)
4. *Dokumenty*, 91.
5. István [Stephen] Borsody, *A Szovjetunió és Középeurópa* (The Soviet Union and Central Europe), *Magyar Szemle*, (Budapest) Vol. 46 (1944), p. 126. (Actually, I first called public attention to Beneš's expulsion plans in a book, *Beneš*, published in the spring of 1943–*S.B.*)

6. Juraj Zvara, *A magyar nemzetiségi kérdés megoldása Szlovákiában* (The solution of the Hungarian nationality question in Slovakia), Bratislava, 1965, p. 43.

7. Beneš, op. cit., p. 17.

8. Ibid., p. 31.

9. Ibid., p. 53.

10. Ibid., p. 62.

11. *Dokumenty*, p. 47.

12. Beneš, op. cit., p. 73.

13. Dr. Edvard Beneš, *Paměti* (Memoirs), Prague, 1947, p. 168.

14. Beneš, *Šest let v exílu*, p. 123.

15. Beneš, *Paměti*, p. 220: "In the second half of December 1939, the Soviet Union informed our ambassador Zd. Fierlinger that his Moscow mission had come to an end. The ambassador left for Paris, and later for London. We expected this, for even beforehand, on September 16, 1939, the Soviet Union had *de facto* and *de jure* recognized the Tiso government in Slovakia and established diplomatic relations with it."

16. *Dokumenty*, p. 84.

17. Ibid., p. 143.

18. Ibid., p. 101.

19. Ibid., p. 102.

20. Ibid., p. 69.

21. Beneš, *Paměti*, p. 161.

22. *Dokumenty*, p. 196.

23. Ibid., p. 200. (A statement made on April 11, 1940.)

24. Cf. Pál Szvatkó, *A visszatért magyarok* (The returned Hungarians) Budapest, 1938, p. 69.

25. Dr. František Koláček, *Zeměpis Československa* (Geography of Czechoslovakia) Prague, 1934, p. 125. Also, *Demografická přiručka* (Demographic handbook) Prague, 1967, p. 45.

26. *Henlein-Hitler a Československá tragédia* (Henlein-Hitler and the Czechoslovak tragedy) Prague, 1945, p. 10. (Czech translation from Swedish of A. Kalgren's book.)

27. Ibid.

28. Klement Gottwald, *Desat' rokov* (Ten years) Bratislava, 1950, p. 367.

29. Ibid., p. 386.

30. *Národnostní kulturní politika a kulturné výchovaní práce* (Ethnic cultural politics and cultural education of work) Prague, 1972, p. 35. (Text of a lecture by Karel Pomajzl.)

31. Beneš, *Paměti*, p. 306.

32. Ibid., p. 330.

33. *Dokumenty*, p. 333.

34. Ibid.

35. Ibid., p. 387. (Notes by Smutný, October 4, 1943.)

36. Beneš, *Šest let v exílu*, p. 199.

37. Juraj Purgat, *Od Trianonu po Košice* (From Trianon to Košice) Bratislava, 1970, p. 172.

38. Beneš, *Paměti*, p. 330.

39. Ibid., p. 330.

40. Ibid., p. 285.

41. Ibid., p. 403.

42. *Cesta ke kvetnu* (Road to May), Prague, 1965, p. 56. (Collection of documents). (Czech Communist Party memoranda regarding the negotiations with Beneš in Moscow.)

43. *Cesta ke květnu*, p. 67.

44. Cf. Samuel Cambel, *Slovenská agrarná otázka* (The Slovak agrarian question) Bratislava, 1972.

45. *Cesta ke květnu*, p. 70. The Rumanian soldiers were encouraged to do the same thing in August 1944: "Fight for the liberation of our brothers in Northern Transylvania. See *Střední a juhovýchodní Evropa* (Central and Southeastern Europe), Prague, 1967, p. 385.

46. Vilém Prečan, *Slovenské narodné povstanie* (The Slovak national uprising) Bratislava, 1965, p. 141.

47. So far only once has public reference been made in Hungary to the Communist exiles in Moscow in connection with the transfer issue: In May 1946, Márton Horváth said in the Hungarian Parliament that during the war Mátyás Rákosi, on Radio Moscow, reported that the Hungarians of Slovakia will be resettled. (K.J.)

48. Klement Gottwald, op. cit., p. 343.

49. Quoted in Purgat, op. cit., p. 201.

50. Václav Kopecký's article in the July 15, 1944 issue of the *Československé Listy*. Reprinted in *Tvorba*, April 16, 1947.

51. *Cesta ke květnu*, p. 184.

52. Ibid., p. 459.

53. J. Purgat, op. cit., p. 206.

54. Ibid., p. 208.

55. *Cesta ke květnu*, p. 418.

56. Dr. Vladimír Clementis, *Odkazy z Londýna* (Messages from London) Bratislava, 1947, p. 191.

57. *Dokumenty*, pp. 749-70.

58. Beneš, *Šest let v exílu*, p. 255.

59. Václav Kopecký, *Gottwald Moszkvában* (Gottwald in Moscow) Bratislava, 1950, p. 43.

60. *Cesta ke květnu*, p. 15.

61. Ibid., p. 364.

62. Ibid., p. 15.

63. Dr. Gustav Husák, *Svedectvo o Slovenskom národnom povstaní* (Witness on the Slovak national uprising) Bratislava, 1964, p. 588.

64. Jozef Jablonický, *Slovensko na prelome* (Breakthrough in Slovakia) Bratislava, 1965, p. 162.

Chapter 3

1. Vilém Prečan, *Slovenské národné povstanie r. 1944* (The Slovak national uprising of 1944) Bratislava, 1965, p. 68.

2. *Obzory*, September 27, 1947, p. 580.

3. *Dejinná križovatka* (Historical crossroads), pp. 120-21.

4. Gyula Szekfű, *Forradalom után* (After revolution), Budapest, 1947, p. 54.

5. *Dokumenty z historie Československé politiky* (Documents on the history of Czechoslovak politics) Prague, 1966, p. 710.

6. Ibid., p. 714. Quoted below as *Documenty*.

7. Václav Král, *Osvobození Československa* (The Liberation of Czechoslovakia) Prague, 1975, p. 22.

8. *Dokumenty*, p. 720. (Notes taken by Jaromír Smutný on August 1943)

9. Ibid., p. 721. (Letter by M. Hanák to Beneš, August 10, 1943.)

10. Ibid., p. 729.

11. Prečan, op. cit., p. 66. (Letter by Viliam Radoković to Beneš, March 12, 1943. Radaković was Secretary of the Czechoslovak Agrarian

Party; he emigrated, and in 1943 became a member of the Czechoslovak State Council in London.)

12. *Horthy Miklós titkos iratai* (The secret papers of Miklós Horthy) Budapest, 1963, pp. 306-307. (Letter by Bárdossy to Horthy, August 26, 1941.)

13. *Historický časopis,* 1967, No. 1, p. 7.

14. Dr. Bohuslav Ečer, *Norimberský soud* (The Nuremberg tribunal) Prague, 1946, p. 197.

15. Prečan, op. cit., p. 48.

16. Ibid., p. 87. (Beneš' instructions to the non-Communist resistance groups, September 3, 1943.)

17. Ibid., pp. 102-103. (Letter by Beneš to the Šrobár group, September 15, 1943.)

18. Dr. Jozef Lettrich, *O Slovenskej národnej rade* (About the Slovak National Council), p. 21.

19. Ibid., p. 14.

20. Jozef Jablonický, *Z illegality do povstania* (From illegality to the uprising) Bratislava, 1969, p. 203.

21. Ibid., p. 205.

22. Prečan, op. cit., p. 243.

23. Ibid., p. 173. (Letter from a non-Communist resistance group, March 14, 1944.)

24. Ibid., p. 183. (Letter sent via Madrid, March 1944.)

25. Ibid., p. 248. (Report by Captain Krátky, July 22, 1944.)

26. Ibid., p. 311.

27. Anton Rašla, *Civilista v armáde,* p. 141. (A civilian in the army.) Bratislava, 1967. (Recollections of the years 1938-45.)

28. Prečan, op. cit., p. 262.

29. *Cesta ke květnu,* p. 177.

30. Zoltán Vas, *Hazatérés,* 1944. (Homecoming, 1944) Budapest, 1970, pp. 101-103.

31. Communication by Colonel Kálmán Kéry who, as the Chief of Staff of the First Army, participated in the negotiations between Béla Miklós and General Petrov and was present when General Mechlis warned the parties about the cessation of the preliminaries. (Statement by Kéry, August 23, 1974.)

32. Éva Teleki, *Nyilasuralom Magyarországon* (Arrow Cross rule in Hungary), Budapest, 1974, p. 50.

33. Prečan, op. cit., p. 509.

34. Ignác Ölvedy, "Adalékok Horthy és a Lakatos-kormány katona-politikájához" (Items concerning the military policy of Horthy and of the Lakatos-cabinet), *Századok* 1969, No. 1, p. 42.

35. Gyula Juhász, "Második világháborús magyar történelmi iroda-lom" (Hungarian historical writing about the Second World War) *Történelmi Szemle*, 1973, Nos. 3-4, p. 322.

36. Vladimír Motoška, *Protifašistický odboj v Novohrade* (Anti-Fascist struggle in Novohrad county) Bratislava, 1974, p. 134.

37. Ibid., p. 135.

38. Ibid., pp. 160-161.

39. *Cesta ke květnu*, p. 204.

40. Ibid., p. 732.

41. Prečan, op. cit., p. 468.

42. Ibid., p. 524.

43. *Cesta ke květnu*, p. 255.

44. Ibid., p. 226.

45. Juraj Purgat, *Od Trianonu po Košice* (From Trianon to Košice) Bratislava, 1970, p. 218.

46. Prečan, op. cit., p. 457.

47. Purgat, op. cit., p. 231.

48. *Pravda*, September 24, 1944. Reprinted in *Cesta ke květnu*, p. 734.

49. *Československá pracovná konferencia KSS v Košiciach ako prínos pri tvorbe vládného programu prvej vlády Narodného frontu Čechov a Slovákov* (Work conference of the Slovak Communist Party at Košice, as a commentary on the government program of the first government of the National Front of Czechs and Slovaks), *Historický Časopis*, 1975, No. 2, p. 183.

50. Jozef Jablonický, op. cit., p. 353.

51. Prečan, op. cit., p. 689.

52. Ibid., p. 622.

53. Ibid., p. 633.

54. Lettrich, op. cit., p. 32.

55. Prečan, op. cit., p. 593.

56. *Cesta ke květnu*, p. 268. (Speech by Marek Čulen, October 13, 1944.)

228 CZECH POLICY AND THE HUNGARIAN MINORITY

57. Prečan, op. cit., p. 734. (The decision of factory council at Podbrezová, October 20, 1944.)

58. Ibid., p. 718.

59. A. I. Puskás, *Magyarorság a II. világháborúban* (Hungary in the
Second World War) Budapest, 1971, p. 297.

60. Dalibor M. Krno, *Maďarská cesta k demokracií* (Hungary's road
to democracy) Bratislava, 1946, p. 77.

61. Prečan, op. cit., p. 827.

62. According to Puskás one million Hungarian soldiers were under
arms in November 1944. Piskás, op. cit., p. 320.

63. *Nové Slovo*, October 28, 1945.

64. *Slovenské národné povstaní: Niemci a Slovensko* (The Slovak national uprising: The Germans and Slovakia) Bratislava, 1971 (Collection of
documents), p. 437. (Dr. Witiska's report to the Reich security agencies,
November 28, 1944.)

65. László Zsigmong, ed., *Magyarország és a második világháború*
(Hungary and the Second World War) Budapest, 1966, p. 434. (Notes of
the Cabinet meeting, August 25, 1944.)

66. Ibid., p. 443. (Notes of the Cabinet meeting, September 8.) Cf.
Gyula Juhász, "Az üszkös pillanat" (The burn out moment), *Új irás,* 1977,
No. 5.

67. Beneš, *Nemzetek forradalma* (Revolution of Nations—Hungarian
translation of Beneš's World War I memoirs), Vol. III, p. 299.

68. Edo Friš, *Povstanie zďaleka a zbizka* (The uprising from far and
near) Bratislava, 1964, p. 67.

69. *Cesta ke květnu,* p. 18.

70. Gustav Husák, *Svedectvo o Slovenskom národnom povstaní,* p.
548.

71. *Nové Prúdy,* January 25, 1948. (Article by J. Lettrich.)

72. *Comunistická Strana Slovenská, Dokumenty 1944-1948* (Slovak
Communist Party, Documents 1944-1948) Bratislava, 1971, p. 185. (Speech
by V. Široký at Žilina, August 11, 1945.)

Chapter 4

1. Ladislav Szántó, *Oktober a moja cesta k marxismu* (October and
my road to Marxism) Bratislava, 1967, p. 223.

2. *Cesta ke kvetnu* (Road to May), Prague, 1965, p. 475. (Collection of documents.)

3. Ibid.

4. Ibid., p. 487.

5. Ibid., p. 491.

6. Samuel Cambel, *Slovenská agrárna otázka 1944-1948* (The Slovak agrarian question) Bratislava, 1972, pp. 76, 99.

7. Jozef Jablonický, *Slovensko na prelome* (Breakthrough in Slovakia) Bratislava, 1965, p. 323.

8. Samuel Cambel, *Revolučný rok 1945* (Revolutionary year 1945) Bratislava, 1965, p. 165.

9. *Cesta ke květnu*, p. 498.

10. *Pravda*, April 17, 1945. (Directive, dated April 12, 1945.)

11. *Generálny register právnych predpisov ČSSSR* (General Catalogue of laws and ordinances of the Czechoslovak Socialist Republic) Bratislava, 1973, p. 814. (Directive 44/1945 of the Slovak National Council, issued May 25, 1945, regulating civil and public service.)

12. *Cesta ke květnu*, pp. 518-20.

13. Häufler-Koröák-Král, *Zeměpis Československa* (Geography of Czechoslovakia) Prague, 1960, p. 236.

14. *Cesta ke květnu*, pp. 384-385.

15. Ibid., p. 383.

16. Ibid., p. 387.

17. Ibid., p. 389.

18. *Prvé kroky po oslobodení* (First steps after liberation) Bratislava, 1970, p. 146. (Essay by J. Purgat.)

19. Rezső Szalatnai, *Kisebbségben és igzaságban* (In minority and on the side of truth) Budapest, 1970, p. 316.

20. Ibid., p. 363.

21. Order of the Council 26/1945, dated April 7, 1945. Reprinted in Cambel, *Revolučný rok 1945,* p. 266.

22. Ibid., p. 271.

23. The text of President Beneš's radio speech in *Čas*, May 12, 1945.

24. Klement Gottwald, *Desat' rokov* (Ten years) Bratislava, 1950, p. 378.

25. Presidential decree 5/45, issued May 19, 1945, regarding the appointment of national caretakers. Published in *Konfiskace, správa a*

převod nepřátelského majetku (Confiscation, management, and transfer of enemy property) Prague, 1947, p. 410.

26. Ibid., p. 6.

27. Ibid., p. 15. Presidential decree 27/45, issued July 17, 1945.

28. Dr. Jozef Lettrich, *O slovenskej národnej rade* (On the Slovak National Council), p. 63. (The date of the order, July 3, 1945.)

29. *Slovník lidové správy* (Dictionary of people's administration) Prague, 1947, p. 297. (Manual for the employees of National Committees.)

30. "While solving these burning issues, conflicts arose between Hungarian and Slovak Communists in the local organs of the Communist Party. . . .Many Communists of Hungarian nationality solved the problem by moving to Hungary where they took an active part in the building of socialism." In Vladimír Motoška, *Protifašistický odboj v Novohrade* (The anti-Fascist struggle in Novohrad), p. 160.

31. J. Purgat's study in *Východné Slovensko pred februárom* (Eastern Slovakia before February), Košice, 1968, p. 104.

32. Stephen D. Kertesz, *Diplomacy in a Whirlpool*, Notre Dame, 1953, p. 122.

33. Lettrich, op. cit., p. 29.

34. Purgat, op. cit., in note 31, pp. 115-116.

35. Juraj Zvara, *A magyar nemzetiségi kérdés megoldása Szlovákiában*, p. 131.

36. Jablonický, op. cit., p. 399.

37. *Prvé kroky po oslobodení*, p. 165. Purgat, op. cit., in note 18.

38. *Komunistická Strana Slovenska 1944-1948* (The Communist Party of Slovakia) Bratislava, 1971, p. 287.

39. Široký's speech, December 5, 1945, as quoted in Purgat, op. cit., p. 120.

40. Cambel, *Revolučný rok 1945*, p. 272.

41. Ibid., p. 181.

42. Cambel, *Slovenská agrárna otázka*, p. 301.

43. Jablonický, op. cit., p. 400.

44. Supplementary note: I found it necessary to expand the section on

45. Ágnes Ságvari, *A magyar kül-és belpolitika néhány összefüggésérŐl a népi demokratikus forradalom ikőszakában* (Certain connections between between Hungarian democratic people's revolution), *Századok*, 1976, No. 6, pp. 1344-45.

Potsdam, as well as the collusion among the communist parties. References to Beneš's intervention are my own hypotheses—*S.B.* Cf. István [Stephen] Borsody, "Potsdam és a magyarországi németek kitelepítése," (Potsdam and the transfer of the Germans from Hungary), *Új Latóhtár* (Munich), XXXII, No. 1 (1981), pp. 103-106.

46. Supplementary note: My hypothesis. Cf. Václav Nosek, as quoted above, from *Pravda* (Bratislava), August 7, 1945. Also, see below, note 47, the Bouček-Klimeš report—*S.B.*

47. Report by Miroslav Bouček and Miloš Klimeš in *Prvé kroky po oslobodení* (First steps after liberation), pp. 28-29.

48. D. M. Krno, *Maďarská cesta k demokracii* (Hungary's road to democracy) Bratislava, 1946, p. 37.

49. See for Hungarian reactions, Sándor Balogh, *Parlamenti és pártharcok Magyarországon, 1945-47* (Parliamentary and party struggles in Hungary, 1945-47) Budapest, 1975, pp. 151-152.

50. Jablonický, op. cit., p. 398.

51. The provisions of the Presidential decree 33/45, affecting the Hungarians, are as follows:

Article 1, Paragraph 1. Those Czechoslovak citizens of German or Hungarian nationality who have obtained German or Hungarian citizenship according to the prescriptions of the foreign occupation forces, have forfeited their Czechoslovak citizenship from that day. *Paragraph 2.* Other citizens of German or Hungarian nationality will lose their Czechoslovak citizenship the day this decree becomes effective. *Paragraph 3.* This decree does not apply to those Germans and Hungarians who at the time of the danger to the Republic, in the sense of the Presidential decree 16/45 of June 19, 1945, declared themselves to be Czech or Slovak. *Paragraph 4.* Members of the Czech, Slovak, or other Slav nations who had declared themselves German or Hungarian during the above-mentioned period, who were forced to do so under pressure in the given circumstances, are not qualified as German or Hungarian according to this decree if the Ministry of Interior approves their certificate of national reliability, issued by the pertinent County National Committee, after examination of the circumstances.

Article 2, Paragraph 1. Those persons who fall under Article 1, but who can prove that they had remained faithful to the Czechoslovak Republic, had never committed offense against the Czech or Slovak nation, and have taken an active part in the struggle for our liberation, or were persecuted by Nazi and Fascist terror, will retain their Czechoslovak citizenship. *Paragraph 2.* The pertinent County National Committee must receive an application to retain Czechoslovak citizenship within six months from the date when this decree takes effect.

Article 3, Paragraph 1. Those persons who have lost their citizenship in accordance with the provisions of Article 1 may request the return of their citizenship within six months from a date specified by an order of the Ministry of Interior. This request must be addressed to the pertinent County National Committee's Administrative Committee. In Slovakia the decisions are handed down by the Slovak National Council. Such applications must not be handled if the person has flouted his duties as a Czechoslovak citizen.

Article 4, Paragraph 1. For the purpose of this decree married women and minors must be judged independently. *Paragraph 5.* This decree becomes effective on the date of publication. It will be applied by the Minister of Interior in conjunction with the Minister of Foreign Affairs and the Ministry of Defense.

52.   Order 99/1945 of the Slovak National Council regulated the dismissal of Hungarian public and private employees.

53.   The exemption clause of the Presidential decree 108/1945 reads: "Those able to demonstrate that they had remained faithful to the Czechoslovak Republic, have never committed offenses against the Czech or Slovak nations, and have either taken an active part in the struggle for liberation, or had suffered consequences of Nazi or Fascist terror."

54.   Speech by Šmidke, *Čas,* October 16, 1945.

55.   *Čas,* November 1, 1945.

56.   Ibid., October 24, 1945.

57.   Ibid., November 8, 1945.

58.   J. Ďuriš's speech in the Provisional National Assembly, November 28, 1945. *Pravda,* December 1, 1945.

59.   Jan Masaryk, *Ani opona, ani most* (Neither curtain nor bridge), Prague, 1947, p. 14.

60.   In January 1942, led by General Feketehalmy-Czeidner, Hungarian troops murdered more than 3,000 Serbian civilians. See Daniel Csatári, *Forgószélben* (In the whirlwind) Budapest, 1969, p. 441. Cf., Stephen D. Kertesz, *Diplomacy in a whirlwind,* p. 209.

61.   Presidential decree quoted in note 25.

62.   V. Jarošová and O. Jaroš, *Slovenské robotníctvo v boji o moc* (The struggle of the Slovak working class for power) Bratislava, 1965, p. 114.

63.   Cf. Cambel, *Slovenská agrárna otázka*, p. 223.

Chapter 5

1.   *Nové Prúdy*, January 20, 1946.

2.   *Pravda*, January 20, 1946.

3.   Cambel, *Slovenská agrárna otázka*, p. 223.

4.   *Čas*, January 6, 1946.

5.   Ibid., January 15, 1946.

6.   Mr. Davies evidently responded to rumors of Hungarian origin, widely circulated in the Western press, that church services in Hungarian had been forbidden in Slovakia. *S.B.*

7.   *Čas*, January 20, 1946.

8.   Ibid., January 24, 1946.

9.   Dalibor M. Krno, *Jednali sme o mír s Mad'arskem* (We negotiated with Hungary about peace) Prague, 1947, p. 47.

10.   *Čas*, February 26, 1946.

11.   Ibid., February 28, 1946.

12.   Ibid., March 26, 1946.

13.   Juraj Zvara, *A Magyar nemzetiségi kérdés mególdasa Szlovákiában* (The solution of the Hungarian nationality question in Slovakia) Bratislava, 1965, p. 36.

14.   *Zprávy štátneho plánovacieho a štatistického úradu*, (Bulletin of the Government Bureau of Planning and Statistics) Bratislava, August 1, 1946.

15.   *Új Otthon* (Budapest), August 1, 1948. The presence in Hungary of 477,000 Slovaks was also cited at the Paris conference by the Czecho-slovaks (Krno, op. cit., p. 125). Twenty years later, the *Pravda* of Bratislava still referred to 300,000 Slovaks in Hungary (*Pravda*, February 28, 1968).

16.   *Új Otthon*, January 31, 1948.

17.   Cf. Dr. Jan K. Garaj, *Slováci a Češi* (Slovaks and Czechs) Prague, 1946, pp. 28, 73, 84, 131.

18.   Cambel, *Slovenská agrárna otázka 1944-1948*, p. 251.

19. *Rok Práce* (The year of work) Bratislava, 1946, p. 85.

20. Zvara, op. cit., p. 40.

21. *Demografická příručka* (Demographic handbook) Prague, 1966, p. 44.

22. *Soupis obyvatelstva v Československu v letech 1946 a 1947* (Census of the population of Czechoslovakia in the years 1946 and 1947), State Statistical Office, Prague, 1951, pp. 548-549. It was made public only in 1951.

23. Krno, op. cit., p. 41. (I compared the text of speeches on Hungarian problems at the peace conference quoted from Krno with that published by the Hungarian Ministry of Foreign Affairs and made adjustments, whenever necessary, for the sake of accuracy.) Cf. *Hungary and the Peace Conference,* Budapest, 1947, vol. IV–*S.B.*

24. Ibid., p. 43.

25. Ibid., p. 47.

26. Ibid., p. 52.

27. In May 1940, I requested an eyewitness, Dr. V. Blaha, a physician of Slovak nationality from the neighboring Komjatice (Komját), to tell the true story of the volleys fired at Šurani [Nagysurány]. Dr. Blaha's account of the incident is as follows: "In the early hours of December 25, 1938, the rumor spread in Nagysurány, that the Roman Catholic priest will deliver an anti-Hungarian speech of exhortation in the church. The community's Slovak population filled the church, while Hungarian soldiers and gendarmes surrounded the church. The local Hungarian gendarmes were reinforced by a military unit under the command of a young officer. When the excited crowd leaving the church noticed this, they began to throw stones at the soldiers . . . . The young officer, inexperienced and confused, kept looking around and, when hit by a stone under the eye, he ordered the troops to fire into the crowd."–*K.J.*

28. *Čas,* August 18, 1946.

29. Ibid., August 23, 1946.

30. Krno, op. cit., p. 60.

31. Ibid., p. 122.

32. Ibid., p. 125.

33. Ibid., p. 126.

34. Ibid., p. 130.

35. Ibid., p. 132.

36. Ibid., p. 145.

37. *Otázky mezinárodniho práva a medzinárodni politiky* (Problems of international law and international politics) Prague, 1935, pp. 61, 63. (Speeches of Academician A. Y. Vishinsky.)

38. Krno, op. cit., p. 148.

39. Ibid., p. 164.

40. Ibid., p. 282.

41. Ibid., p. 177.

42. *Čas,* October 6, 1946.

43. Ján Masaryk, *Ani opona, ani most* (Neither curtain, nor bridge), pp. 13-14.

44. Krno, op. cit., p. 249.

45. *Nové Prúdy,* October 6, 1946, p. 434.

46. Ibid., October 25, 1946, p. 466. (Article by Ibl.)

47. Ibid., October 25, 1946, p. 468 (Article by K. Argus.)

48. Ibid., November 8, 1946. (Article by Dr. Martin Hano.)

49. *Obzory,* October 19, 1946, p. 659.

50. *Čas,* November 5, 1946.

51. *Pravda,* January 29, 1946.

52. *Čas,* November 20, 1946.

Chapter 6

1. *Východoslovenská Pravda,* November 3, 1946.

2. Cambel, *Slovenská agrárna otázka,* p. 318.

3. *Čas,* October 23, 1946.

4. *Práca,* November 13, 1946.

5. *Československý Východ,* November 24, 1946.

6. *Čas,* January 8, 1947.

7. Gyula Duba, *Vajúdó parasztvilág* (Peasantry in Travail), pp. 91-92.

8. Purgat, *Za nové Československa,* p. 191.

9. *Slovník lidové správy* (Handbook on people's administration), p. 325.

10. Václav Prúcha, *Hospodárske dejiny Československo v 19. a v. 20. storočí* (The economic history of Czechoslovakia in the 19th and 20th centuries) Bratislava, 1974, p. 275.

11. *Čas,* November 29, 1946.

12. Ibid., November 26, 1946.

13. Ibid., November 29, 1946.
14. *Nové Prúdy*, Christmas 1946, p. 613.
15. *Práca*, December 19, 1946.
16. *Pravda*, December 22, 1946.
17. *Čas*, Christmas 1946, ("Where Does Terror Reign?")
18. *Práca*, February 10, 1947.
19. *Katholické Noviny*, 1947, No. 33. The Catholic paper's statement was attacked as "un-national" by *Národná Obroda*, August 21, 1947.
20. *Partizán*, 1947/15, p. 5.
21. *Nové Prúdy*, February 9, 1947.
22. *Práca*, February 2, 1947.
23. Ibid., February 7, 1947.
24. Ibid., February 9, 1947.
25. Ibid., February 10, 1947.
26. Ibid., February 15, 1947.
27. *Čas*, February 13, 1947.
28. Ibid.
29. Ibid.
30. *Práca*, January 25, 1947.
31. *Nové Prúdy*, June 8, 1947.
32. *Magyarok Czehszlovákiában* (Hungarians in Czechoslovakia) Bratislava, 1969, p. 218. (An essay by Juraj Zvara.)
33. Cambel, op. cit., p. 318.

Chapter 7

1. *Obzory*, January 25, 1947.
2. *Rol'nická Nedel'a*, January 19, 1947.
3. *Obzory*, January 4, 1947.
4. *Práca*, February 28, 1947. (Article by Dr. Andrej Sarvaš.)
5. *Pravda*, March 25, 1947 (Article signed "Pb.")
6. *Obzory*, March 15, 1947.
7. *Čas*, March 25, 1947.
8. *Práca*, March 27, 1947.
9. *Čas*, March 25, 1947.
10. Ibid., April 12, 1947.
11. *Československý Východ*, April 27, 1947. (Article signed "Kin.")

12. *Nové Prúdy,* April 8, 1947.

13. *Čas,* April 13, 1947.

14. Ibid., June 22, 1947.

15. *Národná Obroda,* April 27, 1947. (Editorial by L. Novomeský.)

16. *Nové Prúdy,* April 27, 1947. (Article by Štefan Pleško.)

17. *Čas,* June 22, 1947.

18. *Naš Národ,* September 7, 1947.

19. *Obzory,* October 25, 1947.

20. *Čas,* December 31, 1947. (Article by Ján Štrba.)

21. *Národná Obroda,* May 22, 1947.

22. *Čas,* May 13, 1947.

23. *Práca,* May 30, 1947.

24. *Nové Prúdy,* Christmas 1947.

25. *Náš Národ,* September 7, 1947. (Article by J. Miklo.)

26. *Čas,* August 9, 1947.

27. Ibid., May 22, 1947.

28. *Obzory,* November 1, 1947.

29. *Čas,* June 27, 1947.

30. Ibid., July 1, 1947.

31. Ibid., August 5, 1947.

32. *Nové Prúdy,* August 31, 1947.

33. Ibid., July 20, 1947.

34. *Z dejín odborového hnutia na Slovensku, 1946-48* (From the history of the trade union movement in Slovakia, 1946-48) Bratislava, 1971, p. 13.

35. *Tvorba,* October 15, 1947.

36. *Dnešek,* August 21, 1947.

37. *Cíl,* December 5, 1947.

38. *Obzory,* October 11, 1947.

39. Ibid.

40. Ibid.

41. *Čas,* April 6, 1947.

42. *Tvorba,* March 19, 1947. (Statement by Dr. Vladimír Procháska, Communist Representative of the Constitutional Assembly.)

43. *Tvorba,* June 18, 1947.

44. Ibid., August 20, 1947.

Chapter 8

1. Anton Rašla, *L'udové súdy* (The people's courts) Bratislava, 1969.
2. *Pravda*, March 20, 1948. (Statement by Dr. Julius Viktory.)
3. Rašla, op. cit., p. 153.
4. *Obzory*, May 3, 1947.
5. Rašla, op. cit., p. 71.
6. *Cíl*, June 27, 1947.
7. *Východné Slovensko pred februárom* (East Slovakia before February), Košice, 1958, p. 112. (Article by Juraj Purgat on the Hungarian minority).
8. *Čas*, December 22, 1946.
9. *Nové Prúdy*, February 15, 1948.
10. The inhabitants of Southern Slovakia were Hungarian citizens by international law (after the Vienna Award, November 2, 1938). Tiso Slovakia was recognized by the Soviet Union, September 16, 1939 (Cf. Beneš, *Paměti*, p. 200). The official mission of the Czechoslovak Ambassador to Moscow, Zdeněk Fierlinger ended, January 1, 1940, at the request of the Soviet Government (Cf. Beneš, op. cit., p. 104). Despite these facts, the theory of Czechoslovakia's "legal continuity" was applied retroactively to 1938. Beneš himself, actually formulated the theory only in exile in 1942.–*K.J.*, supplemented by *S.B.*
11. *Čas*, April 17, 1947.
12. Ibid., January 22, 1947.
13. Ibid.
14. Ibid.
15. *Dnešek*, January 2, 1948.
16. Ibid., November 13, 1947.
17. *Národná Obroda*, April 27, 1947.
18. *Tvorba*, July 25, 1947.
19. *Dnešek*, January 8, 1948.
20. Ibid., January 15, 1948.
21. *Čas*, March 16, 1947.
22. Martin Vietor, *Dejiny Okupácie* (History of occupation), pp. 367-68.
23. *Čas*, September 18, 1947.
24. Éva Teleki, *Nyilasuralom Magyarországon* (Arrow Cross rule in Hungary), p. 120.

25. Cf. Zoltán Fábry, *Stószi délelőttök*. See Chapter 1, note 30.
26. Vietor, op. cit., p. 349.
27. Cf. M. Lackó, *Nyilasok, nemzetiszocialisták* (Arrow Crossists, National Socialists), p. 283.
28. *Pr \pevky k dejinám východného Slovenska* (Contributions to the history of East Slovakia) Bratislava, 1964, pp. 385-86. (Essay by Ladislav Olexa.)
29. Vladimir Motoška, *Protifašisticky obdoj v Novohrade* (Anti-Fascist resistence in Novohrad), Martin, 1974, p. 159.
30. *Predvoj,* April 25, 1968.
31. Dr. Daniel Okáli, *Matica Slovenská a národnosti* (Matica Slovenská and the nationalities. In *Narodné Výbory,* 1969, No. 9.
32. *Tvorba,* May 14, 1947. (Article by Dr. Jozef Štěpánek.)
33. Ibid., October 8, 1947. (Article by same, critical of the Minister of Justice, Dr. Prokop.)
34. Ibid., July 25, 1947. (Intervention by the Communist Deputy Karol Bacílek.)

Chapter 9

1. *Čas,* January 11, 1948.
2. *Nové Prúdy,* January 25, 1948.
3. *Čas,* January 28, 1948.
4. *Nové Prúdy,* February 8, 1948.
5. Ibid., February 22, 1948.
6. *Sloboda,* January 23, 1948.
7. *Obzory,* January 31, 1948.
8. Ibid., February 21, 1948.
9. *Tvorba,* February 4, 1948.
10. *Pravda,* March 9, 1948.
11. *Tvorba,* May 1, 1948. (Report on comments by the French paper, *Le Populaire.*)
12. József Rávay, *Élni tudtunk a szabadsággal* (We knew how to live with freedom) Budapest, 1949, p. 375.
13. *Pravda,* November 28, 1948.
14. The census of 1950 found 13,441 Hungarians in the Czech lands; if not all, but the majority of them were the deportees who chose to stay.

Cf. *Demografická příručka*, 1966, p. 45.

  15. *Uj Szó*, February 26, 1949.

Epilogue

  1. Juraj Zvara, *A magyar nemzetiségi kérdés megoldása Szlovákiában* (The solution of the Hungarian nationality question in Slovakia) Bratislava, 1965.

  2. Maria Lavová's review of Zvara's book in *Historický Časopis*, 1967, No. 2.

  3. Lavová, op. cit., p. 301.

  4. Ibid., p. 305.

  5. *Új Szó* March 1, 1951; *Pravda*, April 8, 1951.

  6. *Új Szó*, April 25, 1954.

  7. See, in particular, the works of Samuel Cambel (*Slovenská agrárna otázka*, 1972) and Juraj Purgat (*Od Trianonu po Košice*, 1979), as quoted several times.

BIOGRAPHIES

KÁLMAN JANICS (YAW-nich), the Hungarian author, is a physician and a sociologist. Born in 1912, he is one of the few Hungarians of the older generation with a higher education who survived in his homeland, the post-war Czechoslovak policy of population expulsion of the national minorities. Well known at home and abroad as a Hungarian writer on minority problems, Dr. Janics has been a target of denunciation and harassment in Slovakia. Since 1970, he was unable to publish in his homeland. From the summer of 1978 to March 1981, he was barred from practicing his medical profession.

GYULA ILLYÉS (DYU-la EE-yea-sh; middle syllable rhymes with "yea and nay"), author of the introductory essay, is an internationally known Hungarian poet and writer. Born in 1902, he is the grand old man of contemporary Hungarian literature. Although recipient of several official prizes, the Hungarian Communist authorities have suppressed his recently published book of essays because of his outspoken views on the Hungarian minorities.

STEPHEN BORSODY (BOR-sho-dee), author of the English Version, is a historian and publicist. Born in 1911, he was a Hungarian journalist and diplomat before becoming an American college professor, now retired. Among his books, *The Triumph of Tyranny* (London, 1960), retitled in the American edition as *The Tragedy of Central Europe* (New York, 1962), has recently been reissued by the Yale Concilium on International and Area Studies. It deals with subjects closely related to Dr. Janics' book.

BROOKLYN COLLEGE STUDIES ON SOCIETY IN CHANGE
Distributed by Columbia University Press (Except No. 5)
Editor-in-Chief Béla Király

WAR AND SOCIETY IN EAST CENTRAL EUROPE
A Subseries